THE WOUND IN THE HEART

THE WOUND

ALLEN GUTTMANN

IN THE HEART

AMERICA AND THE SPANISH CIVIL WAR

 THE FREE PRESS OF GLENCOE

To Johann Friedrich Guttmann

PREFACE

On the night of July 17, 1936, at Melilla, Ceuta, and Tetuán, the garrisons of Spanish Morocco rose in armed rebellion. Their leaders hoped that a *pronunciamiento* would overthrow the Spanish Republic as *pronunciamientos* had toppled regimes in the past. Instead, the Spanish nation collapsed into thirty-two months of civil war. No public event of the years between 1919 and 1939—excepting the Great Depression itself—moved Americans as did this Spanish conflict. My concern here is not to recreate these thirty-two months of crisis nor to settle the historical controversies that have arisen nor to justify one or another of a multitude of contentious factions. My concern is analysis. How did Americans see the Spanish Civil War? Why did they, in Camus' phrase, "feel the Spanish drama as a personal tragedy"? Why has the Spanish war become the last great cause?

In attempting to answer these questions, I limit myself, for the most part, to the years 1936 through 1939. I use as sources books, pamphlets, magazines, newspapers, propaganda releases, letters, films, paintings, drawings, cartoons, speeches, and radio broadcasts. Because the Spanish war cannot be understood through American sources only, because American interpretations were influenced in part by foreign opinion, and because comparisons and contrasts often dramatize a point, I have used, on occasion, foreign sources. I hope that these efforts at casting a wider and finer net have resulted in a rich haul and not in an entangled text.

The variety of the source materials and of the concerns made the problem of organization exceedingly pressing. The virtues of a chronological narrative are many. The chief virtue is that most readers are accustomed to histories that "begin at the beginning" and move to that moment the historian calls "the end." This study is not so organized. There were three major reasons for this decision:

1. Political and social histories, chronologically narrated, are already available.

2. There was surprisingly little variation in the position taken by any single person or group. Most magazines, for instance, did little to modify the editorial stands taken in the first month of the war. Moreover, many of the events that caused the most controversy were controversial only *within* one or another faction or group. For example, the "May Days" in Barcelona were of extreme importance *within* the various radical movements.

3. Most importantly, an analytical study has virtues of its own. By separating and by grouping responses and interpretations, we can see patterns that well might not have been illuminated by other schemes of organization. At the same time, I have tried to avoid gross and needless violations of chronological sequence.

Once I had decided to organize analytically and to relate the Spanish Civil War to the liberal democratic tradition in America, a movement from political right to political left seemed in order. The movement from chapter to chapter approximates a movement from certain irrational responses through conservative and liberal and radical interpretations back to other irrational responses. There is, however, no attempt at rigid categorization within chapters.

Chapter 1 is concerned with the irrational responses that, in a sense, precede or underlie more conceptualized and more logical interpretations of the war. Chapter 2 deals with interpretations that avowedly rejected liberal democratic assumptions and ideals. This chapter includes sections on Fascism and on antidemocratic theories. Chapter 3 is a study of the Roman Catholic Church in the United States and the Spanish war. Chapter 4 is devoted to American "conservatives," to the property-conscious, religiously-oriented bourgeoisie. Chapter 5 includes sections on "Reason and Progress," "Education and the Rule of Law," and "Liberty, Equality, Fraternity." Since the liberal democratic tradition has been dominant in the United States, it seemed necessary, at this point, to ask why this intense and extensive sympathy for the Spanish Republic did not lead to a foreign policy less harmful to the Loyalists. The fourth section of this chapter, "Franklin Roosevelt and the Stalemate of Liberal Policy," is an attempt to answer this question. The next chapter, Chapter 6, is an examination of those groups and those single thinkers who moved, as they saw it, "forward from liberalism" by amending the liberal position in order to achieve more valued liberal ideals at the possible expense of less valued ones. The three sections of this chapter deal, specifically, with Americans dedicated to the ideals of organicism, anarchism, and socialism. The last section includes Stalinists, dissident Communists, and socialists of varying degrees of radicalism. The last chapter, "Primitivism versus Progress," suggests that support for the Spanish Republic led many Americans into a dilemma found in American history as well as in the history of the Spanish Civil War.

It is obvious that no one writes anything on the Spanish

war without running counter to someone else's strong feelings on the subject. Versions of this study have seemed, to one reader, excessively anti-Communistic and, to another reader, excessively pro-Communistic. Furthermore, chapters of this study, especially the earlier ones, seem to emphasize the uglier aspects of the human personality. All one can say to the charge of muckraking is that Milton's Jehovah is the only general whose armies were composed entirely of angels. For the most part, the more grotesque interpretations of the war are, after a brief discussion, laid aside as eccentric. The very paucity of the bizarre interpretations is further evidence for the argument that the liberal democratic tradition is the key to an understanding of the intense and widespread response to the Spanish war.

One further point. Not old enough to remember the war, I know it only from what I have been told and from the historical documents I have seen. Presumably, the loss of direct experience is balanced by a gain in detachment, even when writing of a war from which complete detachment seems to be impossible. This study, at any rate, is intended as an addition to scholarship and to understanding. Uninformed partisanship seems to be getting on very well without belated help.

Materials on the Spanish Civil War are widely scattered. Of the many librarians who aided me in my study of these materials, I wish especially to thank the following: E. Porter Dickinson and Floyd Merritt, Amherst College librarians, who ordered over one hundred volumes on interlibrary loan; Miss Margaret Johnson, Smith College librarian, who did not skin me for the irregular use of valuable magazines; and Howard Gottlieb, Yale University librarian, who permitted me to examine the papers of the late Charles Fenton. I wish also to thank Charles W. Cole and Calvin H. Plimpton, Presidents of Amherst College, who made available money for journeys after unloanable books.

For their many helpful suggestions on the manuscript itself, I wish to thank Professors Clarke A. Chambers, Charles Foster, and Donald Torbert, of the University of Minnesota, and Professor Daniel Aaron, of Smith College. My greatest debts for advice, aid, counsel, and encouragement are to Professors Mulford Q. Sibley, of the University of Minnesota, and Leo Marx, of Amherst College. For much of the dirty work, I am indebted to my wife, Martha Britt Guttmann, and my sister, Betty Guttmann. If my errors of fact and of judgment do not alienate the reader, I should like him to think of this book as one written in the tradition of two great educators: F. O. Matthiessen and Tremaine McDowell.

ALLEN GUTTMANN

It is now nine years that men of my generation have had Spain within their hearts. Nine years that they have carried it with them like an evil wound. It was in Spain that men learned that one can be right and yet be beaten, that force can vanquish spirit, that there are times when courage is not its own recompense. It is this, doubtless, which explains why so many men, the world over, feel the Spanish drama as a personal tragedy.

—ALBERT CAMUS

CONTENTS

INTRODUCTION:

"THE RED NEW DEAL"

When William Lemke ran in 1936 for the presidency of the United States, Father Charles E. Coughlin, of Royal Oak, Mich., cheered him on, and somebody wrote a jingle that appeared in the pro-Lemke newspapers of William Randolph Hearst:

> The Red New Deal with a Soviet Seal,
> Endorsed by a Moscow Hand.
> The strange result of an alien cult
> In a liberty-loving land.

Most historians today are unwilling to credit this interpretation of Franklin Roosevelt's domestic policy, but another accusation has been widely accepted: it is often thought that the Spanish Civil War was one of the great radical causes of the period that Eugene Lyons dubbed "The Red Decade."

Father Coughlin argued that David Dubinsky's contributions to the republican government of Spain were indications of a subversive desire to aid "his communist brothers," and John V. Hinkel condemned each of the various committees

1

established to support the Republic as "Communistic," "Communist," or "Communist-dominated." Of American volunteers to Spain, John E. Kelly wrote, "These men do not go to fight for Spain—they go to serve Communism." Congressman Martin Dies of Texas, chairman of the Committee on Un-American Activities, asserted that membership in one or another pro-Loyalist committee evidenced possible disloyalty to the United States. Citing a representative case, Dies wrote that Attorney General Robert H. Jackson "sent a telegram of endorsement [to] a parade . . . led by two hundred Veterans of the Abraham Lincoln Brigade." After referring to other evidence of this type, Dies remarked that "tabulations such as the foregoing could be extended to fill an entire volume." This seems quite possible. Years later, J. Edgar Hoover, a man often taken as an expert in such questions, argued that volunteers who went to Spain furthered Bolshevism's international greed.[1]

Men like Father Coughlin and Congressman Dies are not thought of as scholars, but Carlton Hayes, an estimable historian and onetime ambassador to Franco's Spain, looks back on the Spanish war with much the same point of view:

The central significance of the Spanish Civil War was its rescue of Spain from the fate which later befell the nations of eastern Europe. . . . The Spanish struggle was a prelude not so much to the Second World War as to the subsequent "cold war" and the struggle in Korea.

Ironically, Communists such as Alvah Bessie and Steve Nelson, both of whom fought in Spain, have further fortified this position. Alvah Bessie's anthology, *The Heart of Spain*, excludes a non-Communist, Ernest Hemingway, for "maliciously" slandering the International Brigades and for presenting an "unforgivable distortion of the meaning of the struggle in Spain." Steve Nelson writes that the Veterans of the Abraham Lincoln Brigade stand "for the cause of world peace, for an end to the war in Korea, and for the liberation of Spain." Ex-Communists such as Sandor Voros and John Gates tell of their experiences in Spain; non-Communists are, for the most part, unwilling to jeopardize their careers by admitting quondam commitment to now unpopular ideals. The impression that the Spanish Civil War was a "Communist cause" is firmly printed on the public mind.[2]

To conclude the indictment it is necessary to add that the Communists *did* lead the way in organizing the committees and the congresses, and the international units as well. But those who joined the committees and went to the rallies were not, for the most part, seeking to advance the Bolshevik cause. The extraordinarily passionate concern that great numbers of Americans felt for the fate of the Spanish Republic was not—for the most part—the result of a movement toward radicalism. It was one more manifestation of the liberal tradition in America. The editors of the *Washington Post* grimly announced during the last days of the war (March 12, 1939) that the "Republic was democratic in its inception . . . and will remain democratic to the end." Most pro-Loyalist Americans agreed. The Loyalist government was supported because it was thought to be legal, constitutional, republican, liberal, democratic. Joseph Warren Beach came as close as any to putting this feeling into a single sentence:

Since the beginning of the civil war in Spain, I have been for the Loyalist Government, because it is the legal, duly constituted government, because it represents republican and representative institutions as opposed to arbitrary and dictatorial rule, because it represents the economic and cultural interests of the great body of the population, and because it gives the greatest hope for a modern and effective organization of society.[3]

Petitions were signed and speeches delivered and lives risked not for the cause of Bolshevism nor for the memory of the October deposition of Kerensky but for a faith in the movements that had dealt with George III and Louis XVI. Spain seemed a last chance for a representative government and a pluralistic society in a Europe that had turned with frightening speed toward dictatorship and totalitarianism. At a time when militant Fascism deified the unreasonable, the Spanish Republic seemed to represent the Enlightenment's faith in reason as the faculty by which men govern themselves.

More specifically, the Republic did not mean *Kolkhoz* and *Stakhanovite;* it meant free speech, a free press, the right of assembly, the separation of Church and State, minority rights, and—in words that should not be surrendered to those who debase them—liberty, equality, fraternity. The surprising thing about the Spanish war is that most American Catholics did *not* rely upon the arguments of the social encyclicals and most American Communists did *not* use the rhetoric of their dialectic. At times, the student suspects both the Vatican and the Kremlin of simultaneous conversion to the liberal doctrines of John Stuart Mill.

This is, of course, an introductory overstatement. There *were* Americans who called themselves Fascists and praised General Franco as a "Blond Beast." There *were* American Catholics who rallied to the banner of Spanish clericalism. There *were* American anarchists and American Marxists who denounced the bourgeois republicanism of Spain's Popular Front as a betrayal of the social revolution. These Americans knew that General Franco was something other than a Hispanic George Washington and these Americans knew that the Republic was not all that its liberal supporters thought it to be. These Americans were radicals and they were, compared to the liberal majority, few. Such generalizations as these are, however, better made in conclusions than in introductions, better received after the presentation of evidence and argument. The first step is to move into the details of the American responses to the Spanish Civil War, to send the rays of political controversy through the prism of analysis, to scrutinize the colors of the political spectrum.

1 ♐

PRELIBERAL RESPONSES:

ASTROLOGERS

AND OTHERS

Sagittarians and the "Powers of Evil"

Although the fabric of American society in the 1930's was not quite ripped to shreds, as was Spanish society, American society had its lunatic fringes. No study of the Spanish war can be complete without noting the existence of bizarre responses that, in a sense, antedate the liberal democratic tradition. Nor can a study be complete without commenting on the sadistic impulses revealed in much of the writing on the war. The bizarre interpretations and the irrational impulses reject, explicitly or implicitly, liberal democracy; furthermore, the irrational impulses have been, for the most part, ignored—unfortunately so—by the proponents of the liberal tradition.

No one departed further from assumptions of natural law

and of man's ability to live a life of reason than did Theodore Heline, a leader of occult movements. In a pamphlet, *Spain: World Ideas in Turmoil,* he explained the Spanish war; his explanation depended upon concepts of national and racial "karma," upon references to his own formulation of "esoteric Christianity," upon a peculiar kind of "color symbology," alchemy, astrology, and upon Rosicrucian lore:

Spain is governed by Sagittarius, the centaurian archer, half man, half beast, with bow and arrow aimed at the stars. General Franco is a Sagittarian. His sun is fiery, his rising sign watery, the two elements in alchemical conflict in war-torn Spain.

Although it is a matter of fact that General Franco's armies did fight under the symbol of the yoke and the arrows, this symbolism was derived from that of Ferdinand and Isabella. Heline's analysis, even when supported by the editors of *Modern Astrology* (London), seems farfetched.[1]

Even more impenetrable to an outsider is the arcane interpretation to be found in the *Theosophical Quarterly.* The "Wanderer," who appears to speak for the anonymous author, places the Spanish Civil War upon the "Screen of Time" and locates it within the larger context of a prolonged and embittered struggle between the "Powers of Evil" and the "White Lodge." The "Wanderer" agrees wholeheartedly with Heline's astrological and alchemical affirmation of General Franco's *Nuevo Estado:*

The government [of the Republic] . . . is Bolshevist seasoned with a considerable sprinkling of Anarchist. Their opponents . . . under Franco represent the more decent element in Spain— a mixed lot— . . . who prefer old-fashioned law and order to the bloody despotism of the Communists and the hell-let-loose of the Anarchists. Anyone with a knowledge of the facts must hope that Franco will win.

It seems proper that the occult writings and secret societies of Madame Blavatsky, the founder and theoretician of the Theosophical movement, bore such fruit as this. Faithful to a mysterious tradition that derives, ultimately, from the "Emerald Tablets" of Hermes Trismegistus, Theosophists protested the aridity of modern civilization. In Franco, they saw an ally.[2]

Naked Nuns and Amazons

Astrology, alchemy, and Theosophy may seem unrelated to the responses of ordinary men and women. Irrational impulses are, however, found in all of us. It is not surprising that, in the stress and tension of a civil war, reason is sometimes abandoned and humanitarian principles forgotten. Men's passions then lead to atrocious actions. I am not, however, concerned here with those who commit atrocities. I *am* concerned with men and women, often an ocean away from the violence of the Spanish war, who seemed mesmerized by the atrocities and the rumors of atrocities. Often, the unlikelihood of the actions ascribed to the enemy suggests that the stories were little more than fantasies, nothing more than the daydreams of the storytellers. In other words, atrocity stories, told mostly by the partisans of General Franco, reveal an extensive and unhealthy fascination, almost an obsession, with the most perverse and nightmarish kinds of violence.

In British publications, supporters of General Franco's *Movimiento Nacional* told gruesome tales of men "maddened by . . . cubist designs," of girls with "tummies slit open with a razor," of wives who received baskets of fruit in which they discovered their husbands' disembodied heads. In American publications, the "Red Terror" was deprecated as the macabre reign of crippled "misanthrope[s] . . . subject to the peculiar perverseness of the deformed," of fiendish simpletons, "disgruntled invalids," weaklings and "sub-human types" who exterminated their betters.

In Madrid the bands of assassins are mostly under the leadership of maniacs, drug addicts, perverts. In Barcelona, a hunchback, puny and degenerate, presides over the Public Safety [Council].

Supporters of the *Movimiento Nacional* did not monopolize the theme of violence. Manuel Komroff, writer for *Esquire* and supporter of the Republic, dramatized a horrible kind of death in a short story published in *Coronet*. When Fascist troops wantonly destroy a Loyalist village, the children watch their parents put to death and then clandestinely poison all the food in the village. "And that night," concludes Komroff, with a kind of glee, "two hundred strong . . . men were rolling in agony." Komroff was one of many writers who projected, in literary forms, a violently pro-Republican vision.[3]

In discussing this obsession with stories of atrocity and tales of violence, Gamel Woolsey, the American wife of Gerald Brenan, noted the credulity of the British in Gibraltar. These British sympathizers with General Franco seemed ready to believe almost anything: "One educated man of reputable position said that he had seen a nun burned alive in broad daylight in one of the public squares of Málaga. . . ." Moreover, such "witnesses" seemed especially entranced by the nakedness of these tortured nuns. Typical of their stories was one in which "naked nuns were being crushed by steam-rollers in the streets of Málaga." Gamel Woolsey refers to such nonsense as "the pornography of violence." Her phrase is apt, for in the fantasies of these hysterical commentators on the Spanish war, we find that combination of sensuality and violence known as sadism. "The dreamy lustful look, . . . the full enjoyment of horror (especially noticeable in reputable elderly Englishmen speaking of the rape or torture of naked nuns . . .), shows only too plainly their erotic source."[4]

The perceptiveness of Gamel Woolsey's observations becomes clear as we examine a frequently cited atrocity story that can be traced to Cornelius Vanderbilt, Jr. In an article written for *Liberty,* Vanderbilt described the vultures, rats, and corpses of a devastated Spanish village. In this "chamber of horrors," "nuns shackled to one another's ankles [were] dragged by lively mules through the cobblestone streets, the whole tops of their heads ablaze." Vanderbilt then added the second theme to the sadistic concert: "The outskirts of Madrid were alive with . . . Red Amazons, many of them actually stripped to the waist, carrying modern rifles, and with blood in their eye." (Having seen no other references to these bare-breasted Amazons, I am skeptical of Vanderbilt's trustworthiness.) The article, like most of those discussed in this chapter, was illustrated.[5]

As Vanderbilt's article suggests, many Americans were fascinated by the females who fought with the Spanish militia in the early days of the war. It may, at first, seem extreme to call this fascination a perverse one. After all, a female militia is—or rather was—quite unusual. Although Mrs. Boone and other frontier wives often defended their homes against Indian attack, women have never formed combat units in English or American wars. It is the *form* of the interest in the "Amazons" that seems perverse. The descriptions, as in Vanderbilt's article and in the anecdotes retold by Gamel Woolsey, were often wildly fantastic. One such description, entitled "Hell-Cats in the Spanish War," was published, like Vanderbilt's article, in *Liberty.* It is a discussion of the "Amazons" fighting on both sides. In *The Fight,* another writer compared the female soldiers of the Spanish war to Homer's "stalwart Amazons, each with a breast removed, the better to poise their bows and arrows. . . ." On two occasions, *Travel* magazine featured pictures of armed women. The first article commented on the "Spanish Amazons of 1936" and quoted from *Don Quixote,* wherein Sancho Panza remarked of a young lady, "I know her well and let me tell you she can fling a crowbar as well as the lustiest lad in town." This is a physical prowess paralleled by the women in Eitaro Ishigaki's painting, *Amazons.* Ishigaki's painting, shown at the 1939 exhibit of the American Artists' Congress, is one in which female warriors vanquish the enemy's bewildered troops in singlehanded combat. (The fascination for Spanish "Amazons" is not a new one. Havelock Ellis described, in *The Soul of Spain,* women "hard as marble" who could outwrestle any would-be rapist.)[6]

Frequently, the image of the Amazon was joined to that of Carmen. In August of 1936, *The Literary Digest* revealed a fevered imagination in its repeated references to "Red Carmens in the Ranks" and to the "all-woman's Amazon Battalion." In the "Dance of Death,"

supple-hipped Carmens of the Revolution, for want of roses, toss bombs as they whirl. Matching stride for stride with their men, the women of Spain march out to fight and die, a song on their lips, rifles on their shoulders. . . .

What hath Bizet wrought?

Other writers described female bayonet charges or the "solid thighs and round bosoms" of the embattled Amazons. The magazines focusing upon Amazons and naked nuns— *Liberty, The Literary Digest, Travel*—suggest a rather extensive fascination in which sex and violence are associated, but no American commentary ever approached the intensity of two British books. In the one, we are told that Communist nurses, spurning the ideals of the chaste Nightingale, led their wounded wards in febrile rumbas that degenerated into nightly orgies. In the other, we are beguiled by naked combats between men and women, by voluptuous dances, by excruciatingly sensuous tortures.[7]

As Mario Praz indicates in his classic study, *Romantic Agony*, this association of sex and violence has been a persistent—perhaps even a dominant—theme in European literature since the time of the Marquis de Sade's *Justine*. Recently, Leslie Fiedler has traced the same association through American literature. Henry Nash Smith's study of the muscular and deadly heroines of dime-novel fiction suggests that popular fiction has paralleled serious literature, that Mickey Spillane's murderous blondes are not uniquely modern phenomena. Such literary studies underscore Freud's association of *Eros* and *Thanatos*.

How conventional then that Hemingway's *For Whom the Bell Tolls* should contain Pilar—the only really successful female character in the Hemingway canon (with the possible exception of the mannish and suspect Lady Brett)! Surely Pilar's fascination for the reader is partially explicable in that she too combines elements of the erotic and the violent. Pilar, the "woman" of Pablo the guerrilla leader, is a matriarch. A kind of Iberian "Earth-Mother" whose lovemaking is, literally, earth-shaking, she becomes, at the same time, the real ruler of the band. She is more manly than Pablo, whose symbolic emasculation is a constant reference. (He is without "cojones.") But phrases like "Iberian Earth-Mother" are obviously inadequate when applied to Hemingway's complex creation. We can better understand the sickness of most accounts of "Red Carmens" by looking for a moment at Hemingway's novel.

In Chapter X of *For Whom the Bell Tolls,* Pilar tells Robert Jordan (the novel's hero) what happened when Pablo and the other peasants seized control of their village from the local Fascists. Pilar describes the descent into savagery and concludes with the assassination of the village's cowardly priest. Pilar watched

the priest with his skirts tucked up scrambling over a bench and those after him were chopping at him with . . . sickles and

. . . reaping hooks and then some one had hold of his robe and there was another scream and another scream and I saw two men chopping into his back with sickles while a third man held the skirt of his robe . . . and then the chair I was standing on broke and the drunkard and I were on the pavement that smelled of spilled wine and vomit.

This episode ends the village's anti-Fascist pogrom. Stunned by the horror, Pilar tells Robert Jordan that she was glad she "did not see more of it. . . ."[8]

Several things must quickly be said about this description by Hemingway of violence and bloodshed. First, the hints of sexual perverseness in this chapter are little more than hints. Second, the violence here is only one aspect of a complex work of art whose end is surely something more than the dramatization of violence. Third, the scene is "realistic" in the sense that it is very like what happened in hundreds of villages throughout Spain. Hemingway did not conjure up fantasies. Having said this much, we can go on to add that Hemingway—unlike the dealers in atrocity stories—seems to understand the dreadful psychology of the moment. Pilar's position is the one that Hemingway wants the reader to share (imaginatively), and Pilar's position is one in which she recognizes both the evil of the situation and her own complicity within the situation. In *not* coming to a similar recognition, Pablo fulfills the description of the authoritarian personality. The same failure is perceptible in the writings of most of those who pledged their allegiance to General Franco.

Perhaps enough has been said to indicate that, at least for readers of such magazines as *Liberty,* fascination with the Spanish Civil War was partly a result of a sadistic impulse, a morbid curiosity, a perverse interest in the nakedness of nuns and the implacability of "Amazons." Surely the circulation triumphs of the *New York Daily News* and the depressing phenomenon of numberless pulp-magazines devoted to sex and violence and violent sex attest to the importance of this aspect of the national character. To say that some Americans were fascinated by this aspect of the war is not, of course, to say that they were uncommitted to the principles they enunciated, or that anyone's commitment to principles was a dispassionate or wholly rational commitment. It *is* to say that no ideological interpretation is sufficient. Surely the most serious defect of the tradition of the Enlightenment, a defect that Melville and Dostoevski were aware of long before Freud and Jung, has been its inability to illuminate the underside of the human consciousness.

2

THE REJECTION

OF LIBERAL

ASSUMPTIONS

Fascists

Nazism is, in one sense, a political manifestation, an institutionalization, of the sadistic impulses discussed above. The "Blond Beasts" whose virility would halt the "seduction of hundreds of thousands of girls by bowlegged, disgusting Jew bastards" seem born of the same imaginations that fixed upon the Spanish Amazons. Although the Marxist view of Fascism as the last gasp of dying capitalism, as exploitation of the worker by open rather than by hidden force, explains many of the economic aspects of Fascism, the Marxist view is too narrow. Fascism is better understood as a complex repudiation of liberal democracy. To speak of freedom to do as the State directs, of equality based on blood or race, of the brotherhood of *Herrenvolk* is to have exchanged Jefferson and Mill for Hitler and Mussolini. In a Spanish context, it is to have substituted Ramiro Ledesma Ramos for Francisco Giner de los Ríos. Behind theories of *Duce, Führer,* and *Caudillo* there is the repudiation of reason and of abstract intelligence. As Adolf Hitler puts it in *Mein Kampf,*

The racial state [educates] the girl on the same principle as the boy. Here too the main emphasis must be placed . . . on physical culture, secondly on the development of spiritual, and lastly on intellectual values.

Abandoning reason, the Fascist turns to man as an animal, to race as "the key not only to world history but to human civilization." The race is expressed not through the individual but through the State. In Benito Mussolini's words, "Anti-individualistic, the Fascist conception of life stresses the importance of the State and accepts the individual only in so far as his interests coincide with those of the State." The *Caudillo's* followers joined their fellow Fascists in opposing the beliefs of the liberal democrat, but, in making room for the Roman Catholic Church, they modeled their *Movimiento Nacional* on the *Duce's* Italy rather than on the *Führer's* Germany.

The first Spanish organization to embrace Fascism was the *JONS (Juntas de Ofensiva Nacional Sindicalista),* formed in October of 1931 by Ramiro Ledesma Ramos and Onésimo Redondo Ortega. The JONS was anti-Semitic and authoritarian. Arguing that liberalism and individualism had weakened Spain, the JONS advocated a Catholic State in which all individuals could integrate themselves, free from elections, free from the Jewish mentality, free from the "Mongoloid-imperialistic Red Stalinists." Two years after the founding of the JONS, José Antonio Primo de Rivera, son of the late dictator, founded the *Falange Española.* In his famous address at Madrid's Teatro Comedia, October 29, 1933, he denounced the liberal tradition and urged "a system of authority, of hierarchy, and of order."

The *Patria* is a transcendent synthesis, an indivisible synthesis, with its own goals to fulfill; and we want this movement of today, and the state which it creates, to be an efficient, authoritarian instrument at the service of an indisputable unity, of that permanent unity, of that irrevocable unity that is the *Patria*.

The Falange and the JONS were merged on February 11, 1934. The combined organization faced, according to its first historian, "a great agony, a denationalized Spain dissolved into all of its parts. . . ." In reaction to the "anarchy and democratic disorder, the anti-militarism and anti-Catholicism of the Republic," the Falange stood for "Authority rather than Anarchy, Militarism and Service rather than un-Spanish Anti-Militarism, and, above all, religious feeling rather than laicism and atheism." When General Franco came to power in Nationalist Spain, he merged the Falange with the Carlists' *Comunión Tradicionalista* and formed, on April 19, 1937, the *Falange Española Tradicionalista y de las JONS,* usually referred to as the *Falange.* General Franco adopted Fascism as his own. His speeches promised an end to the "pseudo-wisdom of the [French] Encyclopedists" and pledged a Spain of "bread and justice" to replace the Spain of "Liberty, Equality, Fraternity." The *Nuevo Estado,* said General Franco, "will be a totalitarian instrument at the service of national integrity."[1]

This brief account should suffice to demonstrate that General Franco's *Movimiento Nacional* was, despite many declarations to the contrary, a Fascist repudiation of the doctrines of liberal democracy. It is necessary to emphasize this point at the beginning. One further point also needs clarification. It was customary, during the Spanish Civil War, to call Neville Chamberlain and Cordell Hull "Fascists." These accusations, like those leveled against the Roman

Catholic Church in America, are instances of an imprecise use of language. These accusations, like those of "Bolshevism" in the White House, are unfounded. Although the Catholic hierarchy in America and, to a lesser degree, abroad backed General Franco's Fascism with very little criticism of its un-Christian features, the Church does not, finally, repudiate human reason or parcel out all human goodness to one race and the heavy load of utter depravity to another. The Church is, moreover, the institutional form of an *international* rather than a national ideal. The distinctions are important ones. If we condemn the State Department and the hierarchy as "Fascist," what terms shall we use to describe the mad dogs of the distant Right?

Since American Fascists, like most American Stalinists, followed their leaders, it is useful to note very briefly the sources of their responses to the war. Hitler's speeches to the Nuremberg Congresses of September 9, 1936, and September 13, 1937, emphasized the Spanish war as but another manifestation of international Jewish Bolshevism. Hitler's invectives seem colorless when compared to Goebbels' tirade:

The Jew, who has been detected and unmasked as the chief agent and trustee of Bolshevism, represents a foreign and parasitic element in the social body of civilized nations. He has created Bolshevism as a favorable soil on which he can flourish. Therefore, the Jews throughout the whole world are against Franco.

No wonder whole units of the *Luftwaffe* "volunteered" for Spain![2]

American Fascists accepted the German view. *The American Bulletin* (New York), a mimeographed publication claiming to represent "The White Man's View-Point," announced that Lenin had planned the Spanish war some fifteen years before its outbreak (a charge echoed by more respectable publications) and asserted that the "patriotic rebels want a Spain for the Spanish and not for the internationalist horde of Jew-Marxists." *The American Gentile* (Chicago) reprinted the Spanish dispatches of Roland Strunk, the correspondent for the Nazis' *Völkische Beobachter,* and warned its readers that the "international-Communist-'Protocolic' conspiracy under our present Roosevelt–Popular Front–Jew-infested government" was preparing America for the fate of Spain:

The average American, thanks to the lies of our Jew-controlled press, is still blundering in total ignorance . . . of this [struggle] for Christian Civilization and against militant Judaism disguised as communism.

This periodical was volubly seconded by William D. Pelley's *New Liberation* (Asheville, N.C.), the organ of the "Christian Silvershirts." Pelley, too, reprinted Strunk's accounts of violated nuns and mutilated mummies, castrations and other exquisite tortures.

The Jewish Reds got into power in Spain by exactly the same processes that they have taken to get into power in the United States. . . . The Christian people of Spain rebelled . . . just as ultimately they've *got* to rebel here.

A subsequent issue quoted "irrefutable" statements by Ludovic Pignatelli to the effect that members of the Third International had been found dead in Spain, with their pockets stuffed full of Russian gold! The frightening tale of Moscow Jewry is related once again, along with the usual quotations from correspondent Strunk, in Orville Brisbane Good's mimeographed pamphlet, *The Truth on Spain!*[3]

Accounts of meetings held to denounce the Jewish invasion of Spain are found in John R. Carlson's *Under Cover.* Although Carlson seems, at times, a little farfetched in his exposé of American Fascism, he is quite correct when he names Merwin K. Hart as one of the leading organizers of

American Fascist support for Franco. Carlson says that Hart organized the American Union for Nationalist Spain "which attracted the Christian Front elements in droves." Hart spoke frequently and was twice reprinted in *Vital Speeches of the Day*. The speeches seem mild when compared with Hart's book-length defense of General Franco—*America, Look at Spain*. Spain's troubles are traced to the liberalism of the Enlightenment:

The parties of the Left had been hypnotized by ideas of the French and American revolutions. They preferred to ignore human nature and construct a government based on wishful thinking.

As in almost all Rightist accounts, Lenin is quoted as having predicted that Spain was next after Russia. And, as in many Rightist documents, there is publication of and excitement over alleged photostatic copies of Communist plans to take over in Spain. Dismissing reports of the bombing of Guernica as a hoax, Hart writes, "Aside from isolated cases, if any, I don't believe the Nationalists have been guilty of atrocities." Hart describes General Franco's plans for a corporate state, interprets the "so-called Wagner Labor Relations Act" as a sign of growing Communistic influence in the United States, and warns us all to act quickly to prevent an American version of the Communistic *Putsch* that had overwhelmed Spain.[4]

Not all American Fascist or near-Fascist apologists were of the alarmingly extreme sort, but even the more moderate relied, like their less respectable brethren, almost completely upon foreign sources. This fact, in itself, tells us a great deal about the weakness of the reactionary tradition in America.

The Examiner, a quarterly published in Bethlehem, Connecticut, was very close to the Fascist position. Erik R. von Kuehnelt-Leddihn anatomized the Leftist for the magazine, and found the Leftist concerned above all else with Spain, where, one gathers from the article, birth control, euthanasia, pacifism, sexual reform, and Communism were going to their collective doom. Franco's New Spain was opposed only by "the dead-end kids of the New York waterfront, Scottish duchesses [a reference to the pro-Loyalist Duchess of Atholl], Soviet aviators, Park Avenue hostesses and *New Republic* readers" who applauded "the delirious atrocities of Communists as the democratic expressions of the people's will." In the same issue, William Fitzgerald accused André Malraux of peddling a "stream-lined Byronism" (a bad thing) in his novel, *L'Espoir*. In an earlier issue, A. D. Corliss had exposed Hemingway's documentary film, *The Spanish Earth,* as as "impressive falsehood" and condemned Walter Wanger's film, *Blockade,* as a "dishonest manipulation of historical fact." Malraux, Hemingway, and Wanger had all taken the Loyalist side.[5]

The most distinguished of the American flirtations with Fascism was surely Seward Collins' *American Review*. Having been an editor of Douglas Jerrold's *English Review* (a near-Fascist publication), Collins turned naturally to the European reactionary and asked for an analysis of the Spanish Civil War. Jerrold, who had been involved in the plotting of the war and in the flying of General Franco from the Canaries to Spanish Morocco, responded with two articles that rank among the least accurate accounts of the war. Jerrold asserted that documents had been captured that proved the existence of a Communist plot ("In May of last year the detailed plans were laid for a Communist rising . . . in June or July"), denied that Guernica had been bombed ("Every count in the indictment against General Franco is a lie"), refused to admit any wrongdoing by General Franco ("There have been no atrocities on the Nationalist side"), attested to the murder, by the Reds, of 4,000 priests, and implicitly disagreed with Mussolini on the role of the Italian army in the capture of Málaga (Mussolini admitted the Italian triumph).

In view of the ignorance of most writers on the Spanish war, it would be pointless to list Jerrold's misspellings of Spanish names and his gross obliviousness to facts.

Jerrold went on, in *Georgian Adventure,* to admit that Franco's government might have erred "on the side of informality, of clemency and of casualness to friend and foe." In *The Future of Freedom,* he developed his ideas on the Christian state, which will, if Jerrold's predictions are correct, replace the anarchy, moral disorder, and Judaism of the modern world. (Jerrold lacked the imagination of another Briton, Francis Yeats-Brown, the author of the *Lives of a Bengal Lancer.* Yeats-Brown informed his American readers that the GPU in Spain hypnotized and tortured prisoners by using metronomes, maddened sleepless men by confronting them with "cubist designs," questioned captives under bright lights, and dosed them with castor oil until they wallowed miserably in their own excrement.) One suspects that such descriptions tell more about the psychology of British Fascism than about the practice of the GPU.[6]

In reprinting such analyses by British Fascists and in denouncing the "Judaism" and "Communism" of the Spanish Republic, American Fascists supported General Franco's attack on liberal democracy and his attempt to restore Spain to her pre-Encyclopedian greatness. The evils of liberal democracy were to be destroyed; political liberty and the reforms of the liberal revolutions were at last to be exposed as the delusions of a handful of fanatics. It is depressing to read these men, but it is, after all, encouraging to remember that not even *The American Review* was a successful magazine. Uncensored, it had its say and disappeared from the American scene. Most of the maniacal periodicals, mimeographed on the poorest paper, are slowly rotting to pieces in the inner sancta of the New York Public Library. There never was an *American Gentile Reader.*

The Pro-Franco Argument: Antidemocratic Theories

Fascists are, however, not the only ideologues to reject the assumptions of liberal democracy. It is possible to cherish *some* of the goals of the liberal tradition—the use of reason, liberty—without accepting the more democratic ideals, or so it has been argued in American history from the time of Alexander Hamilton and Chancellor Kent to that of Irving Babbitt and Walter Lippmann. Many of the spokesmen for antidemocratic theories have been studied in David Spitz' book, *Patterns of Anti-Democratic Thought.* Although none of these spokesmen for antidemocratic ideals attempted to make a full-scale justification of General Franco's *Nuevo Estado,* several did comment, in one way or another, on the Spanish Civil War. Their remarks are an indication of the attitudes of the conservative tradition in America.

Lawrence Dennis wrote, for *The American Mercury,* an analysis of the Spanish war; he did not, however, take this opportunity to develop his concept of the elite class. Instead, he confined himself to a denunciation of the evils foaming from the fountain of international communism. The word "communism," or a derivative of it, appears one hundred and six times in a twelve-page article—not counting its use in quotations from Communists. "The significant peculiarity of the Spanish civil war," wrote Dennis, "is that it is actually a fight to the finish between Communism and nationalism on Spanish territory." In its failure to discuss the positive achievements of General Franco's rule, the article is representative of the conservative position throughout the entire war. (This will be especially apparent when the position of the Roman Catholic Church is discussed.)[7]

Ralph Adams Cram, the architect who attempted at West Point and with Princeton's Graduate College to forward his

"Gothic Restoration," argued that great building was impossible in any but an "organic" society—and a Christian organic society at that. He wrote, hopefully, *The End of Democracy*, in which liberal democracy was found inferior to the Corporate State, in which a belief in Progress (a staple of the liberal's thought) was thoroughly denounced, in which the "High Democracy" of the Middle Ages was found preferable to the "Low Democracy" of the society produced by the English, American, and French Revolutions, in which the Spanish Civil War was laid to the immoral control of the "Communist-Socialist, anti-religious, masonic 'Popular Front.' " Believers in "High Democracy" could not be expected to countenance such control. "Once more," wrote Cram, "the better sort, both military and civil, rose in revolt." (One wonders if Eduardo Torrojo y Miret's extraordinary achievements—in the reinforced concrete of the International Style—represent, in architecture, the "Gothic" fruits of General Franco's victory.) The best that can be said for Cram is that he did not attempt to conceal his position behind a façade of accusations, nor did he—like some writers discussed below—try to pass General Franco off as a rotund version of Abraham Lincoln.[8]

Although George Santayana and Ezra Pound—two antidemocrats more noted than either Ralph Adams Cram or Lawrence Dennis—both shared the hospitality of Mussolini's Italy, neither made extended comments on the *Duce's* Spanish adventures. Both men did, however, say enough to add something to the statement of the conservative position. Santayana's opinions, expressed in a personal letter, were formed on the basis of whatever news reached him in Fascist Italy. These opinions cannot, therefore, be taken as the public and conclusive statements of a philosopher who had exhaustively studied the problem. Nevertheless, the letter indicates the temper of a tough-minded antidemocrat. It gives some of the reasons why an honest man might have supported General Franco.

Santayana wrote to Robert Shaw Barlow, on November 3, 1936, that he had no inside knowledge of the Spanish Civil War; he felt, however, that it could easily represent a turning point in the history of the world:

Since the triumph of Christianity, and again after the Reformation and the English, American and French revolutions, our part of the world has been governed by ideas, by theories, by universalistic sects like the Church, the Free Masons, the Free Trade Industrial Liberals, and last of all the Bolshies. Such influences are non-natural, non-biological; whereas the agricultural, military, and artistic life of nations is spontaneous, with ambitions that impose morality, but are not imposed by morality of any sort.

It was possible, Santayana thought, that the world was returning to such an ideal after two thousand years of hypnosis by "medicine-men and prophets." The argument is similar in many respects to Ralph Adams Cram's opposition of "High Democracy" and "Low Democracy." The enemy, however, has become something more than the liberal democratic tradition. The enemy here is *all* traditions that attempt to make the Idea universal.[9]

Considering the prominence given by some to the political and social theories of T. S. Eliot and Ezra Pound, one expects to find these writers volubly pleased by the possibility of the establishment in Spain of the "Christian society." They were not. Their statements were scarcely more public than Santayana's. Their French hero, Charles Maurras, was enthusiastic over the Fascists' refusal to "dissociate" the ideals of patriotism from those of religion, the traditions of morality and society from those of the Church; their English-speaking cohorts, Wyndham Lewis and Roy Campbell, applauded the way that General Franco handled the Communist menace

of "Don Moses Rosenberg" (Marcel Rosenberg, Soviet ambassador to Spain) and denounced pro-Loyalist writers as
"antediluvian lounge-lizards"; but neither Pound nor Eliot
had very much to say about the Spanish Civil War.

Amidst the conflict and the side-taking of the 1930's,
Eliot seemed to defend the last turret of the Ivory Tower.
Questioned on his view of the Spanish war, Eliot remained
aloof and refused to surrender his neutrality: "I . . . feel . . .
that it is best that at least a few men of letters should remain
isolated, and take no part in these collective activities." Ezra
Pound was only a little more responsive to the questionnaire
sent out, as a collective activity, by the *Left Review:* "Questionnaire [on the Spanish war] an escape mechanism for . . .
fools who are too cowardly to think; too lazy to investigate
the nature of money. . . . You are all had. Spain is an emotional luxury to a gang of sap-headed dilettantes." Pound was,
at this time, obsessed with the problem of usury in Western
history. Unimpressed by the fiscal aspects of the Spanish war,
Pound had nothing more to say. If the American theorists
who sketched designs for the *Nuevo Estado* expected the literary Right to fill in the gaps in their blueprint, they had to
look abroad—as did American Fascists—to find their drafts-
men.[10]

The antisemitism of the Dem/Libs is anti-Catholicism.

3

THE CATHOLIC CHURCH

AND

THE SPANISH WAR

The Roman Pontiffs and the Errors of Liberalism

Writing home from Spain, in the summer of 1937, John Fitzgerald Kennedy observed that, at the beginning of the Spanish Civil War, "the government was in the right morally speaking" in that "its program was similar to the New Deal." The Republic's attitude "towards the Church *was* just a reaction to the strength of the Jesuits who had become much too powerful—the affiliation between church and state [was] much too close." To say that neither the hierarchy nor a majority of the laity of the Catholic Church in America shared these sentiments is to utter a commonplace, but to move from this commonplace to an accurate description of the Catholic position on the Spanish Civil War—this is quite another matter. The intellectual response of the Church was

29

The Church is authoritarian about abortion. However, the U.S. Supreme Court is even more authoritarian.

a very complex one. It was *not* an affirmation of Spanish Fascism. It was not even, for the most part, an affirmation of the doctrines of the social encyclicals of Leo XIII and Pius XI. Setting aside for the moment the large minority (of the laity) that supported the Republic, we discover that the Catholic response was, for the most part, a denunciation of "Communism" and, surprisingly, an affirmation of General Franco's *Movimiento Nacional* as liberal, democratic, and in the tradition of the American Revolution. The response of American Catholics to the Spanish war, divided as it surely was, tortured as it often was, is in itself a fascinating subject. It is, moreover, a subject that leads, by intricate twistings and turnings, to the problem of an authoritarian church in a pluralistic society.[1]

?? This leads to relative truth.

Although this is not the place for an elaborate attempt to decide the historical relationship of the Church to liberalism, the reaction of the Church (American and European) seems more nearly understandable in light of Pius IX's celebrated *Syllabus of Errors* (December 8, 1864), Leo XIII's *Rerum Novarum* (May 15, 1891), and Pius XI's *Quadregismo Anno* (May 15, 1931). Pius IX's quarrel with liberalism was based, apparently, on liberalism's emphasis upon human reason. The third error reads as follows: "Human reason, without any reference whatsoever to God, is the sole arbiter of truth and falsehood, and of good and evil; it is law to itself, and suffices, by its natural force, to secure the welfare of men and nations." From this basic error, the other errors flow—freedom of choice in the question of religion, separation of Church and State, the lawfulness of rebellion against legitimate princes, divorce. The last four errors are specific castigations of modern liberalism, and the last of all seems the most sweeping. It is an error, wrote Pius IX, to argue that "the Roman Pontiff can, and ought to, reconcile himself, and come to terms with progress, liberalism and modern civilization." The *Syllabus* is, of course, a negative statement in that it condemns errors. Leo XIII's *Rerum Novarum* is a critique of the misuse of private property *and,* like Pius XI's supplementary encyclical, an argument for practical Christianity in the social world. In summing up his predecessor's social doctrine (on the fortieth anniversary of the promulgation of the doctrine), Pius XI wrote that Leo had

sought no help from either Liberalism or Socialism, for the one had proved that it was utterly unable to solve the social problem aright, and the other, proposing a remedy far worse than the evil itself, would have plunged human society into greater dangers.[2] *Dem Libs have no lasting core values.*

The fortieth anniversary of *Rerum Novarum* came only one month after the Spanish liberals and socialists had joined forces to expel Alfonso XIII and to prepare for the establishment of the second Spanish Republic, a republic whose constitution seemed almost to be negatively based upon Pius IX's *Syllabus,* for the constitution affirmed almost every one of the doctrines condemned by the nineteenth-century pontiff. *Quadregismo Anno* was not the Vatican's only response to the establishment of the Spanish Republic. On June 3, 1933, Pius XI sent forth *Dilectissima Nobis,* in which the Republic was accused of animosity toward the Church, an animosity based upon a hatred "of the Lord and His Christ. . . ." The Republic was warned that separation of Church and State is a "serious error" and a "particularly repugnant" error in Spain "where the Church has always and rightly held the most important and most beneficially active part in legislation, in schools, and in all other private and public institutions." Other aims of the Republic were also denounced in this encyclical.[3]

It is clear then that, when the generals and their supporters among the Spanish civilian population revolted in July of 1936, the Catholic hierarchy in Spain had good reasons for supporting them, and except for the Basque clergy the Spanish prelates were, indeed, with the rebels. In the holocaust that ensued, the clergy suffered greatly. Hugh Thomas, the most generally reliable historian of the Spanish Civil War, gives the following estimate of clerical dead: bishops, 12; priests, 5,255; nuns, 283; monks, 2,492; novices, 249. Afflicted by these losses, Pius XI, in an address to the Spanish Nationalists who sought refuge in Italy, denounced the Communists for their "truly Satanic hatred against God and against humanity redeemed by Him. . . ." An even fiercer attack was contained in the encyclical against Communism, *Divini Redemptoris* (March 28, 1937):

Every vestige of the Christian religion was eradicated [in Spain]. The fury of Communism has not confined itself to the indiscriminate slaughter of bishops, of thousands of priests and religious of both sexes; it searches out . . . those who have been devoting their lives to the welfare of the working classes.

The leaders of the Spanish Republic had tried to build a nation on the "bases of liberalism and laicism." Now their Republic crumbled "as everything must crumble that is not grounded on the one corner stone which is Christ Jesus. . . ." The general indictment by the Pope was substantiated by a Pastoral Letter from the Spanish Bishops. Because the America Press and The National Catholic Welfare Conference published these papal and episcopal statements in pamphlet form, American Catholics had available to them ample evidence and ample theoretical justification for defending General Franco's movement from a Catholic point of view. By and large, *they did not do so.*[4]

The bellicose attacks on Spanish liberalism and on the democratic tendencies of the Republic came mostly from foreign Catholics writing in American journals. The mere publication of foreign denunciations of Spanish liberalism could be taken as indicative of *the* American Catholic position—if American Catholics had not so often insisted on the

liberalism and the democracy of the *Movimiento Nacional.*
As a matter of fact, it is difficult to find American Catholics
attacking Spanish liberalism. Wilfrid Parsons, editor of
Columbia, denounced "pseudo-liberals" as "strictly non-
rational animal[s] without any power of thinking." He implied that *true* liberals, in Spain and in America, would
sympathize with General Franco. Benjamin Masse asked
"Christian liberals" to help the Church defend "the ideals
of . . . democracy." Most American Catholic spokesmen for
Franco seemed to agree, as I shall demonstrate in the section
of this chapter entitled "Lionel Washington and His
Friends", that Franco's movement saved Spanish democracy
from Communism and anarchism.[5]

The major exceptions to this generalization are Francis
X. Talbot, Francis X. Connolly, and Joseph F. Thorning (of
the clerics), and William P. Carney and Owen McGuire (of
the laity). Although Carney, a reporter for the *New York
Times,* reached the largest audience (his dispatches were
reprinted, or quoted, in *The Catholic Mind, Catholic
Digest, The Brooklyn Tablet, New World, Our Sunday
Visitor,* and other Catholic publications), Talbot, Connolly,
and Thorning were the most forceful condemners of liberalism at home and abroad.[6]

Talbot dismissed as a "hiss of hate" the Open Letter
written by American Protestants in reply to the Pastoral
Letter of the Spanish Bishops: "American liberals who care
nothing about Spain . . . have seized on the Joint Letter of
the Spanish Bishops as a pretext for a renewed attack on
Catholicism. . . . These Christian liberals are always Catholic
baiters." Talbot was among the handful of Americans who
wrote for *Spain,* a magazine published by the Nationalists'
Burgos government.[7]

Another contributor to *Spain,* Francis X. Connolly, defended Franco in *America* and in *The Franciscan.* He also

contributed a preface to the *Labor Charter for New Spain,*
one of the few documents to provide accurate information
on the nature of the *Nuevo Estado.* (The thirteenth article
of the charter is typical: "The Syndicalist Organization of
the State will be inspired by the principles of Unity, Totality
and Hierarchy. All the economic elements will be joined
together in vertical Syndicates formed according to branches
of production or service. . . . The hierarchies of the Syndicates will necessarily be formed of militant members of the
Traditionalist Spanish Phalanx Party.") Still another contributor to *Spain,* Joseph F. Thorning, was (and still is) the
most prolific and vehement of the American defenders of the
New Spain as a *Catholic* State. In Spain he found a paradise
based on the papal encyclicals. Franco told him that

both employers and employes will receive a share of the fruits
of industrial production. . . . Our corporatism will be indigenous,
domestic, Spanish. . . . Spain guarantees complete religious liberty, as opposed to mere religious toleration, to all who believe
in God.

Even here, however, Thorning prefers to let Franco speak
for himself. (The same technique—quotation and republication of speeches—can be seen in William Carney's *New
York Times Magazine* article, "Franco Tells What He Plans
to Do for Spain," and in William F. Montavon's pamphlet,
Insurrection in Spain.)[8]

Owen McGuire was quite unrepresentative when, in his
own voice, he praised the New Spain in Edenic terms.
McGuire found "peace, plenty, prosperity, normalcy, gaiety,
and contentment . . ." but these praises leave one unsure of
the political and social principles under which the New
Spain was governed. It is mainly from foreign Catholics
writing in American periodicals that we learn of the actual
goals of the Nationalists, and only from José María Gil
Robles, the former leader of *Acción Católica,* that we can

derive a nearly accurate picture of the Nationalists' ideology. It is useful to turn to the writings of foreign Catholics.[9]

Aileen O'Brien, an Irish girl, became famous by publishing articles in *America, Catholic Digest, Commonweal, The Sign,* and other Catholic journals. She described General Franco's Spain as a peaceful land where all the classes labored together in harmony and justice, where the soldiers were consecrated to Christ the King. She dramatized her convictions about the *Nuevo Estado* in several short stories. In one of them, an unknown private "with . . . aristocratic hands" reads Aristotle between forays. A corporal dedicated to this same crusade carries a manuscript on Santa Teresa as he goes to his death in battle. Aileen O'Brien's compatriot, Bernard Wall, was even more outspoken about the failure of the Republic and about the need for a "radicalism of the Right" based on the social encyclicals. Paul McGuire, an Australian, was confident that the New Order would resemble that of neighboring Portugal, that the new welfare state would be characterized by mercy and justice: "Franco has adopted a policy of conciliation, bygones are allowed to be bygones, unless they are too gross to be ignored." In *America, Catholic Digest, Columbia,* and *The Sign,* McGuire sang the praises of the *Nuevo Estado.*

The Sign also carried Catherine de Hueck, a Hollander, who entitled her piece, "The Spirit of New Spain." Describing the fields where "picturesque peasants worked hard at threshing mounds of golden grain" and "children, brown and dark-eyed, stopped their singing and playing to gaze in admiration at our big car," she seems to have discovered in Spain another flowering of the Golden Age. She was assured that "all the Moors love Christ, for they say He was a great Prophet." Her last impression of Spain was that "the Mother of God was bending over bleeding Spain." Catherine de Hueck, however, failed to reach the rhetorical heights of Nena Belmonte, a Spanish Marquesa, who rhapsodized the

New Spain in *America, Catholic Digest, The Catholic Mind, Commonweal, The Sign, Today,* and even *Current History.* Her *Commonweal* article is the most illuminating. She described charity for all the needy, education for all children, free clothing for "all children and adults who are in need," maternity homes to assure "a strong, healthy race," and an end to domestic bitterness.

The new Spain does not recognize class differences. All the people are closely united in serving the welfare of the country. . . . The new State does not admit the class struggle. Youths of all classes are united as never before in the great work of building a prosperous and free Spain.

To my knowledge, no American Catholic commentator on Nationalist Spain ever reached such heights as these.[10]

These articles by foreign Catholics were, for the most part, descriptive of life in Nationalist Spain. There was little said about the political and social theories of the *Nuevo Estado.* Most of what *was* said about political and social theory was said by the Burgos Government itself, through the agency of its Peninsular Press Service. This organization published the Duchesse de la Rochefoucauld's *Spanish Women,* Manuel Torres' *The Social Work of the New Spanish State,* and the *Labor Charter for New Spain.*

The best articles on what was actually happening in Nationalist Spain were written by José María Gil Robles. These articles, printed in *America,* and reprinted as a pamphlet, do provide a broad theoretical justification for the revolt against liberal democracy. Gil Robles defended the New Spain as an "organic," rather than a liberal, democracy. He argued that, as head of *Acción Católica,* he had advocated control of government through constitutional means, by democratic education, by "giving an organic structure to Spanish society." He divided the needs of Spain into four categories: *(a)* The Strengthening of Authority, *(b)* An Organic Concept of Democracy, *(c)* Disappearance of the Class Struggle, *(d)* National Unity and Regional Variety (a variety that did, however, include the regional autonomy the Republic had granted the Basques and Catalans). This program of Gil Robles' was very like Mussolini's Corporate State, but Gil Robles seems to have been honest in his desire to further the religious ideals of Catholicism. His Organic Democracy was not the flight-from-reason of Fascism. It is also worth noting that Gil Robles' moderate views were put forth from exile in Portugal. Spanish Fascism had already moved beyond the program of Catholic Action.[11]

This then is the situation: the journals of the Catholic Church in the United States and the publishers of Catholic books (Bruce; Sheed & Ward; etc.) were not, it seems, very much interested in the theories of Spanish Fascism and only slightly more interested in the theories of Spanish Catholicism. (It is ironic that Pemartín Sanjuan's *¿Que es "Lo Nuevo"? Consideraciones sobre el Momento Español Presente* was reprinted, in part, by the Republican government as a portion of its anti-Franco propaganda.) What little was said, in America, about the nature of the *Nuevo Estado* was said mainly by foreigners writing in, or quoted by, the American Catholic press. Our own Catholic press developed a pro-Franco argument based mainly on condemnations of the Republic as "Red Communism" *and* on an alleged similarity between the *Movimiento Nacional* and the classic movements of liberal democracy.[12]

Martyrdom and Conversion

Rather than attempting to discuss here the hundreds of American Catholics who saw the Loyalists as "diabolical, blood-crazed enemies of God," I shall turn to *literary* conventions. In this way, a few pages of testimony can suggest the intensity of the emotional response, and the paucity of ideological commitment, to the Rebel cause. (Since the poems and stories of European Catholics reprinted in American magazines are almost indistinguishable from the poems and stories of Americans, they are included in this discussion.)[13]

Two conventions, two archetypes, predominate: conversion and martyrdom. These two archetypes are apt. They are the traditional archetypes of the saints' tales, and they give the experience, symbolically, of Jesus and his disciples. The resemblance was not missed by Catholic writers. As an Irish Catholic noted,

The Government [of the Republic], like Pilate, yielded to the demand of the mob and delivered the priests to them to suffer like their Master the tortures and pains of Calvary, including, in many cases, actual crucifixion. Men . . . sunk to the lowest depths of human passion and degradation, cried out once more for the blood of Christ and His priests.

Numerous references, in other authors, make the same point.[14]

The number of plays, poems, and stories dealing with these archetypes is very large. In Ruth Burdin's play, *Incident*, the heroine is a radical pyromaniac named "The Flame" who accepts Catholicism and saves the priest and the church she was about to destroy. In stories by other writers, we find the same rather simple pattern. Brutal pilots of the Loyalist air force return from an air raid that killed eighty children in Nationalist Spain. They discover, in the arms of a statue of the Virgin, a dead girl and her dead child. The destruction wrought by General Franco's bombers causes them to realize the monstrosity of their own actions. They repent and baptize the baby. In another story, a priest, disguised as a Republican militiaman, is caught while performing a secret Mass. Fortunately, his discoverer—a ferocious terrorist named "El Matador Rojo"—converts to Catholicism, confesses his sins, and "covers" the priest's escape "towards Franco and safety." Still another story combines the themes of conversion and martyrdom. Padre Bernardo del Rey is murdered at Mass, but the murderer repents, tells his bloodthirsty fellows that they have killed a saint, and suffers martyrdom himself.[15]

Nuns were, in other literary works, forced to dance in cabarets or to seek shelter in brothels, but the attempted escapes were usually unsuccessful. Martyrdom was nearly always the inevitable end for the nuns. "Maria's Grand Finale" is an American Catholic's story of a concert singer turned nun. When the feral Reds break into her hospital in Spain, Maria sings them into an amiable mood, but the exertion is too great. Out of practice, she sinks to her death. In another story, Sister Teresa is killed without even this moment of triumph. The unrepentant Reds loot her convent. Her fate was not worse than that of priests in stories by American and by foreign Catholics. In El Paso's *Revista Católica*, Rogelio Pérez Olivarez wrote of the heroic death of a priest about whose head the setting sun threw "an immortal golden crown of glory." In Jerome Maher's " 'Unimpeachable Sources,' " a saintly priest and a harmless professor are vilely assassinated while a British news commentator continues to broadcast contemptible distortions. In another story, Father Brennan is axed to death by a mob of renegade Catholics (of "puny muscles") and university, or "Left Club," intellectuals. His assassins include a "rabid no-Popery man and Bible-thumper."[16]

In one of the many poems on the martyrdom of Spanish nuns, we are told that the "murdered nuns . . . cry out: how long?" There is no answer: "The Roman soldiers, just like Negrín's, had no eye/To see the crime committed on God's Being." Crucified Spain itself was the theme of Hugh de Blacam's "For the Spanish Martyrs" and of Herman Benedict's "Song for Spain." Another American Catholic poet, Leonard Feeney, called upon an unusual trinity to witness Spain's martyrdom: "O God! O Christ! O Franco!"[17]

As this summary of mine doubtless suggests, the literary merit of these productions was not high. Even a great poet, the French Catholic Paul Claudel, wrote a very bad poem, "To the Spanish Martyrs," in which he compared the Spanish Republicans to Henry VIII, Nero, Diocletian, Robespierre, Lenin, Calvin, Voltaire, Renan, Marx, Judas Iscariot, and other miscreants. Nevertheless, it would not do to imply that no good book has ever been written from the point of view of the Right—Stefan Andres' novel, *Wir Sind Utopia,* written long after the war, is an extremely moving statement of conversion and martyrdom; José María Gironella's celebrated novel, *The Cypresses Believe in God,* is a fair statement of both sides by a Spaniard who accepts the *Nuevo Estado.* Michel Del Castillo's *The Disinherited* is a better one by an expatriated Spaniard.

Finally, it must be admitted that the literature of the Right is crippled by the lack of any book as good as several written from the point of view of the Left (where, of course, books could be written as badly as on the Right). One reason for the inferiority and the stereotyped simplicity of the Right's literature can be seen in four lines by Sister Mary St. Virginia, an American who spoke for many American Catholics when she admitted that the political and social aspects of the struggle were beyond her:

> I know but little of the ultimate reason
> Which is besieging this bewildered Spain,
> But simple truths are clear in any season:
> Christ was away and has come back again—

Too many writers (on both sides) were convinced that simple truths were available, a point of view that does not lead to a very complex art.[18]

On the other hand, an awareness of the complexity of the Spanish Civil War led many American Catholics to agonized indecision. They were caught in a desperate dilemma: they wanted, at one and the same time, to affirm their Catholicism and also to affirm their loyalty to the liberal democratic tradition in America. Before turning to these more sophisticated Catholics, it is necessary to show the degree to which Catholics *did* adopt the rhetoric of the liberal tradition in America.

Lionel Washington and His Friends

Imagine, suggested Reverend M. D. Forrest, an America ruled by the Soviet Union through a puppet-president named "Trickster." Imagine then a "Popular, Lawful, Praiseworthy Revolt" led by a certain Lionel Washington. Having foxed his reader into accepting these *données*, Forrest then unbags his cat:

Trickster & Co. represent the Spanish gang that took the reins of government in February, 1936, while Lionel Washington stands for the brave, chivalrous, patriotic Francisco Franco. . . . Any democratic, liberty-loving American who cherishes the memory of George Washington must, with equal or greater reason, admire and praise General Franco.

Bernard Grimley was another who compared General Franco to General Washington, and John E. Kelly went even further: "Blasted by propaganda such as General Washington never dreamed of, Franco stands forth serene, victorious, deserving of high place in any category of human greatness." William Walsh, writing in the Burgos Government's *Spain,* contended that General Washington would have understood and sympathized with General Franco and the "other 'rebels' who have prevented the complete subversion of Spain by the

Jacobin spirit of Soviet Communism." He went on: "The 'Rebels' of Franco, like the Rebels of Valley Forge, represent the aspirations of a people, aspirations long since reduced to principles by the oldest democracy in Europe. The obligation of the framers of the Declaration of Independence to Spanish tradition has often been demonstrated." When the priests and laity of the Catholic Church in America answered the Protestant's Open Letter (itself written in response to the Spanish Bishops' Pastoral Letter), they went even further in stressing the similarity of the *Movimiento Nacional* and the war for American independence:

The principles for which the Spanish bishops stand are the principles common to all humanity. They are the principles enunciated by George Washington and the founders of the American Republic and embodied in our democratic laws and institutions: the freedom to worship God in peace, freedom to dedicate one's children according to the dictates of one's conscience, freedom from the interference and tyranny of foreign states and alien agitators.

It is interesting that, in this most important of American Catholic statements, it is George Washington—the general and the man of action—who is credited with the enunciation of American principles. Neither Jefferson nor Madison nor Hamilton are cited.[19]

Reverend Joseph B. Code, a prolific supporter of General Franco, emphasized both the American analogues for the New State and the democratic basis upon which it was allegedly erected. With some justice, Code denounced Fernando de los Ríos, Spanish ambassador to the United States, as another propagandizing Citizen Genêt. Mr. Code explained the atrocious anticlericalism of the Spaniards as the work of a few who did their work unhindered because "the lesson of Christian nonresistance and obedience to authority . . . had developed in the faithful a spirit of passivity."

Code condemned radicalism of all sorts and concluded his pamphlet with a fervent plea for liberal democracy and the Dies Committee. Since atheistic Communism, according to Code, attacks "religious and civic liberties in the United States" by denying "to the Spanish people liberty of conscience and other *inalienable rights*," Catholics should rouse other Americans to the "pressing need [for] a congressional investigation of . . . radical groups."[20]

Code was but one of the many to stress liberty of conscience and other inalienable rights. Fulton J. Sheen defended General Franco by quoting from the Declaration of Independence. He went further: "The truth is that America did not have a greater reason for protesting against the English than the Spaniard had against the Popular Front." Umberto Oliveri, writing in a series prepared by the Spanish Relief Committee of San Francisco, set Thomas Jefferson's theories of democracy against Joseph Stalin's and concurred with Mr. Code that no true democracy would allow religious persecution of the sort practiced by the Spanish Republic. Edward Lodge Curran, leader of the International Catholic Truth Society, praised the rebels for fighting to restore "constitutional and republican government in Spain" and for their dedication to "social justice." Curran saw in "the Spanish struggle of 1936-1937 a replica of our own struggle against British . . . tyranny in 1776. . . ." He went so far as to praise the rebels as leaders of the Spanish proletariat:

The Nationalist Cause is [the] proletarian cause. The Nationalist Cause is for the benefit of the workers and the middle class and the poor. . . . The cause of the Nationalists is the cause of all opposed to the godlessness, the immorality, the tyranny, the brutality, the bigotry, the dictatorship of Communism.

Father Charles E. Coughlin lamented that we had "lived to see the day when one who upholds democracy, the right of private property and the freedom of religion is classified with the Benedict Arnolds of civilization!" Still other writers told their readers that the Rebels fought for "world democracy" or "Christian Democracy." Reverend Joseph F. Thorning, who sometimes wrote as though he approved of Franco's attack on liberalism, informed readers of *Spain* that all "clear-eyed, democratic, liberty-loving citizens" were in favor of maintaining the American embargo against exports to either side.[21]

Of all the books on the Spanish Civil War, F. Theo Rogers' *Spain: A Tragic Journey* was the one most admired by Catholic reviewers. Rogers, who claimed to be the world's leading authority on the Spanish war, argued that Franco was chosen intuitively by the people as their leader in a "democratic uprising against cruel oppression." Although Rogers never saw "an Italian soldier or officer" in Nationalist Spain, he assured us that the "Soviet dictatorship" of the Reds was maintained by "entire regiments of Russians, officered by Russians." In such a state of Red anarchy, says Rogers, "the Washingtons, Franklins, and Lincolns of Republican Spain" prayed for protection and found an answer to their prayers in the person of General Franco. It remained only to assert that the Spanish monarchy had been a model of liberal democracy. This was done by Julio Altabás Yus in a book, published in New Orleans, entitled *The Struggles of Spain:*

The monarchs were constitutionalists, and the people enjoyed absolute liberty to express their opinions; journalists wrote upon any subject they wished; teachers imparted knowledge in the form they approved; politicians criticized with perfect immunity; and there was no institution . . . that hindered or limited free intellectual expression. There was liberty of trade, of labor and of education; liberty of the press and of public assembly; inviolability of the home and of the mails; . . . religious tolerance and personal security.

Other historians have described Spain's *ancien régime* in less sanguine phrases.[22]

Considering these rather ingenuous references to Lionel Washington and his followers, and the inadequate development of the Catholic defense of the *Movimiento,* we are faced with a problem in explanation. Did the hierarchy actually believe that General Franco was bringing liberal democracy to Spain? The Caudillo's own statements make this hard to believe. Were these men, on the other hand, cynically weaving propaganda nets? Although they were, to be sure, striving to place their case in the best possible light, it is hard to believe that the hierarchy was, by and large, insincere in its arguments. Here then is the dilemma. The key to the dilemma is, apparently, found in the situation of an authoritarian church in an open society.

The Catholic Dilemma

The whole effort of many members of the Church to accommodate themselves to American society, an effort that can be traced back to men like Isaac Hecker, Bishop Ireland, and Cardinal Gibbons (to name only three), seemed, in the era of the New Deal, about to succeed. Americans of Catholic faith found themselves on the winning side politically, voting for a well-descended, Harvard-educated Episcopalian backed by James Farley and Cardinal Mundelein. Catholics found themselves reaching positions of political power; they had, in the 1930's, an importance they had never enjoyed in any other administration. Surely Woodrow Wilson's two terms were, ethnically and religiously, a world away, and the humiliation of Alfred E. Smith's defeat could be forgotten, for a little while, in the pride over Ambassador Kennedy's appearance at the Court of St. James and in the economic gains of the New Deal.

Then, during the Spanish Civil War, Catholics found themselves once again in the minority, the only large group to oppose the will of the dominant Protestant stock. One suspects that the failure to discuss the principles of the *Nuevo Estado* was, at least partly, based upon an unwillingness to admit that the unbridgeable gap seemed to be opening once again. The clergy's effort to gloss over the situation and to explain it away seems not so much an effort to deceive the Protestant opposition (or the Catholic laity) as to persuade *itself* of the compatibility of the two worlds.

Evidence for this interpretation is at hand, for there *were* Catholics—men and women quite unlike Code and Thorning—who were willing to admit that the Spanish Church had not done all it could have done. Even the Reverend Wilfrid Parsons, who was to become one of Franco's most voluble supporters, admitted in the early days of the war that the Church had indeed contributed to the cataclysm. The great tragedy of Spain, wrote Parsons, was that the working classes, made desperate by destitution and injustice, had apostatized from the Church: "They got to hate the Church because they hated the friends of the Church, who exploited them and whom the Church did nothing to rebuke or correct." Had the Church listened to Leo XIII, "the poor would today be fighting on The Church's side, instead of against it." Similarly, *Catholic World*—the magazine founded by Father Hecker—seemed for a short time to waver between two views. The editors found certain difficulties in the position of the Spanish hierarchy. They were especially troubled by the devout but fiercely anti-Franco Basques:

Were not the pages of Catholic magazines given over rather often to rhapsodies about the beautiful and wonderful faith of the Basques? How comes it then that they fight side by side with Communists and atheists? . . . Of all the unreasonable and impossible explanations the most unsatisfying is that a handful of agitators came to Madrid from Moscow and . . . won over a population of a million good Catholics. . . . What were the priests doing . . . while the agents of Moscow were selling atheism to the people? There was something wrong in Spain.

As the propaganda war grew hotter, the editorials of *Catholic World* grew more perplexed. They asked why so many Spaniards had "joined hands to repel with fierce and bloody zeal the insurgents under Franco, engaged we are told in a holy crusade to rout atheism and Communism and anarchy? . . . Franco's slow progress . . . seems to indicate that a considerable percentage of the people . . . have remained lukewarm or even hostile to his crusade on their behalf." Articles by doubters, however, gave way to articles by the convinced. Perplexity over the war gave way to a conviction of the rightness of the Spanish Nationalists. F. Theo Rogers' book, *Spain: A Tragic Journey,* was praised as the confirmation of General Franco's point of view: "This war . . . is a war [on the part of the Left] against religion, especially against the Catholic Church." Articles by Robert Sencourt and by Gertrude Godden—two fanatically pro-Franco Britons—began to appear in *Catholic World.* Father Joseph McSorley was permitted to dismiss, one after another, eminent European Catholics who testified against General Franco. Jacques Maritain, Georges Bernanos, Antonio Ruiz Vilaplana—such men found Franco's crusade less Christian than they had anticipated, but McSorley felt that Bernanos could not be trusted, that Ruiz Vilaplana's *Burgos Justice* failed to justify its publication, and that Maritain was gullible; McSorley gave to Joseph B. Code the praises he denied to these "misguided" accounts.[23]

Commonweal, a lay magazine with liberal tendencies, took European witnesses much more seriously than did McSorley. On March 5, 1937, Barbara Carter discussed "European Catholics and Spain." The following month, in

"Some Reflections on Spain," George Shuster noted that the Pope had asked for Catholic neutrality, that Miguel de Unamuno had renounced the Right before his death, that the Spanish people *had* fallen from the Faith, and that the Church could not be too closely linked to the "apostles of violence." An interview with Jacques Maritain touched off a prolonged controversy, which turned into a denominational Donnybrook when, on June 24, 1938, the editors of *Commonweal* formally announced a policy of neutrality on the Spanish war:

One government . . . has instigated, or at least permitted, the murder of priests, nuns and lay people. . . . Its alliance with Russia implies some . . . degree of identification with the evils of the Soviet regime. . . . The second government . . . repeatedly and despite protests from the Holy Father, destroys defenseless civilians, particularly by its air raids upon cities. . . . Many of its leaders give utterance to totalitarian views. . . . Its alliance with the Fascist and Nazi nations implicates it to some . . . extent in the evils of those regimes.

This was a long way from the pro-Franco position taken in October of 1936. The editors were not, however, unanimous. Michael Williams was outraged. He had organized a huge, fiscally disastrous, pro-Franco pageant in Madison Square Garden and had carried on, in *Commonweal,* a bitter campaign against the "lies" of the secular and the Protestant press. Faced by this change in *Commonweal*'s position, he dissented vigorously and urged Americans to support General Franco's opposition to an "anti-God revolution." He offered, as authorities, the Spanish hierarchy, whose "definite, objective testimony" came from "men whose sacred responsibility was higher than that of any other group of Spanish leaders."[24]

Williams' disavowal of *Commonweal's* shift was mild compared to *America*'s disgust. Francis X. Talbot had already denounced editor George Shuster for his "Some Reflections on Spain" and informed Shuster of his own erudition. (Said Talbot, "My head is stuffed as full of Spanish knowledge as the skin of a Malaga grape is full of Spanish juice.") The Jesuit weekly now charged that *Commonweal* had "willed not to consider the Spanish conflict comprehensively." John La Farge compared the editors to Nero. Despite these rebukes and despite outraged letters (". . . the Spanish war is a revolt of the God-loving people against a government of oppression inspired and financed by Moscow and its Arch Devil Stalin"), despite the loss of 25 per cent of its subscribers, *Commonweal* held its course. On February 3, 1939, *Commonweal* printed an interview with Jacques Maritain, who condemned Franco's "White Terror" and denied being a Jew or a Mason or a Communist. (He had been accused, because of his stand on Spain, of all three.) Although one reviewer took an unfavorable view of Bernanos' anti-Nationalist description of the Italian conquest of the Balearic Islands, George Shuster himself wrote a strong recommendation of the book for the *New York Herald Tribune* (December 11, 1938).[25]

Only one other Catholic magazine in the United States was neutral on the Spanish war. That other magazine was the small anarchist and pacifist publication, *The Catholic Worker*. Catholic pacifists had become, along with many other Catholics, extremely distressed by the bombing of cities. For many Catholics, General Franco's willingness to utilize the *Luftwaffe* against Madrid, Barcelona, and—most horrifyingly—Guernica, destroyed Franco's claim to moral superiority. Cardinal O'Connell felt that the March 17, 1938, bombing of Barcelona "must have been a military manoeuvre" and Cardinal Hayes found himself unable to believe that Franco would "do such a thing" and Joseph Keating wrote that "we cannot with justice denounce the [bombardment] of military centers . . . however much civilians have to suffer in consequence," but many Catholics drew back in horror. Jacques Maritain stated his position with striking directness: "Christianity will remake itself by Christian means or it will unmake itself altogether." Reprinting articles by Maritain, by Cardinal Verdier of Paris, by Emmanuel Meunier of *L'Esprit,* by Don Luigi Sturzo of the liberal Catholics exiled from Italy, Dorothy Day—editor of *The Catholic Worker*—agreed that violence and Christianity were incompatible:

As long as men trust to the use of force—only a superior, a more savage and brutal force will overcome the enemy. We use his own weapons, and we must make sure our own force is more savage, more bestial than his own.[26]

It seems very clear that the dilemma of the American Catholic was a real one, and that the experiences of magazines like *Catholic World* and *Commonweal* illustrate the problem. It is unfortunate that, unlike English and French magazines, no clerically controlled periodical was able to maintain a neutral position. Only *Commonweal* and *The Catholic Worker* received Nationalist propaganda with enough skepticism to achieve a relative impartiality, and both of these magazines were controlled by the laity. It is also, if one professes a lingering faith in the vitality of the liberal tradition, upsetting to see that neither clergy nor laity could produce a leader to rally the 30 per cent of the Catholics who refused to follow the hierarchy's lead, who actually supported The Republic.

Anne Fremantle published a fine story from the Loyalist point of view, Shaemas O'Sheel supported the Republic by saying that he refused to "identify Franco with Saint Michael"; Kathleen Norris wrote an introduction to a mimeographed pamphlet of letters from Loyalist trenches; Westbrook Pegler condemned air raids ("If I were a Spaniard who had seen Franco's missionary work among the children, I might see him in hell but never in church"). But no leader appeared of the stature of Maritain, Bernanos, Verdier, of Georges Duhamel, François Mauriac, Angel Ossorio y Gallardo, or José Bergamín, and no organization was created as the American counterpart of the French Committee for Civil and Religious Peace in Spain.[27]

Perhaps this is merely another way of saying that American Catholics have not produced a sufficient number of outstanding intellectuals, that Cardinal Gibbons and Isaac Hecker have not been followed by men of equal eminence, that the hidden fears of the hierarchy led to feelings of insecurity and to a shutting off of criticism. Looking back on the Spanish war, one wishes that a more flexible position had been assumed, that *Catholic World* had been able to keep up an unbiased attitude and to become a kind of citadel to which less hysterical elements could have retired. On the other hand, scholars today, speaking with the detachment of the unthreatened, wonder what John Foster Dulles, paragon of Protestantism, was doing in the ranks of General Franco's lawyers. At any rate, it is clear from the current *New York Times* that Reverend Joseph F. Thorning is still defending General Franco's regime. One wonders if John F. Kennedy still disagrees with such defenses and, if he does, what effect this will have on American support for the *Nuevo Estado* and its elderly *Caudillo*.[28]

[handwritten margin note: Dulles' son is a Jesuit.]

[handwritten note at bottom: Why did the Spanish liberals murder so many Catholic priests?? It is politically incorrect in America to be a practicing Catholic.]

4

AMERICAN

"CONSERVATIVES"

AND

THE NUEVO ESTADO

The Temptation of the Bourgeoisie

Conservatism in America seems solidly based on property rights and a belief in a morality derived ultimately (if not directly) from God. This is, at any rate, one reading of Russell Kirk. It is possible to argue that conservatism in America, fixed upon laissez faire economics and lacking the Burkean sense of the past, is very different from European conservatism. Lacking a feudal past, we are all products of the liberal tradition. In other words, it can be maintained—by the dogmatic liberal—that American conservatives are really nothing more than fossilized liberals whose beliefs

53

reveal the skeleton of property rights but not the living ideals of rationality and progress, men so obsessed with liberty (for the property owner and the churchgoer) that they forget all other (and more democratic) ideals.

A study of American magazine and newspaper opinion on the Spanish Civil War suggests that American conservatives *are* a part of the "liberal consensus." Such a study also suggests that the bias toward property is not as strong as some have charged. The magazines and newspapers of the conservative and predominantly Protestant middle class were

Carey Orr: "The Red Hand of Moscow." A conservative view of the Spanish Civil War as a catastrophe in which the Soviet Union is primarily responsible. (Copyright 1936 by Chicago *Tribune.*) (Reproduced by permission of the Chicago *Tribune.*)

strongly tempted to announce their support for the *Cau-dillo,* for many felt that the Nationalists were fighting against a Spanish version of the New Deal and against the forces of atheistic Communism. Nevertheless, although commitments to the sanctity of property and the prerogatives of religion brought American conservatives to the very gates of Franco's camp, they did not enlist in the *Movimiento Nacional.* Other factors, either a commitment to liberal democracy or a deep dislike of Roman Catholicism—or both—kept most conservatives from declaring themselves partisans of General Franco.

Nelson Harding: "Bolshevik Russia's Fire Department." An example of the conservative's interpretation of the Spanish Civil War as a conflagration worsened (if not caused) by the actions of Soviet Russia. (Reproduced by permission of the Washington *Times.*)

But the temptation was real. On July 30, 1936, the *Chicago Tribune* warned that the Republic was "rapidly going into a commune." On August 4, 1936, the *Dallas News* reported that "expropriation of private industrial property" was indicative "of an imminent turn to complete socialization." Conservative newspapers—such as the *Chicago Tribune* and the *Washington Times*—ran cartoons in which the Soviet Union fanned the flames, or watered the seeds, of destruction.

"Imperial Hearst" was convinced that the Nationalists were to be preferred on the basis of their respect for property and for religion. The Hearst publications were, of course, strongly opposed to collectivization. The *New York Journal,* for instance, wrote that news of a

Communist dictatorship in Spain [ordering] confiscation of all religious institutions and buildings, as well as the control of private industry, should surprise no one with intelligence enough to recall the Russian revolution.

The relative weight given by the *Journal,* in this editorial, to the religious issue reflects a constant tendency in the Hearst publications.

The Reds in Spain . . . are putting their victimized country through the fiery flames of revolution. . . . 50,000 killed . . . churches . . . desecrated. . . . Nuns and priests shot down.

Arthur Brisbane, writing in Hearst's *Cosmopolitan,* took the same position:

The so-called rebellion is a protest against the establishment of "Red" government along Russian lines, centered at Madrid; a protest also against the overthrow of religious respect and authority, and especially against the criminal destruction of Spain's most beautiful historical monuments.

(Since the monuments were endangered more by the protest than by the Republican government, this seems an odd argument.) The proclivity of the Hearst papers to emphasize any sort of violence, catastrophe, or depravity ("human interest") makes the papers unconvincing evidence for a conservative rationale for General Franco, but the sentiments are fairly familiar ones. Much the same thing can be said for H. R. Knickerbocker's portrayal of Francisco Franco as kind, brave, austere, suave, anticommunistic, and "heavily-muscled." (*Cosmopolitan* printed Knickerbocker's description when General Franco became "Cosmopolite of the Month" in July of 1937.)[1]

Vincent Astor's magazine, *Today,* was like *Cosmopolitan* in that it ran a number of articles by men and women who supported or sympathized with the Spanish Nationalists, but none of these articles—by Nena Belmonte, H. R. Knickerbocker, Raymond Moley, or Rosie Waldeck—does very much more than assert the heroic quality of General Franco or the demonic aspects of Communist rule. This assertion is, however, enough to place *Today* within the rough category of conservative pro-Nationalists.[2]

Of all pro-Nationalist magazines, *The National Republic,* "A Magazine of Fundamental Americanism," seems closest to the ideal type of a property-conscious, religiously-oriented, Protestant, extremely conservative journal. In September of 1936, *The National Republic* took its stand: Spain had fallen victim to a Communist conspiracy. *The National Republic*'s interpretation was elaborated in a monthly section called "The Enemy within Our Gates." A subtitle suggests the tone of the series: "American Communists and Roosevelt Supporters Send Funds to Spanish Reds" (September, 1936). At this point, the Reds were charged with confiscation of property; the Nationalists were credited with a zeal for true democracy. According to *The National Republic,* those opposed to Communism claimed to want to "set up a democracy and restore church, industrial and personal property to the original owners." The following month, Walter B. Steele

warned that Americans were also in danger of "bloody uprising, confiscation of property and the establishment of a
militant dictatorship." That month's "Enemy Within the
Gates" contained stories of Spanish girls forced into the
front lines. The Rebel cause was the cause of Christianity
and of free enterprise. (The Christianity, however, had to
be of the fundamentalist and not of the "modernist" variety.)

Carey Orr: "Proclamation for World Revolution Bears
Fruit." The tree of world revolution bears "Radical Government, France" and "Communist Government, Spain."
Russian Communism waters the tree. (Reproduced by permission of the Chicago *Tribune*.)

In the June issue of 1938, the Reverend Raymond J. Mc-Williams described his visit to Nationalist Spain. He found "order instead of chaos, people fed and clothed, normality and tranquility instead of shiftlessness and uncertainty." McWilliams' bias is evident in his "investigation" of an atrocity story. Lawrence Fernsworth of the *New York Times* had reported the murder of 3,000 civilians in Teruel. "I made," said McWilliams "careful inquiries about this in Seville, where it was denied as pure fiction. . . . In fact, the Marquis de Larios declared to me: 'On my honor, that is absolutely false.' " McWilliams did not impugn the Marquis.[3]

The position of *The National Republic* was illustrated by cartoons from the *Chicago Tribune* and the *Washington Times,* and by photographs of government vehicles labeled "LENIN" and "POUM" *(Partido Obrero de Unificación Marxista),* the names, we were informed, of two Soviet leaders! Graphic interest declines from this point: the picture of one burning church appears, variously labeled, on September, 1936; October, 1936; February, 1937; June, 1937; and October, 1937.

The American Mercury, a more respectable magazine than *The National Republic,* featured exposés by Fletcher Pratt and by Lawrence Dennis (whose article has already been discussed), but even as *The American Mercury, Cosmopolitan, The National Republic,* and *Today* were lining up on the side of the conservative rebellion in Spain, most of the popular press (periodical and daily) was taking a pro-Loyalist position. Although articles such as Jaime Castellano's "I Lost My Parents in the Spanish Revolution" and Orrin Bell's "I've Stopped Killing for Money" suggest the persistence of "human interest," the mass-circulation journals, after variously worded caveats on the dangers of collectivization, were surprisingly in accord in their opposition to the *Movimiento Nacional.* Despite the merit of certain articles and authors (e.g., Martha Gellhorn's series in *Collier's*), it would be tedious to attempt a discussion of the entire popular press. The general argument of this chapter is better substantiated by a look at the so-called "news magazines" and by a word on the strange career of Ellery Sedgwick.[4]

The *United States News,* lukewarm toward Franco, hotly denounced the Spanish "Reds" for their "reign of terror," which the Republican government was unwilling or unable to check. By August 3, 1936, the magazine joined most newspapers in alarmed commentary on the dangers to American property in Spain. *Newsweek* shared this fear for American interests. After an article providing much inaccurate background, *Newsweek* announced, on August 8, 1936, that "the Soviet had come to the land of Loyola, Cervantes, and Carmen." Two weeks later, Francisco Largo Caballero's "crimson henchmen" controlled Madrid. "They Sovietized major industries. . . . Mobs sacked churches and convents, and massacred priests and nuns." By September 14, 1936, *Time* joined *Newsweek* in denominating the two sides—as General Mola had suggested—"Reds" and "Whites." Two days earlier, *The Literary Digest*—which had been rather less inclined to Franco than these other magazines—had condemned "Red Terror in Spain" and commiserated with Pope Pius: "Nowhere do the horrors of the Spanish civil war strike more heavily than in a palace high among Italy's Alban Hills, where an aging man has grieved to the verge of illness."

Time and *Newsweek* were both ecstatic over the successful resistance of the Rebels in Toledo's Alcázar, but, as more information became available, *Time* became increasingly disenchanted with General Franco's tactics and quite antagonistic toward his German and Italian allies. In this, *Time* resembled—increasingly—the pro-Loyalist *Review of Re-*

views. Newsweek remained sympathetic to the Nationalists for a longer time; as late as November 14, 1936, the magazine castigated Largo Caballero for not surrendering Madrid:

Instead, Spain's might-have-been Lenin launched a grandstand counter attack in which ill-piloted planes and obsolete Russian tanks proved as worthless as the desperate, half-trained anarchist troopers.

As the defense of Madrid began to seem a little less quixotic, General Franco felt himself impelled to bomb Madrid and other cities. This seemed to make a great difference in the attitudes of American journals. During the first ten days of May, 1937, *Time* angrily condemned the bombing of the Basque village of Guernica, *Newsweek* reprinted G. L. Steer's passionate denunciation of the attack, and *United States News* disapproved of the massacre. As the bombings continued, as Hitler's ambitions ripened in Austria and Czechoslovakia, *Newsweek* followed *Time* into a pro-Loyalist position. As *The Literary Digest* put it on June 12, 1937, "To the prospect of a Fascist Europe most liberals prefer to take their chances with a possibly sovietized Spain." By the end of the struggle in Spain, *Time,* which had in its first dispatch referred jauntily to the "obese," "blotchy," "frog-faced" president of the Republic, became eloquent about the "Fall of the City": "White flags began to flutter wanly over the ramparts of Madrid, the last symbol of the Spanish resistance to Fascism."[5]

Although *Time's* sister magazine, *Life,* did not begin publication until the winter of 1936 (when *Time* had already begun to show a change of sentiment), *Life* followed a similar pattern. Whatever sympathies for the Rebels existed ("The Spanish Rebels have at least one virtue that the Socialist Government conspicuously lacks: a love of discipline and order.") vanished before an increasingly pro-

Loyalist policy. Commemorating one year of war on July 12, 1937, *Life* excoriated the Spanish Church and pointed out that the

ruling classes of Spain were probably the world's worst bosses—irresponsible, arrogant, vain, ignorant, shiftless, and incompetent. . . . The reason for the civil war was simply that the people . . . had fired their bosses for flagrant incompetence and the bosses refused to be fired.

By April 3, 1939, *Life* had come to refer to the Spanish Civil War as "an heroically tragic epic."

The pattern we can trace through the popular periodical press was violated—in a very instructive way—by the career of Ellery Sedgwick, the distinguished editor of *The Atlantic Monthly*. The *Atlantic*, like *Harper's*, had—up to the time when Sedgwick threw his editorial bombshell—printed essays by partisans of both sides and, like *Harper's*, shown a distinct bias for the Republic. Then, in June of 1938, Sedgwick "canonized" the least likely Nationalist general (Queipo de Llano, whose obscene broadcasts over Radio Seville disgusted even Falangists) and praised the Spanish Nationalists as members of the great tradition of outlaw justice. Although Sedgwick himself was a member of the "Brahmin" class of New England, he lauded the Nationalists not for their conservatism but for their radicalism, for their ability to break through legal nonsense in order to establish real justice. Of Queipo de Llano, Sedgwick wrote:

Here is a judge who would hold Don Quixote harmless for freeing the galley slaves, and Jean Valjean for stealing the silver candlesticks. . . . Canonized or no, Don Gonzalo Queipo de Llano is ensconced as patron saint of Andalusia, firmly and finally as El Cid Campeador.

He will remain "patron saint" of Andalusia "as long as uninstructed people prefer the irregularities of Robin Hood to the virtues of the excellent Sheriff of Nottingham." This argument, the rising above society's law in order to affirm a higher law, was not one emphasized by American conservatives, but this argument does represent one element of the Protestant tradition. From Sedgwick's point of view, it is possible to place the Spanish Rebels not only in company with such fictional heroes as Don Quixote, Jean Valjean, and Robin Hood but also in a tradition that begins with Luther's breaking from the Church of Rome and proclaiming the priesthood of all believers and culminates with Emerson and Thoreau breaking from that most permissive of sects, the Unitarians.[6]

Sedgwick's view of the Nationalists would surely place them in this tradition of "antilegalism," but Sedgwick seems to have been alone in this interpretation of the Spanish Civil War. Other writers urged that Franco was not really a rebel or that he was justified in his rebellion against "chaos," but no one else had quite this sense of radical Protestantism's affirmation of the higher lawlessness. Sedgwick's reward for having taken this position was a hubbub that began immediately, lasted through his resignation as editor of the *Atlantic,* and was discernible even in his obituary notices of twenty years later. The most interesting and instructive thing about the whole affair is that the bourgeoisie that subscribed to the *Atlantic* refused to accept Sedgwick's view of the Spanish Nationalists. Americans who were unable to believe in General Franco as the bringer of law and order were even less capable of believing in General Queipo de Llano as the voice of quixotic redistribution.

Finance Capitalists for the Republic?

My argument that the great majority of American conservatives were, at best, lukewarm in their support of General Franco's *Movimiento* is borne out by a brief survey of the financial press and by a study of the Gallup Polls. One would expect, if the economic factor were at all important in American opinion on the Spanish war, the financial press to have been strongly pro-Franco. It was not. The financial and business press was, on the whole, even less tempted by the *Movimiento Nacional* than was the popular press. *The Wall Street Journal* remained nonpartisan. The *Journal* feared that the moderate elements in Spain were losing ground to extremists of Right and Left. The *Journal* accepted the American embargo and the Neutrality Act of 1937, but with many reservations about the rights of business. Some of the reservations were expressed on May 1, 1937: "What we do not know is whether [in a hypothetical clash of major powers] we should be willing to pay the price in abandonment of export markets."

Other periodicals were frankly hostile to Franco's *Nuevo Estado*. *Business Week* commented frequently on the economic hopes of the Germans and Italians; *Barron's* and *The Journal of Commerce* denounced the Nationalists for the bombing and shelling of civilian populations. Although *Business Week* approved of American neutrality legislation, *The Commercial and Financial Chronicle,* on January 2, 1937, denounced the projected embargo as quite unjust to the Republic: "In view of the friendly diplomatic relations which are supposed to exist between the United States and the Madrid Government, it is a question whether the Department of State has not violated diplomatic propriety by publicly arraigning a private shipment of arms intended . . . to enable that Government to cope with a formidable rebellion." The strongest opposition to Franco came, however, from the editors of *Fortune*. In a series of six articles published from March through August of 1937 (and then printed as a part of the book, *The Background of War*), the editors castigated the "heirs to the ruins of feudalism in Spain" (i.e., the Church, the Army, the landlords) and declared their sympathies for the Republic: "The issue is presented by the history of the people. Its significance is plain."[7]

The opinions of these periodicals are reflected in the responses of businessmen to polls. Businessmen and "professionals" were *more* strongly pro-Loyalist than skilled workers, unskilled workers, or the unemployed. In the first poll taken, the pro-Loyalist percentages were as follows: businessmen, 31 per cent; professionals, 41 per cent; skilled workers, 27 per cent; unskilled workers, 30 per cent; unemployed, 25 per cent. Although businessmen were slightly more prone to favor the Rebels than were skilled workers, they were less inclined toward them than were unskilled workers or the unemployed. (The percentages are, respectively, 18 per cent, 16 per cent, 20 per cent, 22 per cent.) Subsequent polls indicated that business sympathy for the Republic increased and that business sympathy for the Rebels decreased. Interestingly, there was more pro-Loyalist feeling among Landon supporters than among Roosevelt supporters—the poll of February 3, 1938, showed 51 per cent versus 49 per cent.[8]

One explanation for the faintness of pro-Franco sentiment among businessmen and professionals is that American conservatives are—as I have been arguing in this chapter— still more or less a part of the "liberal consensus" and, as such, they found Franco's Spain ideologically repugnant. (Additional evidence toward this thesis is implicit in the next chapter.) Equally important as an explanation is the so-called "religious issue." In a sentence, differences in religion were more important than differences in income. Of Catholics polled, 39 per cent were for General Franco; of Protestants, 9 per cent; of Jews, 2 per cent. One scarcely need comment that the average income of American Catholics is lower than that of American Protestants and Jews.

The priority of religious over economic motivations is

shown dramatically by the role of the labor unions during the Spanish war. They did not, en bloc, support the Republic; while the predominantly Protestant American Federation of Labor was pro-Loyalist in sympathy and in print, the CIO was badly split. Heywood Broun raged against General Franco and David Dubinsky's largely Jewish ILGWU was solidly pro-Loyalist, but John L. Lewis and Phillip Murray, leaders of predominantly Catholic unions, vetoed any expressed support for the Republic and justified their veto by references to the Catholicism of their followers.

The same dramatic split is evident in the colleges. Traditionally wealthy New England colleges such as Amherst, Bennington, Harvard, Smith, Williams, and Yale showed overwhelming student and faculty support for the Spanish Republic; the Catholic University of America, despite the lower-class (economically speaking) origin of many of its students, showed an equally overwhelming preponderance of student and faculty support for the Spanish Nationalists. With such evidence as this in mind, one is no longer surprised to find, in the journal of the DAR, a lament for the Spanish Republic.[9]

It is very difficult to speak of the personal views of the "finance capitalists" and the great "monopolists" of American industry. As noted above, financial and commercial journals were not pro-Franco. Personal letters, which might show a bias toward Spanish Fascism, are not yet available. The NAM's publications are of no help on this question. Nonetheless, the few bits of evidence available to me indicate that religious affiliation was *at least* as important as any tendency of capitalists to stick together. Although Texaco supplied smuggled oil to General Franco, although a very tenuous connection can be traced between General Franco and the E. I. Du Pont Corporation, it is a fact that Joseph Kennedy—a Roman Catholic—is the only important financier known to have inclinations toward the *Nuevo Estado* and that Bernard Baruch—a Jew—is the only important financier known to have given large sums of money to pro-Loyalist organizations. (Henry Ford's notorious essay, "The Jewish International," was at this time translated into Spanish, but the essay—written in 1920—is surely insufficient evidence for an indictment of Ford as pro-Franco.) Had American investments in Spain been as large proportionally as they were in Batista's Cuba, economic motivations might have played a larger role. As it was, International Telephone and Telegraph—the most important American-owned corporation in Spain—served both sides. Its Madrid headquarters, the Telefonica, became a symbol of the Loyalist resistance to Fascism. Had the possibility of "war profits" been greater, the business community might have—as *The Wall Street Journal* hinted—been less pleased by the American embargo. But such speculations are risky. The evidence suggests that, in the formation of American opinion on the Spanish Civil War, economic considerations played a distinctly secondary role.[10]

As I noted at the beginning of this chapter, American conservatives withstood the temptation of the *Movimiento* because of their commitment to many of the tenets of liberal democracy and because of their dislike of Roman Catholicism. Having shown that the bourgeoisie did, indeed, draw back from the lure of the *Nuevo Estado,* having delayed until Chapter 5 my consideration of the liberal democratic tradition itself, I shall now turn to the rather unpleasant task of tracing the vein of virulent anti-Catholicism that runs through much of the pro-Loyalist argument.

The Black Legend of the Spanish Inquisition

Ralph Henry Gabriel's *Course of American Democratic Thought* attempts to explain the extraordinary hatred of

Catholicism that was so notable a part of the America of
Lyman Beecher and the apostles of Know-Nothingism: "National faith needs an adversary. . . . The ogre of American
democracy was the Scarlet Lady of Babylon." If Catholicism
was the national adversary, there is little doubt that Spain
was the epitome of the hated foe. Stanley T. Williams makes
this admirably clear in the first volume of his *Spanish Background of American Literature:*

Hatred of Spain . . . burned deep and lasting in the minds of
the English colonists of the seventeenth century. . . . They shrank
from the legends concerning the terrible Spaniard: his cruelty
and craft, his alleged barbarism . . . in his colonies, his fanaticism
in his dark religion of the Inquisition. . . . This bitterness
endured.

When Americans won their war for independence and
became a nation, they continued to make of Spain a symbol
for the evils of the Old World. Whatever Washington Irving
and Henry Longfellow did to soften our harsh judgment of
Spanish civilization was more than compensated for by
William Hickling Prescott's histories of the conquests of
Mexico and Peru, by Henry Lea's monumental history of
the Inquisition, and by John Lothrop Motley's vigorously
anti-Spanish *Rise of the Dutch Republic.* It is quite possible
that some of the popular enthusiasm for the "splendid little
war" of 1898 was a manifestation of this anti-Spanish tradition. Considering the long line of Protestants who have
written the great American histories, it is not surprising that
the image of a black Spain should exist. Considering the
facts of Spanish history, the image does not seem entirely
unjust.

Catholic leaders have never been unaware of these antip-
athies, and they did not delay before charging that the supporters of the Loyalist cause were merely prolonging an
ugly tradition of Catholic-baiting. I have already quoted

Father Talbot's charge that "Christian liberals are always Catholic baiters." Joseph B. Code decried the "unwillingness of non-Catholic religious bodies . . . to acknowledge the truth" and asserted that this was evidence of their un-Christian mentality. Cardinal Hayes lamented the "anti-Catholic prejudice here and there throughout the United States," but Cardinal Hayes was not worried: "The Church just turns her head a little, sees who it is, and then goes right on." Anthony Clifford hit back at the "devitalized, pseudo-Christian world" for inveterate anti-Catholicism, and Theophane Maguire threatened Protestantism's "Blind Leaders": "We must know who is friend and who is foe. . . . We think once again of the warning of Christ: 'Those who are not with Me, are against Me.' " Catholic complaints were aimed mostly at the Protestant's Open Letter on Spain. Michael J. Ready characterized this Open Letter as a "harsh and hostile diatribe" and the Knights of Columbus found it brimming with "limping logic, devious phrase-twisting, tricky rhetorical questions, and fake solicitude for democracy." Catholics could have gone to many other places to document their accusations. Although most of the Protestant clergy's response to the Spanish war seems prompted by sincere faith in liberal democracy, part of the Loyalists' support *did* come from feelings of animosity toward Catholicism. The arguments of Protestants often betray a deep-seated dislike of Romanism and a barely concealed delight in the sufferings of the Spanish Church.[11]

Consolation, a magazine published by the Jehovah's Witnesses, was aggressively anti-Catholic. On the occasion of the Nationalists' bombing of the Basque town of Durango, *Consolation* noted, "The pope wants Franco to win, and no doubt secretly chuckled over what happened." The magazine accused the Pope of going "out of his way to bless the Moorish, Italian and German army of Franco the Butcher." *Consolation* further charged that the Pope knew of the

Spanish Civil War "long before it started; for his churches
in Spain were the arsenals . . . and . . . almost all the priests
enlisted with Franco's troops." After the bombing of the
village of Guernica, the editors concluded that the "Papal-
'blessed' planes of Herr Hitler" were instruments of the
devil. This conclusion was illustrated by a cartoon in which
Cardinal Hayes blessed Franco even as Franco's bayonet held
the corpse of a child.

In a like fashion, *The Christian Evangelist,* national
weekly of the Disciples of Christ, denounced the "unholy
alliance" of Catholicism and Fascism in an article entitled
"The Pope and General Franco." Earlier, the magazine had
accused the Church of fighting against "Progress" and of
being a "symbol of everything reactionary, privileged, and
plutocratic." *The Messenger of the Evangelical and Reformed Church* castigated the hierarchy, while *Signs of the
Times* (a "Prophetic Weekly") thought of the Inquisition,
the Auto-da-Fé, Torquemada, and the Spanish Armada,
which cruel Philip dispatched to subdue the Protestantism
of Elizabeth's England. The Church of Rome, according to
this author, can be identified as the "Great Beast" of Reve-
lations.[12]

Such polemics can, perhaps, be discounted as the phi-
lippics of a frenzied group of evangelical sects, but more
sober denominations shared this dislike of Roman Catholicism. *The Lutheran Companion,* for instance, gave its
version of the war in a very stringent editorial. In the

background of the bitter struggle may easily be discovered the
sinister shadow of the Roman Catholic Church. . . . It is the
chief ally of predatory interests. It has kept the common people
in a state of ignorance and superstition, and has contributed . . .
to their poverty.

Still, both the Jehovah's Witnesses and the Augustana Synod
of the Lutherans are thought of as fundamentalists. It might

be argued that other sects were less harsh on the Church. But Hubert Herring, in the Congregationalists' *Advance*, used the rigmarole of the "Black Legend" to describe the situation in Spain. The Republic was "on the rack." The Inquisition had

come to life. New Spain, born in travail and fighting back betrayal, is wrenched and torn by the instruments of a new and more fiendish cruelty. . . . It is democracy which is on the rack, with mediaevalism reincarnated in the fascist guise at the screws.

"Living examples of the mind of the Roman Hierarchy." An example of extreme anti-Catholicism, from cartoons in Protsetant magazines.

This frantic article was accompanied by Helen G. Murray's "Jesu-Cristo in Spain," an account of Miss Murray's adventures in a third-class coach. She had explained to the peasants of the coach that Jesus himself had been a poor carpenter betrayed by the grasping priesthood of a corrupt Judean church. On another occasion, the editor of *Advance* contended that the "struggle in Spain . . . was essentially a struggle of republicanism and democracy against aristocracy and landlords supported by Fascist dictatorship and by the Roman Catholic hierarchy." The Unitarians made *their* pro-Loyalist stands in *The Christian Register* and in *Unity*. In the first magazine, Frederick May Eliot—the leader of American Unitarians—took sharp issue with Cardinal O'Connell. To the Cardinal's defense of the bombing of Barcelona, Eliot answered, "It is a plea which we might expect the military and political leaders of the fascist movement to use." In the same magazine, Norman Hapgood accused the "archaic and inhuman" Church of fighting not for freedom but for a "renewal of slavery." The editorial for October 21, 1937, was an all-out attack on the "immorality" of Roman Catholicism. John Haynes Holmes, the editor of *Unity,* steered that journal in a pro-Loyalist but noninterventionist course. Here, too, the Church was abused. Similarly, S. E. Priestly, in the Universalists' *Christian Leader,* gave a brief history of Spain, in which the Catholic Church was the source of all ills. Priestly's point of view is clearer than his theological terminology: "To doubt or think [in Catholic Spain] was a capital sin."[13]

The attitude of the more rationalistic churches was shared by the Neo-Orthodox. *Radical Religion,* a magazine supported by Paul Tillich and Reinhold Niebuhr, denounced Franklin Roosevelt as afraid of the Catholic vote. The Church was dealt with tersely:

Franco's fascism is, from the standpoint of social justice, just as evil as German Naziism. . . . In other words, not being Catholics, we are not under the necessity of judging all political facts in terms of their relation to the visible church.

Niebuhr himself blasted the Church, especially the primate

of the Church in the United Kingdom, for identifying the sufferings of priests with that of Christ, a practice Niebuhr termed "spiritual arrogance of the worst type." The Church in Spain, he went on, is a "political instrument, and one which is committed to reactionary politics without reservation." *The Christian Century,* the leading interdenominational magazine, referred to the "fascist-clerical insurgents" but insisted that nonintervention was the proper course for the United States. The pro-Loyalist stand of American Protestants is obvious in other nondenominational magazines. Reviewing André Malraux's pro-Republican novel, *L'Espoir,* for *Christendom,* Halford E. Luccock, who had signed pro-Republican statements, now praised the Republic for its resistance to Fascism. The *Protestant Digest,* a less speculative journal edited by pro-Communist Kenneth Leslie, was openly anti-Catholic. The first issue carried four articles on Spain. One of them contained a statement from Angel Ossorio y Gallardo, who wrote of "bishops . . . covered with jewels . . . [who] even employ the Holy Sacraments as a weapon to gain the elections" and of priests "fighting with rifles or machine guns." In an article original to the *Digest,* Tom Davin condemned the Church for "patent blasphemy" and flayed the pro-embargo movement as "pseudo-Catholic." "The greater part of the Spanish Catholic bishops," he wrote, "having abandoned Catholicism for the heresy of fascism, openly support this illegal, unholy attack upon the people and the state of Spain."[14]

H. H. Marlin, who wrote for Pittsburgh's *United Presbyterian,* was unusual. He favored the rebels under Franco: "May God prosper these rebels against the chains and degradation and violence and chaos of the leftists, men without reason or conscience or humanity." *The Presbyterian Tribune* took a very different line against the "dark sinister power of Spanish clericalism":

It is a gross untruth to say that the government now fighting for its life and for the principle of government of the people, by the people and for the people has been hostile to religion as such. It has not been opposed to religion or Christianity or Christ but only to the dark sinister power of Spanish clericalism which has been the traditional friend of the military and the ruthless aristocracy and the inveterate foe of every liberalizing tendency.

In another editorial, entitled "Roman Catholicism and Fascism," this magazine deprecated "Roman spokesmen" for justifying the "slaughter of women and children at Málaga, Guernica, Madrid, Valencia, and Barcelona." "There is a close affinity," wrote the editors, "between the Church of Rome and the totalitarian state, whether the latter is fascist or communist in its form." In still another issue, the editors spoke on behalf of the Spanish people "hungering for light that the Roman Church and an autocratic state had denied for centuries."[15]

George Mecklenburg, in the Methodists' *Christian Advocate,* condemned Franco's persecution of Spanish Protestants as "one of the blackest chapters in the history of the world." Another Methodist magazine, *Zion's Herald,* covered the speeches of the Republic's ambassador and the activities of the various pro-Loyalist agencies. Bishop Francis J. McConnell, a Methodist, was a leader of pro-Loyalist opinion.[16]

In a display of Protestant amity, Baptist leaders, such as Edwin M. Poteat, Jr., joined McConnell in condemnation of Nationalist Spain. John W. Bradbury, in the Baptists' *Watchman-Examiner,* spoke for many of his denomination when he apologized for the Republic's burning of Catholic churches used as "snipers' nests" or as "storehouses of ammunition." Southern Baptists seem to have been more strongly pro-Loyalist and anti-Catholic than Northern Baptists.[17]

It was, however, the Episcopal Church that contributed the greatest number of pro-Republican spokesmen. *The*

Churchman condemned the Romans frequently and praised Bishop Paddock for his work on the board of the North American Committee to Aid Spanish Democracy. The editors went to the verge of threats over the deterioration of Protestant-Catholic relations in the United States. At the same time that Catholics were making false assertions about the Republic's attitude toward religion, Protestants were asked

to be tolerant towards Roman Catholics—as they should be. But have we reached the point . . . where toleration means saying nothing to "offend" a church group which is so loudly vocal in behalf of Hitler's and Mussolini's attempted conquests in Spain?

On another occasion, Samuel Guy Inman, in *The Churchman,* denounced the Catholic hierarchy in the rhetoric of the Reformation: "Out of the terrible bloodshed at present let us hope there will finally come to the land of the Inquisition the liberty wherewith Christ will make Spain free." Guy Emory Shipler, editor of *The Churchman,* joined Bishop Paddock and William B. Spofford, editor of *The Witness,* as a signer of pro-Loyalist and anti-Nationalist statements. *The Chronicle,* still another Episcopal journal, editorialized thusly on the Church in Spain: "The Church, as always, is not so much concerned with liberty as it is with its own power." The Church itself, not the Soviet Union, was responsible for the Spanish tragedy. *The Living Church,* despite a belief that Bishop Paddock should not have meddled in politics, indicated that the Roman Catholic Church in Spain was getting what it deserved, "reaping the whirlwind."[18]

Considering the evidence of American Protestant distrust of Spain and of the Catholic Church, it seems appropriate that the Swedenborgians—the strange sect that played so important a role in the lives of Sampson Reed, Ralph Waldo Emerson, Henry James, Sr., and William Dean Howells—

should have stepped into the ranks of their more pedestrian fellows on the question of the Spanish Civil War. Like most Mormons, Freemasons, and Christian Scientists, Swedenborgians supported the Republic.

Gardner Rea: "Oh well, if the Fascists did it, that's different!" *New Masses* takes an unusual view of institutionalized religion. (Reproduced by permission of *Masses and Mainstream*.)

The final irony came from the desire of the Communist Party—committed to the strategy of the Popular Front—to disguise and to de-emphasize *its* very serious quarrel with the Church and to publish statements by Catholics who supported the Republic. Communist publishers, for instance, issued pamphlets such as *Catholic Evidence on Spain* and *Catholics Speak for Spain,* and *New Masses* carried frequent articles by "good" Catholics. James Hawthorne praised pro-Loyalist Catholics and assured his readers that Communism is closer to Christianity than Fascism is. In August, 1937, *New Masses* declared that "the Spanish people distinguish between religion and clericalism." There were no "irreligious" sentiments in Madrid. When *Commonweal* expressed its doubts about clerical policies, *New Masses* applauded.[19]

Anti-Catholic statements *had* been made by Communists: "The Catholic Church hovers over the whole fascist movement." But such statements were made, for the most part, in the first month of the war, before Soviet policy was determined. Kenneth Fearing's poem, "The Program," sets "Act One" in Barcelona:

> (Scenes by Neville Chamberlain
> costumes, courtesy of Daladier
> Spanish embargo by the U.S. Congress
> music and lighting by Pius XI)

Norman Rosten satirized General Franco as "the man of God, the pope's choice, / voted most likely to succeed." But such sarcasm was relatively rare. Occasional cartoons lampooned the Church, but, for the most part, Communists made backbreaking efforts to draw the line between the hierarchy's evil and the believers' good. Anti-Catholic sentiments were voiced by Protestant journals, by popular magazines such as *Life,* by non-Communists such as H. V. Kaltenborn, who belabored the Catholic Church in Spain as the holder of

about thirty percent of the wealth of Spain. The Church is Spain's chief *entrepreneur*. It is the principal banker, factory owner, mine operator, land owner, educator, and moneylender for the Spanish people. . . . The Church represents, in fact, it *is* the "economic royalist" of Spain. . . . Until 1931 the whole educational system was in the hands of the Church; yet fifty percent of the Spanish population is illiterate.

John Mackey: "Hear No Evil. . . ." *New Masses* satirizes the Church. (Reproduced by permission of *Masses and Mainstream*.)

The Church could be denounced by ex-Communists, like Jef Last, but when George Seldes, a fellow-traveler, wanted to flail the Church in *The Catholic Crisis,* he sought a non-Communist publisher (Julian Messner); International Publishers and the Workers Library Publishers seemed to want no part of his invectives.[20]

Briefly, then, it seems that the Roman Catholic Church was, in part, correct to think that Protestant opinion was often anti-Catholic as well as pro-Loyalist. Although it is going too far to call Protestants "pseudo-Christians" or to complain that all Protestant hearts were filled with hatred for the Church, there was, along with a faith in liberal democracy, too frequently a willingness to attribute *all* of Spain's misfortunes to the Church, to defend the Loyalists against every charge of anticlericalism, to take considerable comfort in the disasters of the Church. Christians were harsher with Christians than Marxists were. After all, *The Presbyterian Tribune* remarked, the disestablishment of the Church made marvelous opportunities for winning the Spanish to evangelicalism.[21]

This is *not* to imply that all the smoldering resentment of the Protestants was directed at a blameless Church. The Church's doctrines are not, after all, compatible with all the traditions of liberal democracy, and the Spanish Church had certainly fallen far short of the standards set by the social encyclicals. The best single sourcebook for understanding Protestant resentment is Pierre van Paassen's bestselling *Days of Our Years.* The contrast between riches and poverty—the contrast that has often dismayed Puritans in Europe—was stated in its most extravagant fashion as Van Paassen described a procession in Seville. The priests carried a "golden-diademed statue of the Virgin which was literally buried under jewels, diamonds, rubies, smaragds and other precious stones," and the priests walked in vestments of gold

under baldachins of purple and damask, swinging censers of
silver and filagree, preceded by banners of silk and jewel-studded
croziers, surrounded by lace-wearing acolytes, train bearers and
boys in violet soutanes carrying glittering boxes containing
relics, followed by a monstrance of [a] value of three million
pesetas. . . . And looking on . . . I had seen the hollow-cheeked,
ragged, barefooted Magdalenes, the disheveled women, the un-
kempt, hungry children, the very flesh and blood of Jesus.

Here, in an image, is the Protestant Reformation.[22]

Paradoxically, then, the "radicalism" of many Americans
who responded intensely to the Spanish Civil War was the
radicalism of the Roundheads who smashed the gilded
brothels of the Great Whore of Babylon. The fiercely anti-
clerical morality of the Spanish Loyalists resembled the
determined sanctity of the Calvinists behind Cromwell. It
seemed, to many Americans, that the Spanish people were
revenging themselves upon the institution that had betrayed them. Many American Protestants seemed ready to
say that the Roman Catholics in Spain had sown a sinful
wind and had reaped a richly deserved whirlwind. This
feeling, joined often to liberal arguments, may not be the
democracy of Thomas Jefferson or the liberalism of John
Stuart Mill, but it certainly resembles the radical egalitarianism of the followers of Winstanley and the rabid anti-
Catholicism of Lyman Beecher and the American Protective
Association. Although the more educated clergy and laity
(especially of the less fundamentalistic sects) seemed sincerely moved by a liberal democratic faith, the same cannot
be said of all who showed antipathy toward Catholicism.
Protestant writers, at times, seemed to feel that the churches
of Barcelona and Madrid had, like the cities of Sodom and
Gomorrah, burned for the glory of God.

5

LIBERALISM

Reason and Progress

Despite the wilder accusations of those who see the 1930's as a "Red Decade" of Communist domination of American life, it is not true that Ruth Benedict, Franz Boas, George Counts, John Dewey, Mark Van Doren, Harry Emerson Fosdick, Robert Lynd, Reinhold Niebuhr, Adam Clayton Powell, John Herman Randall, James T. Shotwell, and Harry F. Ward—all signers of statements in support of the Spanish Republic—were intent upon establishing a Soviet in Morningside Heights. If Newton Arvin, Oliver Larkin, former President Meiklejohn of Amherst, President Neilson of Smith, President Woolley of Mount Holyoke, President Angell of Yale, and Dean Weigle of the Yale Divinity School were, in protesting the stand of the Catholic hierarchy or the bombing of cities, instrumental in founding a Bolshevist community in the Connecticut Valley, it has since gone the way of the Shaker settlements. The statements which these men and women signed affirmed a belief in "the forces of democracy and social progress," "popular government, freedom of worship and separation of Church and State," and "our own traditions of education for democracy." These men and women, and the college presidents, professors,

Protestant bishops and ministers, governors, and Congressmen who signed petitions or worked on committees, were
not acting subversively. Although many of those who interpreted the Spanish war as a struggle for liberal democracy
were to some extent misled about the degree of Russian
influence, the task at hand is the analysis of the myriad interpretations of the war; and the longer one looks, the more
closely one sees that for most of those concerned the Spanish
Republic represented a liberal democratic cause.[1]

Spain, for most of those concerned, symbolized the
brightness of the Enlightenment's vision, or, at least, a
beacon of hope in a continent darkened by increasingly
ominous clouds. It was hard, in the late 1930's, not to see
the Spanish war as an invasion of Spain by Germany and
Italy. It was natural to wonder what nation would be next.
To be quite clear about this, most Americans who supported
the Spanish Republic did not do so because they were
Marxists; they did so because they believed in liberal democracy and were willing to join other anti-Fascists in a
fight for their faith. There are, of course, important exceptions to this generalization: they are the subject of Chapter
6. But the question directly at hand is the extent to which
the partisans of the Republic were members of what Louis
Hartz calls a "liberal community."

Beneath the whole liberal movement there are several
fundamental assumptions, of which the most important are
a belief in a universe where laws are discoverable by human
reason and a belief in progress based on a more and more
complete discovery of those laws. Alexander Hamilton and
Thomas Jefferson agreed on these fundamental assumptions.
The law of nature, wrote Hamilton in "The Farmer Re-
futed," is the source of

. . . the natural rights of mankind: the Supreme Being gave an
existence to man. . . . He endowed him with rational faculties,

by the help of which to discern and pursue such things as were consistent with his duty and interest.

Jefferson, who summed up a world view in his reference to the laws of Nature and of Nature's God, went beyond Hamilton in his faith in man's "rational faculties." "Reason and free inquiry," he wrote in Query XVII of *Notes on Virginia,* "are the only effectual agents against error. . . . Reason and experiment have been indulged, and error has fled before them." The idea of progress became in America, in the phrase of Arthur Ekirch, a "dynamic reality." "No longer only a philosophical theory, but also a demonstrable fact, the idea . . . was delivered . . . into the hands of the people." Questing further for quotations would be tiresome, but George Bancroft's panegyric to progress was surely spoken to a receptive America:

The movement of the species is upward, irresistibly upward. . . . No principle once promulgated has ever been forgotten. . . . The world cannot retrograde; the dark ages cannot return.

It seemed in the 1930's that the dark ages might, after all, return. John Elliott noted that the followers of Franco had turned as "resolutely against progress and the free play of the mind" as men had centuries before when they "devised the Inquisition and the Auto-da-fé." Fascism as a "philosophy" was the apotheosis of unreason, as a way of life it was the denial of rationality, and as a fact of history it was not progress but retrogression. To many, Fascism seemed aptly epitomized in the cry of one-eyed, one-armed General Millán Astray—"Death to Intelligence!" American liberals were not unaware of the implications of Fascism when they supported the Spanish Republic. Frank E. Manuel wrote,

The Republic still represents the belief in the power of reason to order life and a desire to improve the physical and spiritual well-being of the entire people.

Sheldon Jones, an American volunteer, wrote home from Spain that he could not see "any basis for anyone failing to support the Spanish people who has the slightest regard for Democracy and all that it implies of possibility for education, progress, and development." Although Joseph Freeman wrote as a Communist rather than as a liberal, his *Never Call Retreat* illuminates brilliantly the antiliberal aspect of Fascism. Praising General Franco as "the warrior of Christ," Father Koch shouts, "Modern liberalism repudiated the City of God and built its secular city on a quagmire of false reason and false hope. . . . What is wrong with liberalism? Its naive faith in human progress. . . ."[2]

Again and again, the idea of progress is a motivating concept behind the appeals of the men and women who sympathized with the Republic. Algernon Black of the New York Society for Ethical Culture said

The struggle is not merely between democracy and feudalism of the past. It involves our faith in progress, in education, in the method of social reform through pressure groups, trade unions, cooperatives, the ballot and legal, constitutional reform.

In *Survey Graphic*, Beulah Amidon praised the Republic for the "effective disestablishment of the church, the fresh impetus to agrarian reform, the education program which struck at ignorance and superstition"; she condemned the rebellion as a barrier to progress. John Dewey urged, in a letter to *The Christian Century*, that Fascist aggression be blocked by the preservation of "the democratic method of progress." Relatively few people dwelled very long on the "feudalism" of the old order. John Reich decried Spain's "feudal shackles," Hubert Herring denounced the "heritage of feudalism," and Frederick Schuman confounded issues with reference to a "medieval, feudal Fascism," but most articles and letters pointed to monarchical blackness in order to show its contrast to Republican illumination. They stressed what Aron Krich called "the first outposts of the future" and were content to let the rear guard of the past retreat into oblivion.[3]

Education and the Rule of Law

Ideals of rationality and of progress represent liberalism on a very abstract plane; on a slightly less generalized level, the liberal democrat believes, as the quotations of this chapter have already shown, in education and in law, in the enlightenment of all mankind, and in progress within the framework of a constitution and a legal system. The drive toward universal education was surely one of the most important of the great reform movements of nineteenth-century America. The tradition of Franklin and Jefferson, both of whom founded schools, and of Horace Mann and the Lyceum and the Chautauqua is a vital part of the liberal democratic heritage. This tradition was "Hispanicized" under the Republic by men like Fernando de los Ríos, Salvador de Madariaga, and José Castillejo y Duarte; this tradition was jeopardized by the spread of Fascism. American educators showed their loyalty to the Republic and its ideals.

In *Open Letter on Culture and Democracy* educators praised the Republic's efforts to raise the people's educational level. James Minifie praised the Republic's schools for soldiers in the *Journal of Adult Education.* The "Schools in Spanish Trenches" were lauded by *School and Society* and by Nancy Bedford-Jones' pamphlet, *Students under Fire. The American Teacher,* published by Jerome Davis' American Federation of Teachers, provided a forum for Fernando de los Ríos; *Educational Forum* printed G. T. Dilla's discussion of educational progress in Spain. In *Clearing House,* a high-school teacher described, for his fellow educators, a class-room re-enactment of the Spanish Republic's struggle against Fascism. (It was a turbulent drama that included physical assaults on the "dictatorial" teacher.) At Teachers College of Columbia University, the editors of *The Social Frontier* took sides on the war by proclaiming their faith in the Republic. *Hispania,* the professional journal of teachers of Spanish, showed a pro-Republican bias that accorded well with its fight against "Fascist" administrators and school boards. Alma Squires, a teacher of "current events," wrote *What of Spain?* in order to provide her colleagues with an "unbiased" defense of the Spanish Republic. Meanwhile, school children read pro-Loyalist essays in their textbooks, in *Scholastic,* and in *World Youth.* Perhaps the best illustration of the pro-Loyalist stand of most non-Catholic educators is the roster of college and university presidents and deans who signed *one* of the many statements and petitions in favor of the Spanish Republic:

Samuel B. Capen, University of Buffalo
Robert G. Clothier, Rutgers University
Ada L. Comstock, Radcliffe College
Frank Graham, University of North Carolina
Roswell Ham, Mount Holyoke College
Franklin Johnson, Colby College
Robert Leigh, Bennington College
Daniel L. Marsh, Boston University
Irving Maurer, Beloit College
Paul Moody, Middlebury College
William Neilson, Smith College
George Norlin, Colorado University
Marion E. Park, Bryn Mawr College
Walter Scott, Northwestern University
Rufus von Kleinmund, University of Southern California
Mary E. Woolley (Emerita), Mount Holyoke College

Leonard Backer, University of North Carolina
Thomas Benner, University of Illinois
Christian Gauss, Princeton University
F. K. Richtmeyer, Cornell University

A list of college professors who supported the Republic would run for pages.[4]

Meanwhile, in Spain, the front lines zigzagged through the campus of the University of Madrid. For twenty-nine months, battles were fought in buildings erected for the study of philosophy and the advancement of science. Robert Capa and Gerda Taro photographed the men of war in the classrooms, and John Sommerfield, a British volunteer, told *New Republic* readers about the academic battlefield:

I learned a new disgust with war in the unfinished laboratories wrecked by shells . . . I saw delicate scientific instruments crushed under fallen bricks, I saw rain beating in through ruined ceilings upon lecture rooms and libraries, I saw indices and notebooks and specimens strewn among shattered furniture, microscope slides on broken floors, the splintered glass starred like crazy paving.

Reading descriptions such as this, looking at Robert Capa's photographs of cannon mounted on laboratory tables, a scholar may wonder if the devastated university was not itself the most tragic symbol of the Spanish Civil War and, for that matter, of all wars fought in the name of civilization. Most liberals, however, assumed that the destruction of the campus was the responsibility of the enemy, of men who did not share their faith in a "liberal" education. For Dr. Walter B. Cannon, noted Harvard physiologist and Chairman of the Medical Bureau to Aid Spanish Democracy, the ruins themselves symbolized the indestructibility of the ideals of the Republic.[5]

Although men's ideals rarely come as separately as the chapters and sections of the books that analyze them, distinctions must be made. Making distinctions, most liberal democrats defended the Spanish Republic because the Republic seemed to them a legal and a constitutional government. To John Gunther, as good a representative of public opinion as any journalist, the Loyalist government was "legally and democratically elected" by a people "groping toward progress." In the Republic's constitution, Gunther smelled "the pure cool aroma of Jean Jacques Rousseau and Thomas Jefferson." Our ambassador to Spain, Claude Bowers, called himself a "Jeffersonian democrat" and defended the Republic because it was "recognized by every democratic nation as the legal constitutional government."[6]

In order to avoid the assembly of a hundred such quotations, a change in tactics is indicated. Legality and constitutionality are, to some degree at least, actualities within the western democracies. The dream of a *world* at law remains a great unrealized aspiration. International law was evaded or ignored, during the Spanish Civil War, by Germany and by Italy, but the United States could do very little about the behavior of other nations (short of going to war). We were not even members of the League of Nations. We *could*, however, have refrained from becoming ourselves the breakers of international law. To many Americans it seemed that our own government was acting contrary to "universally recognized international law" and contrary to specific treaty stipulations. The allegedly unlawful policy was the neutrality policy that led to the erection of an embargo on the export of arms to Spain. By focusing on the embargo policy, we can see how ideals of legality became inextricably involved in the liberal democratic view of the Spanish war.

The Neutrality Act of 1935, in force when the Spanish Civil War broke out, did not provide legislation applicable to civil wars. The Roosevelt administration asked for a "moral" embargo, but the failure of this policy of persuasion became obvious when, on December 28, 1936, Robert Cuse asked the State Department for licenses to export $2,777,000 worth of aircraft materials. As Cuse's ship, the *Mar Cantábrico,* loaded in New York harbor, the administration hurriedly requested a Joint Resolution in order to stop the shipment. Although many Congressmen joined Maury Maverick, a Democrat from Texas, in condemning the resolution,

John Groth: "Behind Enemy Lines." *The Nation* emphasizes the role of Moors, Italians, and Germans. (Reproduced by permission of *The Nation.*)

only one man in both houses of Congress—Congressman John T. Bernard, a Farmer-Laborite from Minnesota—was willing to vote against the administration's urgent request. The Joint Resolution passed the Senate by a vote of 81-0, the House by a vote of 406-1. The resolution stipulated that it was "unlawful to export arms, ammunition, or implements of war from any place in the United States . . . to Spain or to any foreign country for transshipment to Spain." This embargo resolution, which was reinforced by the Neutrality Act of May 1, 1937, became law with the President's signature, January 8, 1936. (The *Mar Cantábrico*, chased by the Coast Guard to the three-mile limit, sailed for Spain.)[7]

The debate over this embargo—and its meaning—was long and fierce. Charles A. Beard, one of the staunchest advocates of neutrality, was caustic in his denunciation of the embargo. It was a transgression of The Treaty of Madrid and

a slap straight in the face of the Madrid government. The Loyalist government had been and continued to be officially accepted in Washington as the lawful government. . . . The belligerency of the insurgents had not been recognized. Under American theory and practice . . . the Madrid regime was entitled to buy munitions and supplies in the United States.

Vera Micheles Dean and Raymond Leslie Buell, two leaders of the Foreign Policy Association, condemned the Neutrality Acts and the Non-Intervention Committee (set up by the British and the French) as instruments of intervention in Spanish affairs. Stephen and Joan Raushenbush thought that the embargo gave "no evidence of a headlong desire to save a democratically elected government in Spain." James W. Garner wrote, in *The American Journal of International Law*, that certain conditions of the Neutrality Act of 1937 "are revolutionary in the sense that they involve an abandonment of certain traditional principles which the United States has always defended, and a reversal of practices which it has uniformly followed from the beginning of its national existence." In the same journal,

Norman J. Padelford published a series of articles marking the various departures from precedent, the numerous infractions of international law. Allen Dulles was joined by Hamilton Fish Armstrong in arguing that our neutrality policies had resulted in a surrender of what Thomas Jefferson had called "inalienable," and Woodrow Wilson had termed "acknowledged," rights. Dulles and Armstrong condemned the embargo as "an abrupt departure from our traditional practice" and as "an instrument in the hands of the German and Italian totalitarian governments." Edwin Borchard and William P. Lage, who were almost desperate in pleading for an end to Wilsonian diplomacy, were also opposed to the Pittman Resolution (as the Neutrality Act was termed before its passage):

This was thought to be neutrality legislation. In fact, it was the precise opposite. International law required [that] the United States . . . treat the elected and recognized government of Spain as the lawful government.[8]

The dispute over the embargo grew intensely heated when Henry L. Stimson, who had been Hoover's secretary of state, entered the fray. In a letter to the *New York Times,* he appealed for an end to the embargo. He developed the legal argument at length and with passion, and concluded by announcing that the "prestige and safety" of the United States was not to be "promoted by abandoning its self-respecting traditions, in order to avoid the hostility of reckless violators of international law." Martin Conboy replied with an erudite argument to which was appended a strongly worded conclusion:

Our preferences, either as to Spain or as to the world at large, may be poles apart, but when it comes to endangering deliberately the peace of the United States over the quarrels of other peoples the solid good sense of the American people is certain to prevail.

This statement was answered by Charles C. Burlingham and Philip C. Jessup in a communication that was in turn answered by Conboy. Burlingham and Jessup contended that the embargo had become, because of Germany and Italy's open intervention, an instrument of aggression and not an implement of neutrality. They urged a "return to our historic policy of avoiding intervention in European civil wars."[9]

This had been the stand taken in Congress by Maury Maverick during the debate on the embargo: "This is a reversal of a policy of the United States Government for 150 years. It is a reversal of international law of four centuries." Eventually, Senator Gerald P. Nye, the very symbol of Midwestern isolationism, was to attempt to undo his own policies, to reverse this departure from tradition: "I am not prompted by the interest of either side . . . I am prompted . . . by a desire to right an injustice . . . which reflects upon our country because of the departure from age-old principles." The emphasis is on the past, on tradition, on precedent.[10]

And, in asking for the repeal of the munitions embargo, the college presidents and deans were acting as liberals rather than as angry young radicals. The same thing can be said of most of the other signatories—of writers such as William Faulkner and Robert Benchley, of musicians such as John Alden Carpenter, Aaron Copland, Olin Downes, Morton Gould, Walter Piston, Wallingford Riegger, Roger Sessions, Fabian Sevitzky, and Lawrence Tibbett, of artists, social workers, doctors, lawyers, and housewives. When Guy Emory Shipler and William B. Spofford (and a number of other Protestant clergymen) announced their support of Spain's "democratic and constitutional government," they wrote of "those liberties and those human rights which the people of America claimed and established for themselves in 1776," and when analogies were sought, most Americans seemed more familiar with the King James Version than with *Das Kapital* or Lenin on imperialism. Barrows Dunham thought of Judas, and Dorothy Thompson called the neutrality legislation the "greatest Pontius Pilate act in history." Their fellow Americans knew what they meant.[11]

In this summary of the liberal view of legality and constitutionality, the opposing views of men like Alfred Bingham, Raymond Moley, and Harold Wright (all of whom thought the American embargo perfectly consonant with American tradition) have been omitted. Nevertheless, it is remarkable how many isolationists and internationalists, Roosevelt supporters and Landon supporters, agreed about the constitutionality of the Spanish Republic and the unwisdom of the embargo against Spain. Although liberal democrats certainly share a respect for law with older and more conservative traditions, they do *not* agree on this question with revolutionary groups. Lewis Mumford based his own opposition to the embargo on much less legalistic grounds: he affirmed the American tradition of opposition "To any fixed and final status, in knowledge, in belief, in doctrine, in the human condition," a tradition of the "universal frontier." Mumford was stressing the progressive aspect of the liberal tradition and warning against a reliance upon the more static aspects. Most liberals, however, chose to follow the pattern cut by John Quincy Adams and Woodrow Wilson. It was not a radical design.[12]

Liberty, Equality, Fraternity

Mumford was right. We trace our national origins back to a band of iconoclasts, and we trace the beginning of our government to a generation of revolutionaries. A concern for law can become obsessive. The scorn heaped by many upon such men as Justice Sutherland was scorn for just such an obsession (which many thought based not on love of law but on love of property buttressed by unfair legislation and propped by unfair interpretations of the law). Although the "Law of the Land" is more often the battle cry than "Liberty, Equality, Fraternity," it is well to remember that laws can be unjust. It is useful to consider the liberal (and even the radical) response to the Spanish Civil War in terms of this classic slogan.

Liberty. The concept of liberty is, after all, at the heart of any *liberal* program, and freedom in the liberal tradition is usually "freedom from." The ideal is that of the free individual. The Spanish war was, in a sense, a war fought to preserve the Spaniard from an authoritarian and established church, from a centralized and unrepresentative state, and from the overwhelming economic power of those whom the state, under the old regime, had favored. The war was fought to preserve the tradition that had flowered in the liberal *Institución Libre de Enseñanza* of Francisco Giner de los Ríos and borne fruit in the Republic of 1931. Liberty was defended by a defense of representative government. (Had not John Stuart Mill written *Representative Government* to show the means by which liberty was to be established and preserved?) American sympathizers of the Republic stressed the republicanism of the Loyalists. Americans were also emphatic on the question of civil liberties. Each group tended to speak most loudly of the liberties it most cherished.

When clergymen of the Baptist, Congregational, Episcopal, Lutheran, Methodist, and Presbyterian faiths signed a declaration in defense of Spain's "liberties and . . . human rights," they specified: "The republic established complete religious freedom in Spain for the first time in the country's history." When fifteen eminent scientists petitioned President Roosevelt to lift the Spanish embargo, they spoke of the advancement of learning: Harold C. Urey and Arthur

Compton—Nobel laureates in chemistry and physics—joined Harlow Shapley of Harvard and a dozen others to maintain that the United States should combat Fascism in Spain and aid "that democratic tradition which has allowed science to advance."[13]

Writers and artists were most interested in freedom of speech, freedom of the press, and—to put the feeling in its most pertinent form—freedom for imaginative creation. "Poets and poetry," wrote Stephen Spender in his introduction to a British anthology of pro-Loyalist poems, "have played a considerable part in the Spanish War, because to many people the struggle of the Republicans has seemed a struggle for the conditions without which the writing and reading of poetry are almost impossible. . . ." Ernest Hemingway spoke for, as well as to, the Congress of American Writers when he denounced the situation of the writer under Fascism: "There is only one form of government that cannot produce good writers, and that system is fascism." The reason given was—in the Age of Stalin—a little too simple: ". . . fascism is a lie told by bullies. A writer who will not lie cannot live or work under fascism." As illustrations for their thesis, Spender and Hemingway had only to point to the roles played by the more famous Spanish artists and writers and musicians: Ramón Sender, Antonio Machado, Rafael Alberti, Pablo Picasso, Joan Miró, Luis Quintanilla, Pablo Casals—they supported the Republic.[14]

The anti-Fascist thesis was further illustrated by the exodus of writers and artists and scientists from Hitler's Germany. The exile of Bertold Brecht, Arthur Koestler, Thomas Mann, Gustav Regler, Ludwig Renn, Ernst Toller, Arnold Schoenberg, Kurt Weill, Lotte Lenya, Walter Gropius, Albert Einstein, and Sigmund Freud suggested —even to the most conservative—that neither art nor science breathes easily in an illiberal atmosphere. The destruction of Madrid's university symbolized, as I have noted, the atti-

tude of Fascism toward science. The murder of the poet
Federico García Lorca symbolized, for William Rose Benét,
William Carlos Williams, and a hundred other poets, the
fate of literature under Franco.[15]

In summary, it can be said that liberal democrats in the
United States saw, in the coming of the Spanish Republic
of 1931, a new birth of freedom; in the rise of Fascism,
liberal democrats saw a threat to freedom in Europe and in
America too. When Fascism threatened the Spanish Republic, such Americans were vehement about their preference
for the Republic.

Equality. The impulse toward freedom, of which artistic
and intellectual freedom is but one example, is represented
by the first part of the tripartite slogan of the French Revolution. The liberal tradition in America, with its concern
for the rights of property, has proved less successful in satis-
fying demands for equality than in meeting requests for
individual freedom. (Fraternity has always been a more
marked aspect of the European than of the Anglo-American
tradition of liberal democracy.) Nevertheless, those fighting
in America for a greater share of equality and a nearer approach to fraternity felt that the Spanish Republic was fighting the same good fight.

It seems almost too obvious to mention, but the statement of the Declaration of Independence that "all men are
created equal" has come to mean that females have the same
rights as males—an occurence not duplicated except in countries marked by the liberal tradition (or by the new radical-
isms of the twentieth century). When the Republic came to
Spain, the most "backward" women had their opportunity
to achieve equality. It seemed that women like Constancia
de la Mora and Isabel de Palencia and Margarita Nelken de
Paul were about to inherit the legacy left by Margaret
Fuller, Elizabeth Cady Stanton, Lucretia Mott, and Susan

B. Anthony—to name only those women prominent in the crusade for women's rights. The Republic made women cabinet ministers and even ambassadors. The convent, symbiotic with the cathedral in the unhealthy fen of the European past, was turned into a sanitorium, closed, or burned. Articles such as Sylvia T. Warner's "Spain's Living Daughters" carried the good news to American women. Magazines such as *Equal Rights* (organ of the National Women's Party) and *Independent Woman* (a journal for the career-minded) praised the Republic for its liberal interpretation of women's rights. In *The Womans Press,* Rhoda E. McCulloch, editor, endorsed the Loyalists. It is difficult to assess such factors, but the roles played by Eleanor Roosevelt and Carrie Chapman Catt suggested that feminine leaders in the United States sympathized with their Spanish counterparts and with the Republic.[16]

It is still more difficult to measure the impact of the Spanish war on American Judaism. If Spain under the Bourbons symbolized the domination of the *señorita* by the *dueña,* it also represented the total exclusion of the Jew. The Republic, counteracting the anti-Semitism endemic in Spanish society, won the plaudits of *The American Hebrew* and *The Contemporary Jewish Record.* When the Falangist press took up the Nazi "line" on the "Jewish mentality," American Jews had little trouble choosing between the Republic and the *Movimiento Nacional.* Wilfred Mendelson, a Communist, surely spoke what many American Jews felt. In a letter to his parents, he said that Spain was a "fit arena" for the settlement of the "Jewish question":

Here it was that the Medieval Inquisition drove the Jews from their homes and their livelihoods. Today Jews are returning welcomed by the entire Spanish people to fight the modern Inquisition. . . . I am sure we are fighting in the best Maccabean tradition.

Meyer Levin, whose autobiography begins with a statement of the problem of "being a Jew," went to Spain as he had earlier gone to the Holy Land. He identified almost as strongly with the "Internationals" as he had with the Zionists of Yagur kibbutz. He felt that "the same people [i.e., Fascists] who were backing Franco were paying for the campaign of Arab terror . . . carried out by mercenary infiltrees into Palestine." Another American Jew, Peretz Hirschbein, noted that Hitler's treatment of the non-Aryan was only a more hideous version of the Spanish expulsion of the Jews in 1492. The presence of German armies in Spain gave Jews a chance to even both scores at once. Many Jews took the opportunity to do just that.

J. B. Mayteson, in *The American Hebrew*, estimated that 35,000 Jews had joined the International Brigades; this is absurdly high, but it is probable that, of the 40,000 men who volunteered to fight in Spain, 3,000 were Jews. *Life* magazine estimated that 10 per cent of the American volunteers in Spain were Jews, and quoted William Harvey: "I am a Jew. I know what Hitler is doing to my people." It would be wrong to argue that Jewish volunteers were motivated primarily by a desire to defend the liberal Republic, but Jews did realize that the Republic's attitude was preferable to Franco's and that the spread of Nazi principles was a real danger. Jews wanted to oppose Hitler. Who can blame them?[17]

One other important minority group in America was able to find in the Spanish Civil War a battleground abroad —the Negroes. The abolitionist tradition of Samuel Sewall and Anthony Benezet, and even of Thomas Jefferson, was thwarted by the invention of the cotton gin and the resulting economic importance of slavery, but the whole abolitionist movement and the partial victory, for which Lincoln has become the symbol, surely establish the legal and moral equality of races as a part of the American tradition (if not

yet a part of the American reality). Because members of
the white race were often unwilling to accept this tradition,
many Negroes turned in the 1930's to the Communist Party
to achieve what had obviously not yet been achieved by
Booker T. Washington's acquiescence or by W. E. B. Du
Bois's intransigence, by the "Atlanta Compromise" or by the
NAACP. In the Communist Party, Negroes like Richard
Wright and Langston Hughes and Paul Robeson hoped to
discover equality before the law and, beyond equality, a
feeling of brotherhood.

Fascism represented the extremities of racism. In this
case, because of the attack on Ethiopia, Italy, and not Germany, was the chief culprit. Although at least one American
Negro fretted over the hatred felt toward the Moors (usually
shown in Loyalist posters as very black), many American
Negroes looked upon the Spanish war as a conflict in which
they could fight for the equality liberals were so very slow
to provide. Edward E. Strong, writing in the periodical of
the NAACP, told of his visit to Spain. He found that the
Republic was for "race equality" and against "race superiority theories" and "new ideas of the Nordic Myth." William
Pickens, in the same magazine, wrote, "There is no color
question in Spain. People are just people." When American
writers were polled on Spain, Countee Cullen, Frank
Marshall Davis, Langston Hughes, James Weldon Johnson,
and Richard Wright announced their support for the Republic. Hughes sought equality as a Communist but his
sentiments were shared by many Negroes who never joined
the Party. In "Negroes in Spain," an article appearing in
Volunteer for Liberty, he told the English-speaking volunteers of the International Brigades that Fascism "preaches
the creed of Nordic supremacy and a world for whites alone;
in Spain there is no color prejudice." Hughes visited Republican Spain and wrote a number of poems about his
experiences; in one of them he exclaimed, "Folks over here

don't treat me/Like white folks used to do." Paul Robeson made the same journey, and sang, appropriately, "Ol' Man River" to the men in the trenches.[18]

The men included a number of American Negroes. One of them is reported to have pointed to Messerschmitts overhead and to have remarked, "Lynch law on wings." Salaria Kee, the subject of *A Negro Nurse in Republican Spain,* is credited with the same motivation, to which was added the invasion and overpowering of Ethiopia by Mussolini's troops. A short story by O. H. Hunter tells of a wounded Negro who gave his reasons for volunteering: "I wanted to go to Ethiopia and fight Mussolini. . . . This ain't Ethiopia, but it'll do." James Baldwin, the Negro novelist, has recently recalled that his first publication (age twelve) was a short story about the Spanish Civil War.[19]

James W. Ford, Negro Vice-Presidential candidate of the Communist Party, stressed the aggressions of Italy:

In Spain, just as in Ethiopia, liberty is being menaced . . . by the unbridled aggression of Italy and Germany. . . . A new friendly ally of the Ethopian people will be born with the success of the Spanish people's democratic government.

Ford's statement seems somewhat less convincing than the comment of Walter Garland, another Negro volunteer in Spain:

We can't forget for one minute that the oppression of the Negro is nothing more than a very concrete form, the clearest expression, of fascism. . . . In other words we saw in Spain . . . those who chain us in America to cotton fields and brooms.

Boris Todrin turned such thoughts as these into the "Ballad of Oliver Law," written for an American Negro killed in Spain: "This is the fruit of the lynching tree/Growing in the cotton fields and risen free!" (Law, who became a captain in the Lincoln Battalion, is reported to have reminded a visiting Southern colonel that such status would have been impossible in the then-segregated United States Army.) In another poem, Langston Hughes commented that Harpers Ferry, thanks to Spain, "Is alive with ghosts today,/Immortal raiders/Come again to town."[20]

Edward Strong's article in *Crisis* reminded us of another aspect of equality:

We visited village hovels . . . inferior to the worst of Mississippi shanties. On the other hand . . . we were in villas and mansions owned by the nobility. . . . For sheer gaudiness, extravagance and uselessness these Spanish palaces far exceed anything to be found on New York's Park Avenue, Chicago's North Shore or Boston's Beacon Hill.

Negroes are discriminated against because of race, but they are also the least wealthy Americans. The Spanish Republic seemed, to Negroes and to whites, a "New Deal" for the forgotten man of Spain. This was, however, one of the few articles to make such a point. The suggestion of the injustice of great differences in wealth was not an important part of pro-Loyalist propaganda. As noted above, the wealth of the Church was abominable to Calvinists like Pierre van Paassen rather than to Communists like Earl Browder—or so it seemed. The tradition of radical egalitarianism associated with Jacksonian America was not emphasized in the propaganda of the Popular Front.[21]

Fraternity. The French Revolution's third battle cry is, in a sense, merely the concept of legal equality made into a social or moral ideal—men should be more than equals before the law; they should be brothers. Here, even more than in the area of equality, the Anglo-American tradition has been deficient. Ideals of the "Melting Pot" and the "Brotherhood of Nations" have been opposed by the DAR and the America Firsters. We point proudly to Whitman's "Song of Myself" and to Huck Finn's raft-board decision to stick by

Jim, but we must admit that the ideals of fraternity have been more often praised than lived by.

Feelings of fraternity were manifested, by the pro-Loyalist manifesto-signers and recruits, in the formation of the International Brigades and in the various humanitarian activities called forth by the war.

Alvah Bessie, an American Communist who joined the Lincoln Battalion, described men singing the *Internationale* in six languages:

Watching them there in that whitewashed room of an old Spanish fortress, these men from foreign lands, you knew [that] they were brothers in the only sense in which the word has meaning.

Since the International Brigades *were* international, hundreds of writers discovered in their very formation a symbol of fraternity, and, once again, in order to avoid cataloguing it is useful to turn to literature.[22]

Erich Weinert's famous *"Lied der Internationalen Brigaden"* expressed the meaning of the volunteer army:

> Born in a distant Fatherland,
> We come, and in our hearts is hatred.
> We have not lost our native lands;
> Our home today is here before Madrid!
> Spain's brothers, to the barricade!
> The peasants' and workers' army!
> Forward, International Brigade!
> Hoist the flag of Solidarity!

(In a poem, Weinert celebrated three recruits to this international army—a Chinese from Korea, a Frenchman from Brittany, and a "young Negro from Connecticut.") In one of the better novels of the proletarian movement, William Rollins, Jr., used the image of international comity in time of war. The last chapter of his Spanish Civil War novel, *The Wall of Men,* is a pageant-like affair in which eight

foreigners meet ten other foreigners. They march along together and sing, in Croatian, Czech, English, French, German, Greek, Polish, and Swedish, "The cannon thunder, the
whole earth trembles,/But at Madrid *they shall not pass!"*
The fraternity was also intranational. Meyer Levin imagined a
movie in which men from various strata of society join together in the fight against Fascism:

A classroom in a California university, and a young professor of
economics, with the shouldry build and the open features of a
football hero; the same young economist to be seen later, an
officer in Spain. A chem lab in Seattle, with a student carefully
packing away his apparatus; a seaman's union hall where we
pick up little long-faced Donavan. . . . The little Greek from the
shoe factory in Connecticut, and the Michigan farmer's son who
went through the General Motors sit-in . . . and the Irish-Ameri-
can newspaperman who had the wanderlust and wound up own-
ing an ice-cream factory in Peru. . . .

All join the International Brigades. This statement of diversity and of unity is, to speak mildly, a cliché, but the
diversity of the International Brigades was, after all, a fact
and a symbolic one. Novels by André Malraux and Gustav
Regler are proof that the theme need not be simple-
minded.[23]

This element of fraternity—which we can liken to Walt
Whitman's "adhesiveness"—is surely nothing new to the
American tradition. Max Lerner had something of Whitman's sense of "adhesiveness" when he wrote that the "common man" the world over was discovering that "what ties
him to men like himself in other crisis-democracies is greater
than what ties him to the ruling economic groups in [his]
own country." Writing an elegy for Arnold Reid, who had
been killed in Spain, Joseph Freeman actually compared
Reid to Whitman. Reid had "realized Whitman's dream
of the manly love of comrades." But, in setting common man

against ruling group, Lerner urged division as well as unity.
In praising Arnold Reid for "taking up a rifle," Freeman
implied something more than love of comrades. The feelings
of fraternity were real, but they were based upon animosity.
As they sang the lyrics of Weinert's song, the men of the
International Brigades admitted that their hearts were filled
with hatred. This is something less than Walt Whitman's
ideal. Romain Rolland begged for an affirmation of "the
fraternity of all the suffering," but most anti-Fascists confined their sympathies to one side only. And most Catholics
who grieved for the martyred priests and nuns seemed un-
concerned for those men and women who died beneath
General Franco's bombers. Few men committed to one side
were willing to testify to the humanity of the other side.[24]

This imperfect impulse toward an international fraternity was articulated largely by writers on the Left, but it is
not fundamentally different, as an impulse, from the humanitarianism that is so notable a part of the liberal democratic
tradition. Although the impulse toward humanitarianism
can also be part of the Augustinian consciousness of the
sinfulness of all men, of our common fate as the children of
fallen Adam, the humanitarianism of the liberal tradition
has different origins and different consequences. The Christian churches in Protestant America have followed the
Arminians, Deists, and Unitarians in de-emphasizing the
sovereignty of God and the depravity of man. We have come
to a point whereupon almost every sect is, for all practical
purposes, universalist. All men are capable of salvation, even
worthy of salvation. Universal progress could have no other
goal. We are heirs to Benjamin Franklin in our churches as
well as in our countinghouses. Such "theologians" as Norman Vincent Peale seem content to leave the study of Jonathan Edwards to literary historians and the disclosure of
guilt to Freudian analysts.

As Reinhold Niebuhr and his followers unhappily admit,

we are living in an age of "liberal Christianity." The United States has, moreover, been the country where the humanitarianism of the liberal tradition has been, in a sense, invested with the religious affections once part of the Puritans' attitude toward the Deity. Although prison reforms stem from Beccaria, it was to Jacksonian America that the French government sent Tocqueville and Beaumont to see what could be done about saving even the criminal for the secular utopia. Benjamin Rush and Benjamin Franklin were both important in prison reform, and reform of prisons was only one avenue on the American march toward universal, if this-worldly, salvation.

No wonder, then, that American readers gasped at the sentiments of Roy Campbell, the South African poet who flung himself into General Franco's crusade:

> The Inquisition in six hundred years
> Pumped not a thousandth of the blood and tears
> As, in some twenty, has the world-reforming,
> Free-thinking, Rational, Cathedral-storming
> Humanitarian with his brother love. . . .

Although General Franco's *Movimiento Nacional* stopped short of the genocide that characterizes German Fascism, the Nationalists' acceptance of the concept of total war seemed, to many Americans, a new barbarism and a repudiation of the humanity of men. There were innumerable acts of horror (on both sides), but the one thing that seized the public conscience, the liberal imagination, was the aerial bombardment of cities. It was this, beyond all other things, that seemed to horrify Americans and this, more than anything else, that brought vast numbers of economically and politically conservative Americans to give their names, their time, their money, to the various committees organized to support the Spanish Loyalists or to condemn the Franco regime.[25]

The experience of an American who flew for the Republic is interesting *because* F. G. Tinker, Jr., the airman in question, seemed to care so very little for ideologies. When the war began, he was not sure "which side was fighting for what." After the Nationalists' heroic defense of Toledo's Alcázar, he was "inclined to favor the Rebels. Then came the aerial bombardment of Madrid, and my sympathies swung to the Loyalists." Tinker's change of heart was one shared by many. Early in 1937, the "deliberate bombing of hospitals, playgrounds, orphan asylums, relief stations and breadlines" was condemned by Maxwell Anderson, Brooks Atkinson, Carl Becker, Robert Benchley, Constance Rourke, Carl Sandburg, Louis Untermeyer, William Carlos Williams, and ninety other writers.[26]

American newspapers were slower to react, but the bombing of Guernica shocked many journals into denunciatory editorials. The *New York Times* condemned the raid in what was for the *Times* remarkably strong language:

None of the other atrocities of this sanguinary civil war has been more conclusively attested than this latest example of ruthlessness. . . . Against the terrorism of fire and destruction from the skies were pitted the quiet courage and deep faith of the people and their priests.

The *Times* quoted from G. L. Steer's famous (and inaccurate) account of the bombing. The *Christian Science Monitor* expressed horror at the "deliberate slaughter of civilians," and the *New York Daily News* announced that the "ruthlessness of Franco toward children, even Red children, will make most Americans sick." During the first week of May, 1937, indignant commentaries appeared in other newspapers. The *Baltimore Sun,* the *Boston Morning Globe,* the *Burlington* (North Carolina) *Times,* the *Hartford Courant,* the *New York Herald Tribune,* the *New York Post,* the *Philadelphia Inquirer,* and the *Washington Post* are a few of the papers that spoke out against the massacre at Guernica. Senator Matthew Neely read the *Wheeling Intelligencer's* editorial into the *Congressional Record*:

There has been terror on both sides . . . but nowhere . . . has one read of such fiendish ferocity as that exhibited at Guernica and Durango, with . . . leaden hailstorm, poison gas, and incendiary bombs let loose on the fleeing populace of the peaceful and piously Catholic . . . country. . . . All other issues in Spain have been sloughed away by this Nazi-Moor-Fascist attack on the Basques.

Senator Nye inserted into the *Congressional Record* a letter signed by seventy-six angry protestants. These Americans condemned the raid on Guernica as an atrocity "outside the pale of morality and of civilization." The signers of the letter included seven senators, two governors, seven college presidents, eight Protestant bishops, and such well-known conservative leaders as Alfred M. Landon, Colonel Theodore Roosevelt, of Oyster Bay, and Charles Taft, II. Congressman John H. Coffee, who did not sign the letter, spoke out in Congress against the "unspeakable infamy of . . . slaughter of innocent women and children by bombs dropped mercilessly from German military planes upon the holy city of Guernica." Senator Borah, who *did* sign the letter, joined the attack: "No language can describe the scene at Guernica, and Guernica was not a single instance: it was simply a culmination of a long line of unspeakable atrocities."[27]

The bombardment of Barcelona in the spring of 1938 brought forth new appeals for an end to the indiscriminate slaughter. When Count Ciano, Mussolini's hardened son-in-law, admitted a sense of horror at what was done to the Catalan city, it is no wonder that Secretary of State Cordell Hull made public his own distress. Sumner Welles read an angry statement on behalf of President Roosevelt, thirty-two mayors joined New York's La Guardia in decrying the attacks on cities, and sixty-one Protestant bishops protested once again. Although the *Indianapolis News* and the *Pittsburgh Post-Gazette* justified the raids, the *Washington Post*

Jerry Doyle in the New York *Post,* May 11, 1937. "Here fascism presents to the world its masterpiece. It has hung upon the wall of civilization a painting that will never come down, never fade out of the memories of men. . . ." Senator William E. Borah. The bombardment of Guernica shocks the nation. (Reprinted by permission of the New York *Post,* copyright 1937, New York Post, Inc.)

and most other newspapers wrote angry editorials against them. With Hearst's front-page editorial setting an example, newspapers deprecated the bombings as "brutal mass murder," a "dreadful assault upon helpless noncombatants," "one of the most pitiable and inexcusable spectacles [in] all history," "butchery with bombs," "slaughter of the innocents." The "ghost of General Douhet," wrote the *New York Herald Tribune,* "grows larger and darker and again overshadows Europe."[28]

In quoting editorials and statements of governmental or educational or clerical officials on Guernica and Barcelona, I have deliberately omitted periodicals as far Left as *The Nation, The New Republic,* and *The Progressive,* deliberately avoided references to such men as Morris R. Cohen, Clifton Fadiman, Arthur Garfield Hayes, Horace Kallen, Oswald Garrison Villard (all of whom signed an appeal, *Bombs over Barcelona,* published by the Medical Bureau and North American Committee to Aid Spanish Democracy). The response of Americans to the bombing of cities was not merely a radical's response. The protest of most Americans was the traditional protest against man's inhumanity to man. The humanitarian's indignation against aerial bombardment was felt by the American people—if ever this amorphous entity felt anything.[29]

Having established the extent of the revulsion against targetless bombardment and indiscriminant shelling, we can look at the comments of three of the protestants. Writing to Freda Kirchway in May of 1938, Thomas Wolfe was indignantly ironic about his intention to avail himself of General Franco's recent offers to reopen Spain's tourist trade. He penned a mock letter of inquiry:

I should like, if opportunity presents itself, to visit the various craters and ruined masonries throughout the town of Barcelona, paying particular attention to the subway entrance where a bomb exploded, and where one hundred and twenty-six men, women and children were killed in one economical gesture. I should like . . . to pay a visit of devotion and respect to the Chapel . . . where General Franco's wife and daughter go to offer prayers for the success of the Defender of the Faith.

(As noted in the previous chapter, ironies at the expense of alleged religious faith more often signified non-Communist than they did Communist affiliation.) Lillian Hellman described the results of a German bombardment of Madrid and commented, "Finding the range on a blind woman eating a bowl of soup is a fine job for a man." Dorothy Parker's comment is equally bitter:

There were two little girls who saw their father killed in front of them, and were trying to get past the guards, back to the still crumbling, crashing houses to find their mother. There was a great pile of rubble, and on top of it a broken doll and a dead kitten. It was a good job to get those. They were ruthless enemies to fascism.

It does not debase these comments to remember how much of the sympathy of Americans (and of western Europeans) has gone forth to animals, to the blind, to the orphaned, to the helpless. A stand against bombing in 1938 was no more radical than a stand against nuclear testing is in 1962. It seems quite appropriate that Helen Keller, the century's most renowned symbol of the redemption of the handicapped, should have appeared at a meeting to commemorate the American dead in Spain.[30]

If it is true that the fraternity that led men to join the International Brigades was limited in that brothers in arms fought and killed other men, it is—alas!—also true that much of the humanitarian impulse was an impulse that went forth to the suffering on one side only. The Loyalists bombed cities in Franco's Spain, but few Loyalist supporters protested. Nor, as a rule, did the drive to succor the injured mean medical aid to both sides. Nevertheless, carried to its logical limits, the ideal of fraternity leads to pacifism, to the conviction that universal brotherhood renders warfare intolerable. Subsequent to the disillusionment that followed World War I, pacifism had, especially in England and the United States, become an important aspect of the political scene. The Spanish Civil War was the first crisis for postwar pacifism.

In the early days of the war, C. E. M. Joad, the English philosopher, asked, "What Is Happening in the Peace Movement?" He found that the war was a vexing problem to many pacifists. Bart de Ligt, one of the foremost advocates of Gandhian *Ahimsa*—nonviolent resistance—argued that the Spanish people should have allowed General Franco to assume powers of government and then, by their refusal to cooperate with him, should have annulled these powers. Nevertheless, in a time when even Jawarharlal Nehru backed the Loyalists and journeyed to Barcelona, the appeals of the pacifists were by and large ignored. Many English pacifists abandoned their beliefs, as did Esmond Romilly (Winston Churchill's nephew), and went to war because they felt other values threatened.[31]

Although the peace movement in the United States had never been as strong as in England, there were many Americans who remained unconvinced by the arguments that swayed Romilly. A. J. Muste urged, as had Bart de Ligt, that the Spanish should have adopted a policy of passive resistance, should have let General Franco establish his *Nuevo Estado* and then, if the new government were a failure, they could have refused to tolerate it. This is also the position taken by Alfred Fisk, of the Fellowship of Reconciliation, and by H. Runham Brown in an article entitled "Spain—A Challenge to Pacifism." Like Brown, Jessie Wallace Hughan and John Haynes Holmes were Unitarians and members of the War Resisters League. They sympathized strongly with the Loyalists and attempted to square some kind of support with their pacifist principles. Hughan wrote of defensive wars such as that waged by the Republic, "If war is ever ethically justifiable, this one is justifiable, but in the twentieth century . . . war is doomed to futility." Holmes, despite his support for the medical aspects of the North American Committee to Aid Spanish Democracy, wrote a number of editorials against American involvement in the Spanish struggle. When Norman Thomas urged American aid to the Republic, Holmes tried to win him back to pacifism:

> You and I, Norman, have been through this business before. We stood fast when the Belgians lifted cries as pitiful as those lifted by Spaniards today, and when Paris was beset no less terribly than Madrid. . . . I appeal to you . . . to save the [Socialist] Party and the nation from this madness before it is too late.

But Thomas, as we shall see, would not listen.[32]

William Floyd, editor of *The Arbitrator,* refused even to join the North American Committee. Insisting that medical aid to one side prolonged the war, he remained aloof. When American journals denounced the bombing of Guernica, Floyd demurred from protest and wrote that he was "shocked by the inconsistency of these supporters of war." He argued that rules for war were nonsensical, that war itself, as an institution, entailed the very atrocities that surprised those who were not pacifists. It is, however, clear that Floyd's own feelings were with the Republic rather than with General Franco's *Movimiento.*[33]

The same combination of official neutrality and unofficial side-taking characterizes the writings of American Quakers. Although the Friends Service Committee was impartial in its assistance to the stricken, and *The American Friend* and *Friends' Intelligencer* were fair in their editorials, it is obvious that many of the Friends sympathized with the Republic. Sylvester Jones, journeying through both

Spains, praised Federica Montseny, the anarchist minister, as a woman who was "plain as any Quaker preacher."

Her simple logic, coupled with a mastery of the Castilian tongue, seemed almost magical in its effect. She said that the great objective is human freedom and with it must go human responsibility.

In the consecration to work and the self-abnegation of the Catalans, Jones found hope for a new religion: "Less artificial than Catholicism, more universal than Protestantism, this new religious expression may move on toward a Christlike fellowship which for simplicity of form and integrity of spirit is too little known in the modern world." Similarly, *The Messenger of Peace* condemned the "fascist rebels" and the "church politicians" who had oppressed the Spanish masses. Howard E. Kershner, looking back on Quaker service in modern wars, wrote that he had seen "the iron jaws of a merciless dictatorship closing upon . . . freedom-loving people." Passionately committed as most Quakers are to libertarian and democratic causes, it is remarkable that they were able to succor both sides impartially.[34]

Most Americans of pacifist inclinations were too involved for such impartiality. They chose sides. The weakness of the pacifist movement during the crisis of the Spanish war is not surprising. The American crusade for peace, led by Elihu Burritt and the Quakers, had faded away with the coming of the American Civil War. The same fate befell the movement of the 1930's. During the years between the two wars, thousands of Americans read *The Arbitrator, Fellowship, Peace Action, World Events,* or one of the many Quaker journals. They themselves were pacifists and participated in peace campaigns and joined one or another of a dozen church groups dedicated to the final repudiation of war. But war came. In the words of one student, "The high hopes of the twenties were shattered by the demoniac hap-

penings of the thirties. Churchmen cried 'peace, peace' even
as the paddy fields of Asia and the rivers of Spain ran crimson with blood." They did not—excepting always the Friends
—cry "peace" very much longer. Nevertheless, in abandoning
the cry of "peace," most pacifists chose to support the Spanish Republic rather than the Spanish Nationalists. By supporting the Loyalists, they hoped that, someday, the liberal
democratic tradition might culminate in a world society
characterized by liberty, equality, fraternity—and peace.[35]

In his most famous monograph, *The Heavenly City of
The Eighteenth-Century Philosophers,* Carl Lotus Becker dis-
cusses the Enlightenment's faith in the possibility of rebuild-
ing Augustine's Heavenly City upon terrestrial foundations.
The faith of the *philosophes* in the idea of progress became,
with the technological revolution, the chief dogma of the
nineteenth century. This faith—one basis for a belief in liberal democracy—and the faith in rationality itself, weakened
as it was by Darwin, Marx, and Freud, were threatened by
World War I. Much of the intensity of the support given the
Loyalist government was, therefore, the intensity of fear. In
a decade of world-wide economic crisis, in a time when Nazi
Germany had replaced the Weimar Republic and Fascist
Italy proved the ineffectuality of the League of Nations, the
resistance of the Spanish people did much to give courage to
the liberal democrat. "It seemed," wrote socialist George
Orwell, "the turning of the tide." The Spanish Civil War
seemed a last hope, a last opportunity for an individual to *do*
something in the face of a world gone mad. Most Americans
turned to the Spanish Republic not because it represented
the social revolution but because it seemed the one contemporary instance of a movement toward and not away from
liberal democracy. The Protestant bishops and the college
presidents, the artists and writers and government officials,
the journalists and the citizens dealt with in this chapter

were not, by and large, revolutionaries. They were, in a sense, reactionaries longing for the more hopeful world of an earlier America. The municipal charter of the Heavenly City of the North American Committee to Aid Spanish Democracy was written not by Karl Marx, nor by Michael Bakunin, nor even by Eugene Debs; it was written by our dean of city planners, Benjamin Franklin.[36]

Franklin Roosevelt and the Stalemate of Liberal Policy

All of which raises a perplexing question. If liberal democrats, reinforced by radicals of the Left, sympathized so with the Spanish Republic, why was American foreign policy so hurtful to the cause of the Republic? Why was the Neutrality Act of 1935 supplemented by legislation specifically intended to bar the Republic (along with the Nationalists) from all purchase of arms from the United States? Why, in the face of enormous agitation, did the Administration maintain its policies until after the conclusion of the war? These questions are best answered by turning briefly from political theories to political action, and by turning directly to the man at the helm, Franklin Delano Roosevelt.

One learns as a child that there are many Roosevelts in our history—Theodore, Franklin, and Eleanor, to name only the most prominent. One learns as an older student that there are many Franklin Roosevelts—the ogre-like Machiavellian, the challenger of our liberties, the opportune patrician, the leonine and foxy politician, the democratic leader, the heroic figure who became the eponym of his age. Nevertheless, despite these and a hundred other dissimilar portraits of the "real" Roosevelt, one can contrast Roosevelt's domestic and foreign policies with those of Adolf Hitler, Benito Mussolini, and Joseph Stalin (or even Léon Blum) and see that Roosevelt belongs within the broad tradition of liberal democracy. Assuming this, one can say that the election of 1936 signified a desire on the part of most of the people to amend and to revise, but not to abandon, the general pattern of American political and economic institutions. Few presidents ever enjoyed so decisive a victory at the polls, and few presidents had a legislative branch so dominated by members of their own party. Yet this president, despite his own sympathy for the Spanish Republic, found himself following a policy that injured the Loyalists and greatly abetted the spread of European fascism.[37]

Why? Basically, for these three reasons:

1. American foreign policy has been, traditionally, greatly influenced by British foreign policy.

2. The vast majority of the people had been, in the years before the outbreak of the Spanish Civil War, extremely anxious to avoid further involvements in "European" wars.

3. The hierarchy of the Roman Catholic Church was almost fanatically determined to block any move that could be interpreted as helpful to the Spanish Republic.[38]

Cordell Hull, the secretary of state, was intent upon following the lead of Stanley Baldwin and Neville Chamberlain, successively the prime minister for the Conservative governments of the years of the Spanish Civil War. Long after Anthony Eden refused to condone further "appeasement," Hull believed ardently in the rightness of British policy. "Britain and France," wrote Hull in his memoirs, "had taken the lead in welding all Europe together into a nonintervention committee" and "it would have been *unthinkable* for the United States to take a contrary course." At almost every juncture in the conduct of American diplomacy, Hull consulted the British Foreign Office. Hull, of course, was not the whole department, but Sumner Welles—often quoted *after* the war because of his regrets—was in fundamental agreement with Hull, and their influence was very important. Ambassador Dodd in Berlin warned of Nazi plans and Ambassador Bowers, in or near Spain, wrote remarkably passionate communications in which he begged (the verb is not too strong) the Administration to change its policy, but the pleas of these two ambassadors were less persuasive than the dispatches of Ambassador Bullitt in France and Ambassador Kennedy in the United Kingdom. Although Bullitt was not, despite charges to the contrary, sympathetic to Franco, his arguments reinforced Hull's; Kennedy, a Catholic layman, *was* sympathetic, and he was more than willing to keep Hull (and Roosevelt) informed of the moods of the British.[39]

The State Department was, of course, only one department, but, charged with the conduct of foreign policy, it was the most important department. Its influence was on behalf of close cooperation with the United Kingdom. It is worth noting, in this connection, that the vainly requested dismantling of American neutrality legislation progressed quickly once the United Kingdom realized the intensity of its own jeopardy. It is also worth noting that the closeness of the cooperation does *not* indicate a conspiracy. The United States, as a nation, is linked to Great Britain by bonds too obvious to mention.

As a factor in the formation of our policy in the middle 1930's, the British lead was probably less important than the predominant mood of "isolationism." Although the tradition of aloofness from "European" quarrels is a long one, going back at least as far as Washington's Farewell Address, it is ironic that American involvement in World War I had been followed by a revulsion felt most strongly by the most liberal segments of the population. Walter Millis's *Road to War* was, in a sense, the complement of Ernest Hemingway's *A Farewell to Arms,* and both books were permeated by a mood of disenchantment with Wilsonian diplomacy. Congressional investigations had discovered that enormous profits had been made in the munitions industry during the war, and many Americans seemed convinced that they had been hoodwinked into a useless war fought on behalf of a handful of cynical bankers and munitions manufacturers. The disillusionment was so widespread that 73 per cent of the voters were, according to one poll, in favor of a national referendum as the necessary condition for declarations of war. The Ludlow Amendment, introduced in 1937, provided for just such a referendum. This crusade to legislate neutrality was defeated in the House by a scant twenty-one votes.

When Roosevelt attempted to stem the tide of sentiment in favor of legislated neutrality, he failed. At Chautauqua, on August 14, 1936, he announced that "we are not isolationist except in so far as we seek to isolate ourselves completely from war," and in Chicago, on October 5, 1937, he urged "peace-loving nations" to "quarantine" aggressors by joining in "positive endeavors to preserve peace." Public response was antagonistic. Newspaper opinion, except for such internationalistic newspapers as the *Christian Science Monitor,* the *New York Times,* and the *Washington Post,* remained very much in favor of a rigid maintenance of neutrality legislation. At the height of the embargo controversy, there were newspapers (such as the *Chicago Tribune* and the *St. Louis Post-Dispatch*) that admitted that the embargo had been a mistake and, at the same time, argued that nothing could be done to rectify that mistake. At approximately this time—during the height of the debate over repeal—only 24 per cent of the population favored changes in the Neutrality Act in order to permit the shipment of arms to the Loyalists. Interestingly, the group least inclined to repeal the embargo was the group categorized as "Housewives." Of "Housewives" only 15 per cent were in favor of repeal; of "Professionals" 34 per cent were in favor of repeal. This strongly suggests that a dread of war prevented many people, despite their pro-Loyalist tendencies, from any but the most indirect demonstration of their sympathies. Roosevelt's decision not to follow his own inclinations was the result of his bowing to public opinion. It was an expedient decision.[40]

Ironically, Ernest Hemingway, who spoke for a generation in *A Farewell to Arms,* came to argue, during the Spanish war, that all causes need not be lost and that some words did, after all, having meanings that mattered; ironically, Senator Nye found himself arguing for the reversal of the very policies for which he had been the moving spirit; ironically, Franklin Roosevelt, whose attacks on the "economic royalists" coincided in part with the Nye Committee's lengthy exposé of the "merchants of death" and their "arms profiteering," found himself unable to convince the people that "collective security" was, in the 1930's, the road to peace.

As important as the mood of isolation, perhaps more important, was the political pressure of the Roman Catholic Church. It should not be necessary at this point to indicate that the clergy were remarkably united and remarkably vehement about their opposition to all measures intended to help the Spanish Republic. The pressures were effective.

Harold Ickes, Roosevelt's fiery secretary of the interior, provides a provocative and vivid glimpse of the behind-the-scenes maneuvering. According to his diary, "Speaker Bankhead, Majority Leader Rayburn, and Congressman Ed Taylor had been in to see [Roosevelt, who] said frankly that to raise the embargo would mean the loss of every Catholic vote next fall and that the Democratic members of Congress were jittery about it and didn't want it done." In his diary, Ickes exploded: "This [is] the cat that was actually in the bag, and it is the mangiest, scabbiest cat ever." Rexford Tugwell, another insider, corroborates Ickes' comments: "During the [Spanish] Civil War, the Catholic interest in the United States had influenced policy against the Spanish Republicans; Franklin's compromise then had been hard to explain

to liberals, and he had never really tried [to explain it]."
In his recent study of the various arms embargo acts of the
1930's, Robert A. Divine concludes that Roosevelt "did not
dare endanger the large Catholic vote that was vital to the
Democratic political machine." For this reason, beyond all
others, Roosevelt chose not to lift the Spanish embargo.
The closest student of the problem agrees that Catholic
pressure was extremely important. To the argument that
pro-Franco Catholics would have stuck with Roosevelt
despite their anger at a (hypothetical) lifting of the embargo, Hugh Jones Parry replies, "The point is less what
would have happened than what Democratic strategists
feared would happen; and they feared [the] alienation of
Catholic votes."[41]

Considering then these three factors—and the absence
of any compelling economic motivation—we can answer
the questions raised at the beginning of this section. The
Spanish embargo remained in effect because most Americans
were, despite their pro-Loyalist sympathies, unwilling to
risk another war and because Catholic voters important to
Roosevelt's domestic progress were determined to keep the
embargo until General Franco's ends were accomplished.
When, in addition, we consider that any move to succor
the Republic would have flouted Great Britain and left the
United States with no support other than that of Mexico
and the Soviet Union, we can see why pro-Loyalist agitation
went for nothing and why Roosevelt chose in this situation
not to act upon his own convictions.

All over America liberal democrats became emotionally
and intellectually involved in the Spanish Civil War. At
the same time, many were still bitter over the tragedy of
World War I or fearful of the approach of World War II.
Thousands of Americans found a compromise between de-
sires to aid the Loyalists and fears of possible involvements

abroad. They agitated, and appealed (for an end to the embargo, or, at least, for an end to bombing raids). For many, the ideal compromise was enrollment in the North American Committee to Aid Spanish Democracy. But Eleanor Roosevelt, a lifelong liberal and the most influential woman of her time, lived in the White House and was wife to the President of the United States and, for that very reason, could not taken even this ineffective step.

6

FORWARD

FROM

LIBERALISM

The Organic Society

When, in 1915, Van Wyck Brooks assailed the division of American life between "high brow" and "low brow," between thought and feeling, between Edwards and Franklin, he wrote as a partisan of a society that was an "all-embracing organism." The atomistic society of liberalism was the enemy. Using romanticism's metaphor for wholeness, Brooks maintained that "the more deeply and urgently and organically you feel the pressure of society the more deeply and consciously and fruitfully you feel and you become yourself." For Brooks, the great symbol of American wholeness was Walt Whitman, who attempted through the imagery of the leaves of grass to reconcile the individual and the society, "the simple, separate person" and the "word

Democratic, the word En-Masse." *America's Coming of Age*
was a germinal book. Waldo Frank read Brooks and wrote
The Rediscovery of America, in which he urged an "organic
order" and "the sense of the Whole." Lewis Mumford joined
Brooks and Frank and, in *The Golden Day,* judged American society harshly for its failure, after the Transcendentalists, to create a more "organic and life-fulfilling world."

Although Brooks had pointed to Don Quixote and
Sancho Panza as types of the divided sensibility, Frank
found, in Spain, a truly organic society. In *Virgin Spain,*
Frank used the word "organic" to explain all aspects of
Spanish wholeness: "The Russian dance is analytic, episodic,
realistic. The Spanish dance is organic and essential." Then
came the Spanish Civil War. As admirers of "the profoundly
whole culture of the Spaniard," Brooks and Frank and
Mumford defended the Republic. It was a government under which men could be whole again. It was a model for
the sort of society that must replace the atomistic society
of the United States. Denouncing England and France as
"gelded democracies," Frank wrote of "organic" Spain where
the people read Marx without forgetting San Juan de la
Cruz, Einstein without neglecting Cervantes:

Spain . . . resolutely moves toward the freedom in which she may
create a society with the measure of her genius: the sense of the
whole man, whose feet are rooted in the Spanish soil and whose
head breathes the airs of the world.[1]

Spain's ambassador to the United States, Fernando de
los Ríos, seemed to join Frank in hoping for a whole man
in a unified society. Spain, he said, sought "to form a new
man. A man whose head, heart and hands would be one."
It is almost as though de los Ríos were attempting to com-
bine Crèvecoeur and Emerson, for the first had written
rhapsodically of the American as the new man and the
second had, in the essay on "The American Scholar," urged

the ideal of wholeness in the image of "Man Thinking." In an exaggerated form, this same ideal appears in Kenneth Rexroth's poems on the Spanish Civil War. The soldiers of the Republic are men who sit up

> All night, talking of trout in the Pyrenees,
> Spinoza, old nights full of riot and sherry,
> Women they might have had or almost had,
> Picasso, Velasquez, relativity.[2]

The figure of the scholar in arms is surely not foreign to a society that grew from a band of Cambridge graduates who cleared the forest, held off the Indians, prayed to God, and built Harvard—all at the same time. And Puritans were followed by *philosophes* for whom the dream of wholeness remained a very vivid one. As a Jack-of-all-trades, Benjamin Franklin became our culture-hero; we think of Thomas Jefferson as one of the builders of the Republic *and* as the architect of Monticello, the capitol at Richmond, and the University of Virginia. Nathaniel Hawthorne's attempt to be a writer, a man apart, a man who could spend twelve years cut off from society, was an enterprise that Hawthorne himself had the greatest doubts about. (In "The Custom House," he imagines the scorn of his Puritan forefathers had they known that their wilderness Zion was to produce a narrow specialist, a "writer of story books!") Henry David Thoreau willingly departed, temporarily, to Walden Pond because he wanted to see what it was like to be a whole man and not simply a "horse-man" or a "herds-man."

In other words, Americans in this tradition have not accepted the division of labor that separates one man from another, nor have Americans in general adopted the rigid class distinctions of European society, distinctions that turned men into peasants or clerics but not, so it seemed, into whole human beings. One aspect of our emotional engagement in the Spanish Civil War was this combination of a desire for wholeness in the man (and especially in the man of letters) coupled with this guilt over the supposed isolation of the artist. During the 1930's, faced with world-wide economic catastrophe and the menace of Fascism, writers were even less able to justify their isolation than Hawthorne had been. The social theories of Karl Marx did not create the ideal of the whole man capable of playing any role in the drama of society. Marx merely emphasized—just as Brooks and the organicists emphasized—the moral obligations of man to society. Society, in the 1930's, demanded attention, and critics worried over the moral responsibility of the artist. Sinclair Lewis and Maxwell Perkins chided Hemingway for his involvement in the Spanish war, but most writers and artists seemed to turn to the Spanish Civil War, as Hemingway did, as a way of saving the world and, with the world, themselves. Spain was both a model of the organic society and a "cause" within which one could be whole. The defense of the Spanish Republic was a social act in which divided or alienated Americans could join together. Janet Flanner, *The New Yorker*'s "Genet," noted at first that the "Spanish civil struggle isn't worth wasting ink on," and took pleasure in announcing, satirically, that Miss Spain had become Miss Europe; but she who scorned from Paris eventually made made her pilgrimage to Perpignan to chronicle the tragic exodus of the refugees from the Catalonian sector of Republican Spain.[3]

The Communists sounded the call. Earl Browder told the second American Writers Congress that it was "indisputably true that literature can be created today only by those who are on the side of the people against reaction, fascism and war." Granville Hicks condemned those "who become eunuchs willingly for the sake of the Kingdom of Art." The Party members were joined by others, by Archibald MacLeish, who had recently been among the leaders, so the Stalinists asserted, of "social Fascism" in America.

MacLeish denied that Spain was a "political allegory" or an ideological drama:

> These actors are not actors. They truly die. The cities are not stage sets. They burn with fire. . . . How . . . can we refuse our help to those who fight our battles—to those who truly fight our battles *now—now,* not in some future war—*now:* now in Spain.

Malcolm Cowley told this same Congress that "one of our jobs today is to see that our . . . books aren't used as barricades to stop the fascist bullets." Martha Gellhorn argued that "a man who has given a year of his life . . . to the war in Spain . . . has not lost or wasted time. He is a man who has known where he belonged."

The same theme was heard at this Congress in the words of A. B. Magil:

> When I hear the sniping that is not directed against Franco, but against the People's Front government, and see these people looking, with microscopes, for pimples on the shining face of the Soviet Union, I wonder, am I crazy or what? Is Spain in flames or is it not?

Spain was, assuredly, in flames, and American men of letters felt morally obligated to do something. Mark Twain had managed to avoid most of the American Civil War, Henry James had been incapable of going, and William Dean Howells had gone off to Venice, but the generation of the 1930's seemed determined to follow the example of Walt Whitman, to *do* something. As Mike Gold remarked, his generation was through with "the rancid atmosphere of the Ivory Tower."[4]

Poetry magazine—not often associated with political events —demonstrates this new social awareness. Poems on Spain by Boris Todrin, Sol Funaroff, David Sachs, and Rolfe Humphries, translations from Federico García Lorca, reviews, debates—they show the new sense of political and social obligation. Reviewing the poems of García Lorca, John Wheel-wright insisted that the martyred Spaniard's poems *couldn't* have been written by a Fascist. Theodore Roethke, a poet seldom thought of as political, reviewed *And Spain Sings* (an anthology of Spanish ballads translated by Edna St. Vincent Millay, Dudley Fitts, John Peale Bishop, and other American poets). Roethke praised the poet as a social being: "This is what the poets of Spain as a part of the people of Spain have written while facing the Fascist guns." Spanish writers, many of whom fought in the Republican army, became the subject of almost countless panegyrics. Men like Rafael Alberti, Manuel Altolaguirre, and Ramón Sender received the accolades of European and American intellectuals.[5]

American writers did not confine themselves to applauding their Spanish counterparts. They signed petitions, organized rallies, gave money, journeyed to Spain to see for themselves, and, finally, joined the ranks of the International Brigades. At times, the references to Spain are oblique, as in Gertrude Stein's ambitious book, *Everybody's Autobiography,* or in Wallace Stevens' comment on the "moralist hidalgo" or in Alan Swallow's poem, "Wyoming" ("*It's cold. And there is war in Spain.*"), but few American poets failed to hear, in the Spanish war, a bell that tolled for them. In the phrase that formed the title of a famous pamphlet on the Spanish war, writers took sides.[6]

And painters joined them. Although Thomas Hart Benton and John S. Curry seemed indifferent to the Spanish Civil War, other painters—Peter Blume, Philip Evergood, William Gropper, the Soyers, Max Weber—used their talents to give visual form to their interpretations of the war. Dozens of lesser artists supplemented their efforts. An editorial in *Art Front* announced that Stuart Davis, Max Weber, Hugo Gellert, Art Young, William Steig, and Maurice Becker were attempting to form an American Artists and Writers Ambulance Corps under the Medical Bureau of the

American Friends of Spanish Democracy. The editorial emphasized the call to arms:

Helios Gómez, Spanish artist, is leading a battalion. André Malraux, French novelist, leads an aviation squadron. Ludwig Renn, German novelist, is an officer in the . . . International Brigade. Ralph Fox . . . was recently killed in action.

The title of the editorial is even more informative: "On to Spain." Artists went, and several were, like Paul Block, killed.[7]

Having before them the example of Pablo Picasso, Helios Gómez, and Luis Quintanilla—and the tremendous precedent of Goya's etchings, *Los Desastres de la Guerra*—American artists painted numerous pictures and carved and cast numerous statues on Spanish themes. Judson Briggs went to Spain and exhibited work done there, and Jo Davidson modeled a fine series of busts of Loyalist leaders. The First Annual Membership Exhibition of the American Artists Congress was dedicated to the peoples of Spain and China. When Pablo Picasso denounced General Franco's *Movimiento*, he was seconded by Paul Manship, Rockwell Kent, Yasuo Kuniyoshi, Max Weber, and Stuart Davis, whose statement—coming as it did from a most unpolitical artist— is representative of the temper of the times: "Picasso's public stand for freedom and democracy against Fascism and war should deal the death blow to the unsound argument . . . that the artist has no concern with public affairs."

One further example should be sufficient to suggest the pervasiveness of the artist's impulse toward political engagement. Sidney Hoff, Fred Ellis, A. Birnbaum, Rockwell Kent, John Groth, William Gropper, and Philip Evergood set up posters in Times Square, Union Square, and Columbus Circle—to raise money for *The Nation*'s ship to Spain—and Helen Hokinson's club ladies (in her *New Yorker* cartoons) listened to talks on Spain, refused sherry not imported from

Loyalist territory, and came in for gentle reproof when they betrayed an interest in Spanish fashions rather than in Spanish politics.[8]

Sidney Hoff: "Thanx, Pop. . . ." Cartoonists become politically involved and draw posters for the Spanish Loyalists. (Reproduced by permission of *Masses and Mainstream*.)

Odd but representative was John Steinbeck's response to the *Monterey Herald* when that newspaper telephoned to inform him that the Dies Committee had denounced him for contributions to the Loyalist cause. Recalling that other California celebrities had also contributed money to Spain, Steinbeck answered, "What's good enough for Shirley Temple is good enough for me." Other cinema stars—James Cagney, Paul Muni, Robert Montgomery, Edward G. Robinson, Orson Welles—supported the Loyalists, and *Life* went to a Hollywood party when Mrs. Oscar Hammerstein III raised money for Spanish children.

Angna Enters, Ida Soyer, and Martha Graham choreographed ballets on Spanish themes derived from the events of the civil war, and Henry Cowell wrote the music for Graham's productions. Martha Graham joined Doris Humphrey and Charles Weidman in performing at the Second Annual Dance for Spain. Another dancer, Janet Riesenfeld, went to Madrid and lost her heart to the Spanish Loyalists: "Looking out of the window I could see Madrid in the early morning rain; sodden piles of mortar, skeleton stone buildings gutted by fire, and before the opening markets endless lines of women in black." She decided that she preferred the "actual world" of political commitment to the "realms of pure fancy and intellect."

Meanwhile, Marc Blitzstein and Virgil Thomson wrote the music for *The Spanish Earth,* a documentary film shown—after its premiere at the White House—at pro-Loyalist benefits in Hollywood. Errol Flynn, Dashiel Hammett, Robert Montgomery, and a dozen others saw the film at Frederick March's home. It was shown privately for Joan Crawford and Franchot Tone, for Darryl Zanuck and John Ford. In New York, Benny Goodman and Burgess Meredith appeared at benefits for Spain; in Cambridge, Massachusetts, Leadbelly sang on behalf of the Republic; in Barcelona, Pablo Casals played, and Ione Robinson, an American painter, recorded in her journal the fate of art in wartime: "During the performance the lights went out. We sat in the dark listening to the bombs and not to Casals." It was a time when many people sat in the dark and listened to the bombs and not to Casals.[9]

Today, when political apathy is likely to be construed as artistic dedication, the fervor is difficult to imagine. Perhaps the scope of this study suggests that the engagement of writers and artists (and others) was more than a beating of wings in a net of alien ideologies. Although the mainstream of American life and art has been characterized by separate channels for "high brow" and "low brow," there have always been men like Emerson, Thoreau, and Whitman, like Brooks, Frank, and Mumford, who have sought a mingling of the waters of our national experience, or, to return to the original metaphor, the whole man within the organic society. The crisis of the 1930's seemed to bring their efforts to fruition. If Ivory Towers were inhabited, it must have been—metaphorically speaking—in order to scan the skies for the approach of enemy bombers.

One of the reasons for the attraction of Marxism as an ideology was the failure of Whitman's ideals—"failure" in the sense that Americans have not as a people lived up to them as he had hoped they would. Liberal democracy in America has been characterized by an excess of laissez faire, and the artist has been as free as the businessman to ignore the social dimensions of his métier. As was the case when Americans turned to Marxism for an affirmation of the equality and fraternity they sought, the inroads of socialist thought were made at the weakest sections of the liberal fencing. Even so, the Marxian influence has been much exaggerated. In England, where Stephen Spender wrote the book whose title gives this chapter its name, the impulse to Marxism was not, in the end, as strong as the dedication

to a more democratic kind of socialism derived, like the
Fabian Society itself and like the British Labour Party, from
the tradition of liberal democracy. Agreeing with much of
the Soviet position on Spain, Thomas Mann wrote that
"politics is everybody's business," and W. H. Auden asserted
that "today is the struggle," but when Stalin's purges in
Russia and in Spain became known, the English Left joined
George Orwell in condemnation of the Soviet Union.[10]

And the same is true for most American writers. The
two most noted of the American writers involved in the
Spanish Civil War, Hemingway and Dos Passos, both reacted against the purges in Spain of Stalin's real or imagined
enemies. Both wrote novels infuriating to the Russian camp.
In *For Whom the Bell Tolls,* Hemingway's hero dissociates
himself from a belief in Marxism and portrays André Marty
(the Communist in control of the International Brigades)
as a maniac. In *Adventures of a Young Man,* a book modeled
on actual experiences, Dos Passos dramatized, in the tragic
career of Glenn Spotswood, the betrayal of the Left by the
Soviet Union. Mary McCarthy presented, in *The Company
She Keeps,* the anti-Stalinist's realization that Stalin's ambitions were leading to Spanish repression. Dissatisfied with
much of the liberal tradition, many American writers were
ready to move *forward* from liberalism; they were not prepared to move *backward* to despotism.

Fortunately, few writers were as fanatical as A. B. Magil.
In an essay, Archibald MacLeish maintained that poetry
could *as poetry* do something to halt the march of Fascism:

Poetry alone imagines, and imagining creates, the world that men
can wish to live in and make true. For what is lacking in the
crisis of our time is only this: this image.

This argument, as old as Sidney's *Defense of Poesie,* suggests
that MacLeish was less committed than many to the belief

that the common calling of citizen implied the abandonment of the particular calling of artist. The artist, in other words, becomes a part of the community because of his art, and not because he joins the army.[11]

Lionel Trilling, defending Hemingway from his critics, clarifies the issue:

We can learn to stop pressing the writer with the demand for contemporaneity when we remember . . . that writers have always written directly to and about the troubles of their own time and for and about their contemporaries.[12]

This position of Trilling's is closer to Emerson's conception of the poet and closer to Whitman's idea of the "Divine Literatus" than to theories of "socialist realism." It is not necessary to minimize the role of Marxism in order to direct attention to the social theories of Americans of the "organic" tradition. Perhaps the fairest statement is this one: the Marxists' call to social commitment reinforced the American tradition that has for at least one hundred years stressed the need for the whole man in the whole society. Emerson did not need Marx to see: "Things are in the saddle/And ride mankind."

In a sense, Brooks and Mumford and Frank and the editors of *Art Front* were naive in their optimism. Spain was a long way from the utopia they dreamed of. The divisions of Spanish life were greater, not less, than those of American life. Nevertheless, the Spanish intellectuals were making an effort to reach the masses and the primitive conditions of much of Spain protected the people from many of the divisive strains of more industrialized countries. The very backwardness of Spain made the efforts of the Republic all the more dramatic, and the violence of the war—the boiling over of the cauldron of change—turned the attention of organicists and socialists and anarchists to Spain. The Scandinavian countries evolved peacefully toward the goals urged by those who dreamed of community, but Spain was in flames, and through the flames Americans seemed to watch the enactment of their personal fates.

Anarchism: From Mother Earth to Comunismo Libertario

Before the eighteenth century had run its course, William Godwin had carried the liberal faith in human nature, in reason, and in progress, forward to a theory of philosophical anarchism. Americans were not far behind Godwin in this perception of a world simplified and glorified by the abolition of political coercion. By 1837, John L. O'Sullivan's *United States Magazine and Democratic Review* announced that "the best government is that which governs least." Shortly after, in his essay on "Politics," Emerson carried his faith in self-reliance to its logical conclusion: "To educate the wise man the State exists, and with the appearance of the wise man the State expires. The appearance of character makes the State unnecessary. The wise man is the State." Henry Thoreau took the impulse toward anarchism even further in his essay on "Civil Disobedience":

I heartily accept the motto,—"That government is best which governs least"; and I should like to see it acted up to more rapidly and systematically. Carried out, it finally amounts to this, which also I believe—"That government is best which governs not at all."

Walt Whitman's *Leaves of Grass* contains this argument in four words, "Resist much, obey little."

The Transcendentalists were part of a Romantic tradition of organicism and their anarchistic tendencies are strongly flavored by an impulse toward primitivism. They were not, however, the only men and women to urge an end to political government. From Josiah Warren to Benjamin

Tucker, Americans developed a theory of individualistic anarchism that had roots in Robert Owen and William Godwin rather than in the Over-Soul. In the first issue of *Liberty*, Tucker announced principles he would maintain for twenty-seven stormy years:

Those who have lost their faith in gods only to put it in governments . . . are foes of Liberty still. The Church has become an object of derision; the State must be made equally so. The State is said by some to be a "necessary evil"; it must be made unnecessary.

With the burning of the office of *Liberty* in 1908, Tucker ceased publishing his magazine and individualistic anarchism lost its American center, but Tucker was succeeded by Emma Goldman and Alexander Berkman, promulgators of a communitarian anarchism that accepts the technological advancements of an industrial age. *Liberty* was succeeded by *Mother Earth,* and, in the figures of Nicola Sacco and Bartolomeo Vanzetti, American anarchists received their martyrs.

Meanwhile, in Spain, the violent anarchism of Bakunin and (indirectly) Sorel received institutional support from the *Confederación Nacional del Trabajo,* a very powerful trade union devoted to the establishment of syndicalism through a social rather than a political revolution. When the Spanish Civil War broke out, the Spanish anarchists proceeded, in Catalonia, to establish their new society of *Comunismo Libertario.* As if to symbolize American interest, Emma Goldman —who had in 1910 organized an association based on the educational theories of Francisco Ferrer, the martyred Spanish anarchist—went to Barcelona to work for *Spain and the World* (an anarchist newspaper). She arranged art exhibits, organized committees (on which served Stella Churchill, Havelock Ellis, C. E. M. Joad, George Orwell, John Cowper Powys, Herbert Read, Rebecca West, and Dame Sybil

Thorndike), and wrote for numerous publications. "In spite of all the compromises and frustrations," says one student of Emma Goldman, "Emma had had a real glimpse in Spain of the New World . . . she had worked for decades to bring into being."[13]

Americans at home were quite as excited by Spanish events. David Lawrence (of *Vanguard*, not *United States News*) imagined Sacco and Vanzetti in Spain: "I saw them . . . with muskets on their shoulders." (There were in Spain anarchists who fought as the "Sacco-Vanzetti Column.") Walter Brooks' tribute to the Spanish comrades is representative of the rhetorical extremes of *Man!* ("A Journal of the Anarchist Ideal and Movement"):

Amidst the sombre and abysmal night of reaction spreading its deadly pall over a submissive world of serfs and eunuchs, you have raised the glaring torch of revolt, O Spanish comrades. . . . The old, decrepit and putrid corpse . . . was brought onto new life thru' a process employing the cosmetics and tinsels of newly concocted social doctrines. It was renamed Fascism.

Describing the events in Spain as a "tragic and epochal Odyssey," Brooks announced that "every heroic exploit recorded by history and mythology fades into inconspicuous pettiness in comparison with the inconceivable exploit of the Spanish people." Brooks' enthusiasm makes Marcus Graham's seem like understatement: "The reaction of the people of Spain to the fascist counterrevolutionary attempt shall always stand out as a beacon light to every individual throughout the world struggling for Liberty."[14]

The Industrial Workers, a publication of the IWW, gave its eager support to the Spanish anarcho-syndicalists, reprinted dispatches from CNT publications, and exposed the illegal shipment, by Texaco, of oil to General Franco. (The Department of State, capable of apprehending individual volunteers as they traveled through French towns, was un-

able, apparently, either to spot the tankers or to discover
the article denouncing the shipments.)[15]

Enthusiasm for the social revolution and a watchful eye
upon illegal tankers did not, however, mean the failure to
consider several theories in conflict. The editors of *Man!*
commented that the *Comunismo Libertario* of Catalonia
was not, after all, "the ideal we have often read about in our
literature." For this hesitation, the editors of *Vanguard* had
scorn. *Vanguard* featured an editorial entitled, "Spanish
Revolution from an Ivory Tower."[16]

The most serious theoretical and practical difference concerned participation of anarchists in the Popular Front (a
problem taken up again further along in this chapter). The
CNT had traditionally opposed such participation and had
followed Bakunin and Sorel in scorning socialists who "ca-
pitulated" and joined parliamentary governments. Now
Federica Montseny was in the cabinet and the CNT was co-
operating with the Popular Front. Federica Montseny asserted, "We are still Anarchists as of old and still pursue the
same ideals," but *Man!* was not convinced. The two anarchist publications split on the propriety of this turn of events.
When, during the "May Days" in Barcelona, the Stalinists
("Marxist gangsters in the service of Spanish and International Capitalism") purged the POUM *(Partido Obrero de
Unificación Marxista)* and halted the social revolution and
assassinated the Italian anarchist, Camillo Berneri, *Man!*
felt itself vindicated. Cooperation with the Popular Front
had, indeed, led to tragedy. (Vernon Richards, the noted
English anarchist, came to the same conclusion after his
extended study of the lessons of the Spanish revolution.)[17]

"Senex," writing for *Vanguard,* had to defend that magazine's policy not only against the anarchists writing for *Man!*
but also against the Trotskyites who condemned the POUM
and the CNT for collaboration in the Popular Front.
"Senex" defended *Vanguard*'s position by citing precedents

from the Russian Revolution and by noting that "the es-
thetic delight of high-towered historic observers at the torch
kindled by a martyred generation of workers, camouflages an
essentially defeatest attitude born out of a sterile romanticism." "Senex" was not above observing that the Trotskyites
who had predicted disaster, who had issued dire warnings,
were themselves reduced to a persecuted and insignificant
minority. At times, it seemed that the angriest fighting was
among the radicals of the Left. It seemed sometimes that the
anarchist journals had nothing in common except the com-
muniqués of Emma Goldman.[18]

Most of this debate went unnoticed in the liberal press.
Despite the literary tradition of radical individualism and
despite names as important as Josiah Warren, Benjamin
Tucker, and Emma Goldman, American anarchists have
been a very small segment in the main line of the liberal
tradition. It is clear that the anarchist movement represents
a tendency within the liberal tradition (or, at least, a logical
extension of liberalism), but it is not a tendency that great
numbers of Americans have felt very strongly. Samuel
Polinow and Hippolyte Havel and L. Frank and S. Morrison
are not, after all, important influences in American affairs,
and their anarchist interpretations of the Spanish Civil War
were read by few and assented to by fewer still.

In a sense this is a great pity, for the anarchists' analyses
of the Spanish war were sometimes more informed and
cogent than the liberals' naive comments upon Spain's complete religious freedom and dedication to capitalism. Still,
the general argument of this study is further supported by
this brief look at the anarchist movement. American support
for the Spanish Republic was, in terms of numbers and influence, not a radical cause. This truth becomes, paradoxically, clearest when we look to the thousands of Americans
who rallied behind the "front groups" and the American
Communist Party.

Varieties of Socialist Responses

Communism as Twentieth-Century Americanism. Prior to Georgi Dimitroff's report to the Seventh World Congress of the Communist International, social democrats were threateningly referred to by the Stalinists as "social fascists." The argument was that their non-Stalinist position "objectively" aided Fascism. Then, at the Seventh Congress, Dimitroff laid out the formula for the Popular Front, for the union of all anti-Fascist groups. Opponents of this strategy pointed out that Lenin had opposed the effort to build socialism around trade unions: "The history of all countries," said Lenin, "shows that the laboring-class by itself is able by its own effort to develop only trade-union consciousness. . . ." But Lenin had also said, when a change in policy seemed necessary, that "the development of the proletariat did not and could not, anywhere in the world, proceed by any other road than that of Trade Unions. . . ." Lenin did not balk even at the entry of socialists into parliaments.

Stalin, then, had ample precedent for a change in strategy. Through Dimitroff, he urged that the "only condition for uniting [with] the trade unions is: Struggle against capital, against fascism and for internal trade union democracy." Spain's *Frente Popular* went beyond this position. *Anyone* qualified, including anarchists and Basque Catholics. This was the government the Stalinists defended. Accordingly, the Spanish Civil War was debated, by the Communists as by the Catholics, with the conceptual tools of bourgeois democracy. The Soviet Union stuck, through the whole turbulent history of the Spanish war, to the strategy of the Popular Front.

American Communists followed suit. Early in the war,

Harry Gannes, of the *Daily Worker,* wrote a pamphlet on Spain. His arguments were those of the Popular Front:

Knowing well that they could not defeat or enslave the majority of the Spanish people, who in the ... 1936 elections had thrown out the Lerroux-Robles-Sotelo fascist-monarchist-feudal landlord ruling cliques, the Spanish militarists and fascist reactionaries ... looked for foreign aid to overthrow the constitutionally elected government.

The last three words jarred readers who had been insensitive to the change in Communist policy. The main line of the Stalinist argument was not to be revolutionary, as it had been two years earlier when the Left attempted a revolution against the Republic, but *legal* and *constitutional.* Gannes, who had commemorated the unsuccessful Left revolution of 1934 in *Soviets in Spain* (1935), joined Theodore Repard, another *Daily Worker* correspondent, in writing the most important American book to discuss the Spanish war from the Stalinist point of view. The "economic roots of revolution" were feudal rather than capitalistic. Accordingly, the "democratic government," threatened by Fascism, "could rally around it all those who supported constitutional rule." The Communists rallied. They discovered that the "old alternative of bourgeois republic and proletarian dictatorship did not face the extreme Left . . . when the revolt broke out or during the conflict." They fought for the bourgeois Republic. Gannes dedicated *Spain in Revolt* to "those who died that Spanish democracy might live." And Earl Browder, Party leader during the Popular Front, spoke of our own "solemn treaty obligations" to Spain and emphasized the legality and constitutionality of the Republic. Other Communists followed this line and frequently omitted even the modicum of economic analysis found in the earliest critiques of the war. *The Communist,* official monthly of the Party, supported the Loyalists with legal arguments:

American reactionaries and fascists are supporting the Spanish fascist mutineers against the legitimate democratic government of Spain. . . . To place the insurrectionists on the same footing with the government is to help the insurrection.

The line established by Dimitroff was redrawn by Clarence Hathaway in a speech delivered in Madison Square Garden (August 18, 1936):

The issue in Spain today is the issue of democracy versus fascism. . . . The fascists are undertaking to overthrow democratic procedure, to institute a fascist dictatorship.

The *Daily Worker, The Fight, New Masses,* and other Communist or "front" publications elaborated this constitutional thesis—with a frequency that would be maddening to document.[19]

Constitutionality was not the only line of defense. The ideological ramparts of capitalism itself were manned with a ferocity that would have warmed the hearts of the Robber Barons. Paying tribute to Joseph Dallet, killed in Spain, Browder wrote that he was one of those who gave "themselves completely to the task of stopping fascism . . . before it [engulfed] the capitalist world." Louis Fischer was lyrical about the Spanish Communist Party's devotion to the bourgeois revolution, and Vincent Sheean described Dolores Ibarruri, the Spanish Communist leader, as she asked her fellow Communists to "support the principle of private property," "liberty of conscience," and higher salaries for the indispensable bourgeois managers. (Sheean, no Communist, rightly attributed this strange speech to the decisions of the Seventh Congress.) As the war continued, the efforts of the truly radical parties to effect a social revolution were squelched by the Stalinists. Joseph Lash wrote to praise Premier Juan Negrín for shunning "Leftist and utopian conceptions" such as "forced collectivization and . . . all efforts to make the peasant the guinea pig of wild social experiments." A long way from the Russian attitude toward the kulak! Eventually, the effort of the "pseudo-anarchists"

Jacob Burck: "I'll Keep Clear of All This." An example of the Popular Front emphasis on "democracy" rather than on Marxism. (Reproduced by permission of *Masses and Mainstream*.)

to destroy the "bourgeois-democratic revolution" by "hasty projects for compulsory 'collectivization'" became a factor in the civil war within a civil war—the tragic week in Barcelona (to which I shall shortly be turning).[20]

Articulations of political theory are, unless clothed with images and made dramatic, naked and unmoving. The clothing in this instance was not from the revolutionary wardrobe of the October Revolution. The Communist Party did not recall the glorious days of the arrival at the Finland Station, of the defeat of Kornilov and Wrangel, of the heroic time of Lenin, Trotsky, and—to suit the Party's newer view of things—Stalin. The Party *avoided* the precedents of the Bolshevik experience. John Cornford's poem, "Full Moon at Thierz," with its references to Dimitroff, the Seventh Congress, and Maurice Thorez, is almost an oddity; the English Communist called for "communism and for liberty." The allusions of the Party-line poets were to Valley Forge and not to Kronstadt. The battle cries were resonant with the rhetoric of the American Revolution.[21]

This rhetoric was a pervasive one. Mike Quin [sic] wrote that Spain was "experiencing her Valley Forge," and Joseph North agreed. Edwin Rolfe's excellent history, *The Lincoln Battalion,* has a chapter entitled "Teruel: Spain's Valley Forge." *New Masses* made frequent use of the same allusion. Norman Rosten's poem, "Fragments for America," became a roll call of American heroes—Benjamin Franklin, Tom Paine, Paul Revere, Daniel Shays, John Brown, Abraham Lincoln. He imagined Sam Adams urging him on to Spain; he sang that "Bunker Hill is now Madrid."[22]

The magic name, Lafayette, and the magic number, 1776, became the touchstones of "radical" writing on the Spanish Civil War. The International Brigades were the "Lafayettes of the modern industrial age" to Louis Fischer, who called upon Lafayette, Byron, Kosciusko, and John Reed. (The reference to Reed is, perhaps, one sign of

Fischer's coming break with the Party.) In another dispatch, Fischer denounced Franco's "Hessians." Anna Louise Strong likened the Internationals to Lafayette, Von Steuben, and the other volunteers of the American Revolution. She denounced the rebels as Hessians and Tories. She asked America to remember 1776 and "the snow at Valley Forge." Don Joseph wrote that militias had "developed [in Spain] in much the same manner as the farmers' militias were organized around Concord, Massachusetts, in 1776." General Franco, to another writer, was associated with Lord Cornwallis. Still another thought of him as Benedict Arnold incarnate. Where, asked William Mangold, "would our own Democracy be if it had not been for the generous aid given . . . by France and by such patriots as Lafayette, Steuben, Kosciusko?" Herbert Kline compared the International Brigades to Lafayette, Garibaldi, Bryon, and John Reed; elsewhere, he thinned his list and thought of them as Paul Reveres waking the drowsy world to the midnight threat of Fascism. The "volunteers of Spain," wrote Joseph North, "are carrying on in the finest traditions of Washington, Lincoln, Tom Paine and Jefferson, giants who founded American democracy." The symbol of the Friends of the Abraham Lincoln Brigade, an organization launched by Browder under the leadership of David McKelvy White, was the Liberty Bell. A pamphlet by White and James Hawthorne, entitled *From These Honored Dead,* quotes the Gettysburg Address in its conclusion and alludes to George Washington, George Rogers Clark, Thomas Paine, Thomas Jefferson, and Benedict Arnold. Harry Gannes warned Americans of the

gangster assistance of Labor's Enemy No. 1, William Randolph Hearst and his ilk, to those in Spain who would rather butcher the very type of liberties which the American people won by the revolution of 1776.

Cartoonists such as William Sanderson and Jacob Burck illustrated the Party's contention that the Spanish war was very like the American Revolution, that the fight was for democracy rather than for Communism.[23]

William Sanderson: "Traditional Americanism?" The Communists stress American history. (Reproduced by permission of *Masses and Mainstream*.)

No one, however, uttered these slogans as often as Earl Browder, who seemed to have forgotten completely the situation's parallels to the events of 1917:

You will remember that, although the overwhelming majority of the American people in 1776 were for democracy, the Tories of that day did not allow them [peaceably] to solve their problems.

In a Madison Square Garden speech, "Lenin and Spain," Browder devoted himself not to Lenin but to Jefferson. Jefferson, said Browder, was for following our treaty obligations to France, for abjuring a cowardly neutrality in the 1790's. Jefferson would not have done as Cordell Hull did:

To avoid embarrassing Hitler . . . our government actually performed an act of war against Spain, against Spanish democracy, and for the alien fascist hordes bombarding Madrid.

Why have we not embargoed Italy? asked Browder: "Let us ask Thomas Jefferson where he stands on this issue." In his recasting of American history Browder found hundreds of "Lafayettes . . . in the front lines of the defense of Madrid." Leon Trotsky, needless to say, has two parts in the drama of Jefferson's career—Benedict Arnold and Aaron Burr. Lenin, of course, was not entirely absent from the speech; he was likened to Jefferson.[24]

Not many statements approach Browder's in their emphasis upon American history, but Leland Stowe (who was not a Communist) seemed determined to push the analogy between Spain and the United States to its ultimate degree:

Like ourselves in 1776, the Spanish republicans have had to develop great military leaders out of farmers. . . . And just as Washington's ragged Continentals were opposed by professional soldiers—and by Hessian mercenaries—so the Loyalists are opposed by experienced army officers and by imported foreign Fascists . . . the Spanish people have found their Washingtons and their Ethan Allens and their Anthony Waynes. . . . If Washington was right in 1776, then Republican Spain is right today.

On another occasion, Stowe denominated Lister and "El Campesino" (two Loyalist officers) as the "Ethan Allens, the Light Horse Harry Lees, and the Mad Anthony Waynes of Spain's heroic struggle against international fascism."[25]

Upton Sinclair's *No Pasaran!* includes the standard line-up. Rudy Messer, the novel's hero, wants to go to Spain, but "there were not going to be any Lafayettes or Steubens or Kosciuszkos going . . . to help the Spanish workers—not if a capitalist State Department and a capitalist Attorney-General could help it!" One can guess, entering the world of *this* novel, that Sinclair was *not* a Stalinist, not a loyal Communist. Convinced that the Spanish Civil War was the "clearest class-alignment in the history of the world," he spoke of "workers" instead of "people" and denounced capitalism as well as Fascism. Throughout the novel, Rudy Messer's potato-chip-manufacturing uncle is satirized as capitalists seldom were in the days of the Popular Front. The war is explained economically (and inaccurately) as the intervention of international capitalism into Spanish affairs: "Franco's revolt had been financed by Standard Oil and by Royal Dutch Shell, each of which had given him fifteen millions of dollars." *No Pasaran!* is a drastically simplified book, but—in an era when Communists like Marcel Acier could speak of "the beloved leader of Madrid's shock police" —Sinclair was laudable for the integrity of his radicalism.[26]

It was obvious, even then, that some of the Stalinists' enthusiasm for the American heritage was forced. No one expressed his disgust more humorously than ex-Communist Charles Yale Harrison, who imagined a group of reporters interviewing Earl Browder "disguised as Paul Revere in breeches and cocked hat, standing beside a spavined palfrey." Browder renounces the dictatorship of the proletariat:

> We believe in American democracy, in the spirit of the frontier, the covered wagon, Buffalo Bill, Steve Brody, Casey Jones and other heroic figures in our nation's copybook past. We appeal to all lovers of popular American history, to all liberals, radicals, socialists, progressive capitalists, stock brokers—and workers—to join the people's front against war and fascism.[27]

It seems clear enough that a great deal of the rhetoric of liberalism was, simply, a lie, a conscious atempt to persuade people that Communism was, indeed, "twentieth-century Americanism." A statement of this sort is not entirely subjective, not entirely a question of belief in one or another spokesman. Those who argued for liberal democracy (in glowing generalities) were sometimes the most illiberal in specific instances. George Seldes, for instance, paused in his eloquent denunciations of the Catholic Church's abridgments of freedom of the press to excoriate *America* for printing a letter to the editor. Seldes found the letter objectionable. Marcel Acier wrote that the "desire for fair play always seems to influence democratic governments and allows participation by the worst enemies of Democracy." Earl Browder, at the American Writers Congress, compared dissent within the ranks of the pro-Loyalists to "the recent uprising against the Spanish government by the Trotzkyites and their anarchist allies. Is it possible for us to adopt an attitude of broad toleration of those who preach and practice such treason?" Clearly, it was not. "Those who, in the sacred name of freedom, would break our unity in the face of the menace of war and fascism, are contributing to the destruction of all freedom." James Hawthorne was still more open about the identity of the sacred cow in the ideological barnyard: "It is impossible to attack the Communist Party without passing beyond that stage to other points of coin-

cidence with the fascists." I have already quoted A. B. Magil
on those who looked "with microscopes, for pimples on the
shining face of the Soviet Union."[28]

The best test case for the problem at hand is the so-called
treason to which Browder referred. The touchstone divid-
ing liberal democrats from shouters of liberal slogans was
the suppression of dissent in Spain and in America. More
specifically, the crucial event was the decision of Stalin (announced in *Pravda*, December 17, 1936) to wipe out the
"Trotskyites" of Spain. The Americans who were most shrill
in their appeals to the memory of Thomas Jefferson were
often the same Americans who were most fanatical in their
charges that the internecine strife in Barcelona (from May
3 to May 8, 1937) was a revolt by the POUM rather than a
crack-down by the PSUC (the Communist-oriented *Partido
Socialista Unificado de Cataluña*).

Browder called the small Trotskyite party the "Trotsky-
ite-POUM agents of Franco, the most dangerous part of the
infamous 'fifth-column' behind the republican lines," "the
slinking masked agent of fascism." James W. Ford accused
the POUM of attracting all the "criminal elements and
provocateurs, who committed acts of sabotage, who engaged
in assassination and, who, wherever possible, tried to weaken
the armed forces of the Republic and war industry." James
Hawthorne, whose fantasies equipped the POUM with
"tanks, armored cars, artillery, machine-guns, rifles, and millions of rounds of ammunition" (all for street-fighting in
Barcelona), announced that "the rising was clearly fascist-
inspired, and national indignation against the Trotskyite
agents of Franco reached fever heat." Robert Minor, a good
cartoonist turned bad agitator, lashed out at the "fascist-
Trotskyist uprising" as one of "declassed adventurers" and
the "riffraff of sectarian grounds" and "professional fascist
agents" from the cesspools of corruption. André Marty
flailed overt and "covert" Trotskyites, and Dimitroff con-

demned them as "a gang of spies, diversionists, terrorists and police provocateurs," "degenerates, on instructions from the fascist intelligence services," but neither of these men reached the speculative depths of Carl Reeve (son of Mother Bloor): "In Spain, it has been proved by documents, Andreas Nin and the other Trotskyites and Lovestoneites of the POUM were paid agents of Franco and were part of his fascist spying and wrecking apparatus." Georges Soria, of *Humanité,* the man who collected the false "documents," must have been pleased by Carl Reeve's addition of Jay Lovestone to the ranks of the "wreckers" in Barcelona. There are times when, in paging such accounts of events in Spain, the reader momentarily loses faith in the very ideal of an honest history. I should not have been surprised to read that Adolf Hitler himself had been in Barcelona to pass out hot coffee and glazed doughnuts to the "Trotskyite wreckers."[29]

The most distressing aspect of this situation is the degree to which Americans were willing to accept the Soviet position on the "May Days" in Barcelona, and, worse yet, to adopt the Soviet position vis-à-vis the problem of dissent. John Gunther noted that the leaders of the Republic "were such profound liberals that they believed in free speech even for those who would destroy free speech." When Mrs. A. Mitchell Palmer and Governor Earle of Pennsylvania banned the film, *Spain in Flames,* both *The Nation* and *The New Republic* cried out against this abridgment of our freedoms. But Loyalist sympathizers rejoiced when pressures were exerted to halt Darryl Zanuck's production of a movie commemorating the Nationalists who withstood the siege of the Alcázar at Toledo. More significant is the statement made by the editors of *The Social Frontier,* a magazine that disseminated the ideals of the Deweyites at Teachers College. They discovered that the Spanish Civil War had crystallized the issue of civil liberties for the undemocratic:

May not the continued extension of democratic privileges to those who scorn them . . . be tantamount to choosing the form in which the death sentence pronounced by the enemies of democracy shall be executed? . . . In both domestic and foreign affairs, democracies continue operating on the assumption that forces inimical to democratic ideals will be susceptible to democratic processes. They forget that democracies can function only among those who believe in democracy.

The very substitution of the phrase "democratic privileges" tells much about a society that once believed in "inalienable rights."[30]

On the other hand, the duplicity of the Stalinists and the ingenuousness of many of the liberals can lead to an excessive disillusionment and skepticism. It is wrong to doubt the sincerity of all of the appeals to the American past or to democratic principles. After all, Lafayette *did* come to these shores, and Jefferson *did* wish to aid libertarian movements abroad. References to Kosciusko, De Kalb, Von Steuben, and the Lafayette Escadrille are to be found even in such anti-Communist publications as the *New York Daily News*. Surely *part* of the fascination of the war was in the feeling that Spanish history was passing through the same stages as had American history, that the impulse to fraternity, equality, and liberty merited our sympathy and help. Lou Ornitz explained that the "Spanish struggle identified itself in my mind with the War for Independence that we Americans fought in 1776." One can hardly refute this. John Peale Bishop, writing to Rolfe Humphries about an anthology of poems written by Loyalist troops, ascribed part of his own interest in the war to his having grown up only a stone's throw from John Brown's scaffold. Asked about *his* position on the Spanish war, Morris R. Cohen answered, "What American, loyal to the principle of government by the people . . . enunciated by Jefferson and Lincoln, can take

any other position" than an anti-Fascist one? Van Wyck
Brooks and R. L. Duffus called upon the names of Thomas
Jefferson, John Quincy Adams, and Abraham Lincoln, and
proclaimed that a pro-Loyalist stand was dictated by "the
simplest principles of our own Revolution." While suspicious of the frenzied allusions of James Lerner and Gil
Green, I feel sure that Ernest Hemingway, once again,
tapped deep reservoirs of feeling when he quoted from the
Gettysburg Address in his Foreword to Joseph North's *Men
in the Ranks,* and when he described Major Milton Wolff
as "tall as Lincoln, gaunt as Lincoln":

He is a retired major now at twenty-three . . . and pretty soon
he will be coming home as other men his age and rank came
home after the peace at Appomattax courthouse long ago. Except the peace was made at Munich now and no good men will
be home for long.[31]

An important reason for thinking that the analogues to
the American Civil War were sincerely felt by Hemingway
is to be found in the novel, *For Whom the Bell Tolls.* In
the novel, Robert Jordan is sustained by the memory of his
grandfather's exploits as a member of Sheridan's cavalry. He
reminds himself that his grandfather fought through four
long years and that he has fought for only one. The novel is,
moreover, complex in that it provides, on the one hand, a
sketch of Communists dedicated to helping the Spanish and,
on the other hand, a portrait of the maniacal Communist,
André Marty. The novel contains, in addition to the harshly
etched portrayal of Marty, an explicit disavowal of Marxism
and an affirmation of the liberal tradition. Jordan reminds
himself that he is not a Marxist, that his fight is for liberty,
equality, and fraternity, for life, liberty, and the pursuit of
happiness. "Don't ever kid yourself," he says, "with too
much dialectics." The writer shows both sides—and some-

thing more—and wins our trust. In this case, I trust Hemingway's analogies to Abraham Lincoln and to the American war.[32]

Finally, although many of the Stalinists might have been cynical in their use of the American tradition of liberal democracy, they were certainly correct in thinking that these symbols and these arguments touched the sources of value for vast numbers of Americans. The impulse toward Spain was an American impulse. The Stalinists were not acting inappropriately when they sought to influence opinion by summoning up memories of Valley Forge and Gettysburg. The best Communists wrote with an awareness of the complexity of the war. They did not reduce the war to a simplistic allegory. Their allusions to 1776 were part of an argument that did not pretend ignorance of the events of 1917. But these writers were few. George Witter Sherman's poem, "Moon over Spain," apostrophizes the moon "sorrowing at Lincoln's tomb in Springfield and/At Lenin's tomb in Red Square . . ."; Edwin Rolfe, in a poem that denies the romantic image of "orange groves," vines, and "steel that sings and bends like a slim girl dancing," concludes with a statement that is, in comparison with most "poetry" of the Communist camp, a very complex statement: "Spain is yesterday's Russia, tomorrow's China,/yes, and the thirteen seaboard states." In an era when Communism was twentieth-century Americanism and Lenin was a Jeffersonian, such poems as these were rare, and rarer still was the Communist speaker or editorialist who acknowledged a familiarity with Russian history or Marxist analysis.[33]

The Non-Stalinist Left. If the average contributor to *New Masses* had doubts about Dimitroff's view of the Spanish Civil War, he kept them to himself. Nevertheless, socialist critiques of the Soviet position were not lacking. It is in the writings of dissident Communists such as Bertram Wolfe and Jay Lovestone that one finds the truly radical, revolutionary interpretations of the war. It is in the writings of the non-Stalinists that one finds the theoretical apparatus of Marxism and the practical experiences of the Russian Revolution employed to analyze the social, political, and economic factors involved in the Spanish situation. And the fiercest attacks on the Stalinists came from a theorist who knew a thing or two about making a revolution—Leon Trotsky.

Rebuking the POUM—which the Stalinists were liquidating as Trotskyite—he called for the conquest of power:

The Bolshevist point of view, expressed in a finished fashion only by the . . . Fourth International, proceeds on the basis of the theory of the permanent revolution and realizes that even . . . purely democratic tasks—such as the liquidation of semi-feudal property—are accomplishable only by the conquest of power on the part of the proletariat.

The POUM did not realize this.

Instead of mobilizing the masses against the reformers—including the anarchists—the POUM sought to convince the *señores* of the advantages of socialism over capitalism.

Trotsky's essays were published in *Partisan Review* and in two magazines of the Socialist Workers Party—*The Socialist Appeal* (New York) and *The New International*.[34]

At this time, the Socialist Workers Party, led by James Cannon, included Max Schachtman, James Burnham, Bernard Wolfe, Felix Morrow, and Dwight Macdonald. This party was almost as concerned about the Spanish war as about the charges leveled by Stalin again Trotsky. "For the Trotskyites," says Daniel Bell, "a 'correct' policy on Spain was the *sine qua non* of the revolutionary policy." Burnham specified Lenin's refusal to cooperate with Kerensky against Kornilov as the "crucial historical example" for his proof that "the attempt of the People's Front to preserve bourgeois democracy . . . is not merely [useless] in the struggle against war and fascism. It makes both inevitable." He called for the turning of the imperialistic war into a class war for the triumph of the proletariat. This course, known technically as "revolutionary defeatism," was advocated by *The Socialist Appeal* (Chicago) in urging the POUM to alter its position in favor of the "line of policy which made possible the victory of the Russian working class in October 1917." From New York, *The Fighting Worker* called for immediate revolution on these principles. Their motto on August 8, 1936: "No Support to Azaña! Create Soviets! Take Power!" This was the position taken by *The New International*—named after Trotsky's Fourth International.

Dwight Macdonald and Bernard Wolfe (not to be confused with Bertram Wolfe) wrote for this magazine, but the most extended Trotskyite analysis of the Spanish conflict was made by Felix Morrow in *The New International*, in *The Socialist Appeal* (Chicago and New York) and in a very important pamphlet. Since Fascism, argued Morrow, is "that special form of capitalist domination which the bourgeoisie finally resorts to when the continued existence of capitalism is incompatible with the existence of organized workers," it was obvious that cooperation with the bourgeoisie was a self-defeating policy. "Spanish fascism is the weapon not of 'feudalism' but of capitalism. It can be fought successfully by the working class and by the peasantry, and by them alone." Although Morrow defended the POUM from the charges of treason made by the Stalinists, he attacked them with all the bitterness of a spurned lover and concluded that the purged party had been filthy with collaboration in a dirty government. Morrow's disgust with the anarchists has already been mentioned. He was equally impatient with the right wing of the "Communist Opposition." Bertram Wolfe's pamphlet, *Civil War in Spain*, was dismissed with revulsion: "The intellectual dishonesty of Wolfe's pamphlet is positively repulsive."[35]

Wolfe's problem was that he belonged to Jay Lovestone's dissident Independent Labor League of America, and Jay Lovestone's attack on the Popular Front owed more to Bukharin than to Trotsky. Or, to suggest a less theoretical basis for disagreement, Lovestone's fierce attacks on the expelled Trotskyites (in 1928) might have irritated men like Morrow and Burnham. Whether the theoretical disagreement was motivated by personal dislike or not, there was a difference of opinion between the right and left wings of the Communist opposition to Stalin. Wolfe agreed in condemning the Popular Front but not in rejecting the POUM. Before the war, he wrote, Spain was

led by two governments: one, the cabinet of bourgeois republican politicans that had proved . . . its incompetence and unreliability, . . . the other a half-formed government of committees, leading the masses, yet only partially conscious of its authority and role.

When war came, the POUM realized that it was to lead in forming this new government. Wolfe's manifesto was prefaced by Will Herberg, who had already analyzed the war with references to Kerensky and Lenin and anticipated the course of events before the war was one month old. Writing in August of 1936, Herberg feared

that the socialist and communist leaderships have so far lost their Marxist sense . . . under the baleful influence of the People's Front bewitchment that they will actually rally behind the liberal bourgeoisie in the crusade to liquidate the revolutionary situation in the sacred name of Democracy.

Herberg's fears became realities.[36]

Meanwhile, despite Lovestone's cry for the defeat of

Fascism, through "working class revolution . . . regardless of and despite the People's Front," despite the Lovestoneite stand of *Workers Age* and *International Class Struggle,* the Communist opposition seemed to achieve nothing more than its own rapid splintering into a vociferous impotence. Hugo Oehler, who had broken with Trotsky and formed the Revolutionary Workers League in 1935 (Bolshevists who condemned the "French Turn" by which Trotsky joined the left wing of the Socialist Party), cursed even the POUM as "pseudo-Marxist." Even as Oehler's followers called for a "Revolutionary Marxist Party" in Spain, a schism developed. Karl Mienov, in the first issue of *The Spark,* announced that he had split with Oehler on "the most important question of the day—the Spanish war. . . . It is impossible to have a false position on Spain and at the same time to have a correct opinion" on any other social question. Mienov vilified the "Stalinists-Socialist-Anarchist-POUM" combination as lackeys of the bourgeoisie and urged "revolutionary defeatism" by turning the imperialist war into a civil war of workers and peasants against the middle class. This would have been an imitation of Lenin's course in 1917. (The opposite argument was termed "revolutionary defensism.") Mienov's followers, however, did not all agree with him. Splits occurred until, it is rumored, Karl Mienov developed a schizophrenic personality and split with himself.[37]

Mienov's was not the last splinter group. A small group of Leninists published *In Defense of Bolshevism* and maintained that they, not the Trotskyites, represented the Fourth International. They strongly opposed the Trotskyite position on Spain: "Disorienting the workers, clogging up their minds with lustrous . . . phrases and engagingly written half-truths and falsifications, the Trotskyites have rendered . . . service both to Stalinism and to capitalism." The Proletarian Party, an offshoot of the so-called Michigan Group

of the Socialist Party, published *Proletarian News,* in which
C. Barone and John Keracher criticized the Popular Front
without suggesting alternatives to it. In its *Bulletin* and in
The Proletarian Outlook, the Proletarian Group condemned
the role of Communism in Spain and elsewhere. *The Industrial Unionist,* of the Industrial Union Party, hit the
Popular Front as "the present day Communist Party pana-
cea" and urged the application to the Spanish war of the
insights of Daniel De Leon. Of these splinter groups, the
Workers Socialist Party was remarkable in accepting the arguments of the Popular Front.[38]

More importantly, V. F. Calverton, revolutionary but
independent, used his *Modern Monthly* as a forum for several radical and dissident groups. Spain was the "skirmish
ground" in a struggle between a reactionary and a revolutionary way of life. In this struggle, asserted the *Monthly,*
the Communist Party and the Socialist Party were both playing the role of the Mensheviks in the Russian Revolution,
and the role was doomed to failure. The true Bolshevists
were the members of the CNT and the POUM. Calverton
printed an important article by Anita Brenner, an Australian Marxist, who used George Orwell's testimony in a
clarification of the antirevolutionary role played by the
Stalinists in Spain. Calverton himself wrote that the war
"is bound to be won by Franco unless it is turned into a
revolutionary war."[39]

Similar to *The Modern Monthly, Partisan Review* was
a rallying point for anti-Stalinists of the late 1930's. Philip
Rahv, who was with William Phillips a founder of the magazine, demonstrated the degree to which excellent critics had
been pushed by the pressure of events. Consider his review
of André Malraux's novel, *L'Espoir*:

A cleverly composed party-pamphlet in the guise of objective fiction, its consummate rhetoric serves only to swell its illusions. Its pretentious political-intellectual dialogues represent nothing but the fantasies of a fellow-traveler . . . no longer capable of thinking for himself. . . .

Leon Trotsky also criticized the novel, in a letter published in *Partisan Review,* as composed of "lying reports from the fields of battle." F. W. Dupee—another excellent critic—berated Malraux for creating a hero who was "the type of liberal Comintern lobbyist thrown up by the stooge politics of people's-frontism." It is surely wrong to accuse such men of being dupes of the Kremlin. The anti-Stalinists of the radical movement were the severest critics of Stalinism. Sidney Hook claimed to be "anatomizing" the Popular Front. "Vivisecting" would have been a more appropriate word for his devastating analysis.[40]

As one moves from Cannon's *New International* through Lovestone's *Workers Age* and Calverton's *Modern Monthly* to *Partisan Review,* one discovers undiminished denunciation of the weaknesses of the Popular Front and fewer references to the experiences of the Russian Revolution and an increasingly vague sense of what was to be done. This tendency is even more obvious when one looks at the socialists' center, at the organizations and periodicals that derive not so much from the Communist Party created after 1917 by Louis Fraina, Benjamin Gitlow, and Charles Ruthenberg as from the Socialist Party of 1901 created by Morris Hillquit, Victor Berger, and Eugene Debs, the party of evolutionary rather than revolutionary socialism.

Using Max Weber's distinction between living "in" the world but not "of" the world, Daniel Bell has isolated the dilemma of the Socialist Party in the 1930's. "It was forced to take stands on the particular issues of the day. But it . . . rejected completely the premises of the society which shaped these issues." The Spanish Civil War illuminated the dilemma in a cruel light. As Bell notes, the Socialist Party had to call for "workers' aid" when the desperate need was for government (i.e., capitalist) aid.[41]

The pages of *The Socialist Call, The American Socialist Monthly*, and *The Socialist Review* reflect the dilemma. Herbert Zam, Sam Baron, Liston Oak, and others reproved the Stalinist repressions but urged continued efforts to vanquish the Fascists. In a series of articles, Luis Araquistain, political ally of Francisco Largo Caballero, urged the formation of class consciousness and the struggle for the social revolution. Norman Thomas felt that the "Fascist rebellion must be defeated," but he drew back from the thought of foreign intervention on either side. His difficulties appear in the very title of his book, *Socialism on the Defensive*. Although Thomas harshly criticized the absence of freedom in the Soviet Union and was especially severe toward the great purges then in progress, he still insisted that the U.S.S.R. was a "proletarian state" free from the "Aryan" myth, with a "relatively pacific foreign policy," with an "avowed belief in socialism," with a determination to stand by the Spanish Republic. In the tradition of Eugene Debs, Norman Thomas maintained that the coming of war would mean the end of democracy and that American foreign policy should be one of neutrality. Thomas, however, allowed for one "seeming exception" in that we should embargo aggressor nations but not their victims.[42]

Norman Thomas's dilemma became most intense when American Socialists attempted to form a volunteer unit for Spanish duty. Despite their grave misgivings about the Popular Front in Spain, V. F. Calverton, James T. Farrell, Sidney Hook, Upton Sinclair, and Norman Thomas called for the formation of the "Eugene V. Debs Column." The reaction of the pacifists in the Socialist Party was one of dismay. As we have already seen, John Haynes Holmes wrote an impassioned letter to Thomas and urged him to remain faithful to his principles. Thomas felt torn between conflicting beliefs and attempted to justify his course by arguing that aid to "our Spanish comrades" would help "stop Franco's war and by stopping it greatly increase the world's hope of avoiding the catastrophe of a second world war far worse than the first."[43]

Holmes' letter to Thomas brought forth agonized commentaries from *The New Leader* as well. This periodical was the organ of the Social Democratic Federation, a small conservative group that had left the Socialist Party upon the short-lived union of the Trotskyites with the Socialists. On January 2, 1937, *The New Leader* printed Holmes' letter to Thomas. They agreed that it was improper to use the name of Debs for a military group. Having said this much, the editors approved of force used against Fascism: "Franco and his gangsters are not going to be converted into decent members of a civilized community by Tolstoyan preaching." Five months later, on June 5, 1937, the editors once again raised the problem of violence. While acknowledging the pull of pacifist and isolationist arguments, they insisted that the real danger came from the "continuous and systematic use of violence by armed janizaries, directed by military officers and clerical bigots, in the service of a degenerate landowning class." *The New Leader* continued regularly to denounce the "Franco-pagan-Nazi-fascist-totalitarian-'infidel'-Moslem insurrection" and to call for action by the United States "in concert with the democratic nations of Europe." Embarrassed by a small American following, the editors continued to print the analyses and dispatches of such European Socialists as Clement Atlee, Louis de Brouckere, Erika Mann, Herbert Morrison, Pietro Nenni, and Ellen Wilkinson.[44]

From Oklahoma and from Kansas, *The American Guardian* and *The American Freeman* (the once-powerful *Appeal to Reason* renamed and degraded to a question-and-answer tabloid) supported the Popular Front. *Common*

Sense, a magazine that included Theodore Dreiser, Paul Douglas, and John Dos Passos among its supporters, carried a number of strong statements of neutrality by Dos Passos and by John Chamberlain. Noting that anti-Stalinists had been excluded from the American Writers Congress, Chamberlain argued that American progressives should quit working "for very special . . . interests in the far-away diplomatic corridors of Europe and Asia." Dos Passos suggested a combination of "quarantine and medical aid" and proclaimed that the place to fight Fascism is "in your own home town." His novel, *Adventures of a Young Man,* is pro-Loyalist but anti-Stalinist. Theodore Dreiser was quite willing to go to Spain and to speak against the bombing of cities, but, in the words of an exasperated organizer of anti-embargo protest, "the old dope" was for enforcing the embargo rather than lifting it. *The Progressive* noted that Americans who condemned the atrocious bombing of Barcelona did so without examining their own position. It was suggested that we strengthen our neutrality laws by embargoing Germany and Italy. *The Freeman,* a magazine dedicated to the single-tax theories of Henry George, all but ignored the Spanish Civil War but did find time to note that inequalities of land-ownership were at the bottom of Spain's troubles and that a devoted Single-Taxer in Tarragona was continuing his efforts to spread the word among the then preoccupied Spanish. In brief, men like Dos Passos and Dreiser and the younger La Follettes seemed to have taken a more moderate stand than many liberals who felt that democracy was international or nothing.[45]

On the basis of this rapid survey of the Left, several observations can be made. Well-organized and hard-working, the American Communist Party appealed, rather hypocritically, to liberal democratic and even capitalistic traditions. The Party became the most important single group to rally pro-Loyalist opinion. The "organic" society preached by Van

Wyck Brooks and his followers represents an important element in American life, but not a movement that has attracted any considerable numbers—even among intellectuals. The "organicists" cooperated with the North American Committee to Aid Spanish Democracy and with other pro-Loyalist committees supporting the Popular Front. American anarchists have attracted an even smaller following. The traditions of Thoreau and Emerson, of Tucker and Goldman, seemed extremely weak during the years of the Spanish war. Although the anarchists, unlike the "organicists," had their own magazines, they reached few readers. American socialists who put forth a truly radical interpretation of the Spanish Civil War did so in the teeth of Stalinist opposition (and the opposition of other radical groups with differing views). Norman Thomas and his followers participated in committees as part of the American support for the Popular Front, but the radical Left found such a compromise with principles impossible. Still others—men like Calverton, Hook, Macdonald, Rahv—were able to Americanize Marx and to use Marxism as a basis from which to make an independent stand. If one wishes to maintain that American Marxists were a powerful force intellectually if not numerically and that, therefore, the Spanish Civil War *was* a truly radical and even a subversive cause, then one must admit that it was *not*—among the revolutionary Left—a cause typified by a blind devotion to the man in the Kremlin.

Furthermore, the influence of Marx on American life has probably been overestimated by nostalgia on the Left and by hysteria on the Right. *The Appeal to Reason* sold in the Middle West to Populists who had never heard of the dialectic; and books like Bellamy's *Looking Backward* (which sold over 600,000 copies), Gronlund's *Co-operative Commonwealth,* and Lloyd's *Wealth against Commonwealth* did more to articulate dissatisfaction with capitalism than did all the polemics of the American Communist Party.

Debs, De Leon, and Gompers were all readers of Bellamy, and both Bertram Wolfe and Jay Lovestone came to Communism through De Leon rather than through Marx. All of which is but another way of saying that socialism is not an alien ideology.

Although the Spanish Civil War was surely a socialist cause *as well as* a liberal cause, one can say that—for most Americans supporting the Republic—the factors that made the war the emotional center of the 1930's were Fascism's threat to liberal democratic values and the optimism generated by Spain's resistance to Fascism. The Soviet Union was an extremely important aspect of the situation, but the radicals discussed in this section were certainly not conniving to extend the Comintern's dominion. They were, on the contrary, desperately fearful that Stalin's perversions of socialism would prove to be exportable and that the heresy of Stalinism would supplant the orthodoxy of Marxism. The weakness of the truly radical movement can be seen dramatically in the relative size of two New York rallies held to commemorate a year of war in Spain. Three hundred people met in Union Square to hear Liston Oak expose the Stalinist role in Spain; 20,000 met in Madison Square Garden to help Earl Browder and Norman Thomas celebrate the preservation of bourgeois democracy.[46]

7

PRIMITIVISM

VERSUS

PROGRESS

Ernest Hemingway's Vision of "Mechanized Doom"

The Spanish Earth, a documentary film written by Ernest Hemingway and directed by Joris Ivens, begins with the camera focused upon the soil itself. From the very beginning the film is an assertion of an intimate relationship between men and the land: "This Spanish earth is dry and hard and the faces of the men who work on [this] earth are hard and dry from the sun." The land must be defended against an enemy armed, in the film as in reality, with the most up-to-date mechanized weapons. The land is defended, and the film ends with the waters rushing through the newly constructed irrigation ditch, bringing life to the sun-baked soil. Floods of American aid never reached the Loyalists of Spain,

Permission to reprint "Mechanized Doom: Ernest Hemingway and the Spanish Civil War," granted by *The Massachusetts Review.*

but that is history's irony, not Hemingway's. In *For Whom the Bell Tolls*, there is a similar structure in that the novel begins and ends with the ''pine-needled floor of the forest.'' In the novel as in the film, there is a struggle between men and machines.[1]

Considering the historical facts, it is not surprising that there should be this element common both to the novel and to the film. When the Spanish army revolted on the afternoon and evening of July 17, 1936, the Republic was saved from immediate destruction by the action of poorly armed and often unarmed civilians. As massive shipments of German and Italian equipment reached the Rebels, it became obvious to military observers that mechanized weapons were likely to be a decisive factor. Military historians studied the war as a testing ground for the newest theories of mechanized warfare: General Duval wrote *Les Leçons de la Guerre d'Espagne;* Hoffman Nickerson commented upon the obsolescence of the unmechanized "mass armies" in *The Armed Horde,* and Basil Henry Liddell Hart, in a series of books and articles, analyzed the new importance of *Blitzkrieg* and *Panzerdivision.* As documents captured after the fall of the Reich testify, Hermann Goering was particularly anxious to test his newly created *Luftwaffe.* Popular magazines such as *Time, Life,* and *The Saturday Evening Post* discussed Giulio Douhet's theory that methodical bombardment would demoralize civilian populations.

Because the London Non-Intervention Committee and the American embargo were effective in reducing the imports of the Republicans and quite ineffective in halting the flow of men and munitions to General Franco, the disparity in equipment grew increasingly greater. It was, therefore, perfectly natural that bombing planes and armored tanks should become, in the writings of Loyalist-sympathizers, symbols for the enemy; the symbols corresponded to the historical situation. At a time when, as we have seen, much of the American public was stunned by the horror of aerial bombardment, it was natural that pro-Loyalist writings should emphasize the plight of the badly armed or unarmed Republicans, especially when these Republicans were the peasants whose primitive conditions of life left them almost completely helpless when attacked by the weapons of a technological civilization. It is, therefore, not unnatural that, in *The Spanish Earth* and in *For Whom the Bell Tolls,* a symbolic struggle between men and machines forms an important part of Hemingway's vision of reality, a vision that is, in the complex way that art is related to the rest of experience, based upon the historical facts. This chapter is an attempt to treat two questions:

1. To what degree was Hemingway's interpretation of the fight against Fascism dramatized and particularized in the struggle of men against machines?

2. Can Hemingway's interpretation be helpful in exploring other interpretations and in suggesting another of the multifarious sources of the extraordinary concern thousands of Americans felt for the fate of the Spanish Republic?

The first step is to look at Hemingway's work. From his earliest stories, from the Nick Adams episodes of *In Our Time* to the fable of *The Old Man and the Sea,* Ernest Hemingway has dealt with man in the natural landscape. Even within the general lostness of *The Sun Also Rises,* the characters find themselves briefly while fishing in Spain, near Pamplona. For Hemingway, Spain is an elemental symbiosis of man and nature. What are the rituals of Hemingway's paean to bullfighting, *Death in the Afternoon,* if not a stylized representation of man's organic relationship to nature? Remembering the proverb about Europe's being cut off at the Pyrenees, Hemingway looks upon Africa and Spain as a unit and, in *The Green Hills of Africa,* shows the mechanized world entering insidiously to destroy the hitherto uncorrupted world of nature. The book opens with a hunt ruined by the passing of a truck. This is put into the simplest possible language: "The truck had spoiled it." Later, the theme is generalized:

A continent ages quickly once we come. The natives live in harmony with it. But the foreigner destroys. . . . A country wears out quickly unless man puts back into it all his residue and that of all his beasts. When he quits using beasts and uses machines, the earth defeats him quickly. The machine can't reproduce, nor does it fertilize the soil.

What Hemingway seemed to discover in the Spanish war was that the machine is not merely passively destructive in that it cannot perform biological functions; the machine can also became an agent of destruction. In a dispatch printed in *The New Republic,* Hemingway wrote

There is nothing so terrible and sinister as the track of a tank in action. The track of a tropical hurricane leaves a capricious swath of complete destruction, but the two parallel grooves the tank leaves in the red mud lead to scenes of planned death worse than any the hurricane leaves.

Before dramatizing the conflict between the values associated with the natural landscape and the values associated with the tank and other machines, Hemingway wrote four short stories and also a play—all concerned with the Spanish Civil War. Three of the stories, set in Madrid, deal with the correspondents and the "Internationals" who made Chicote's bar their place of rendezvous. Hemingway himself felt that these stories are inferior in technique and refused requests to print them anew. The fourth story, "The Old Man at the Bridge," dramatizes the flight of the peasant from the artillery and the planes of the Fascists. This story has become a part of the Hemingway canon.

The play, *The Fifth Column,* was written at the urging of the foreign correspondents in Madrid. Set in Madrid's

Hotel Florida, it is a wooden play about a Vassar girl (with long legs) and a counterspy for the International Brigades. If the play has any enduring meaning, it is to make clear that Hemingway could not dramatize the Spanish war with these stick figures; the play violates its author's own often repeated rule—the writer must always tell the truth as he sees it, and the truth for Ernest Hemingway was not to be seen in Chicote's and not to be seen in the Hotel Florida. It was not even in Madrid; it was closer to the peasants and gypsies, closer to the earth, closer to the pine-needled floor of the forest.[2]

The first thing one notices about *For Whom the Bell Tolls* is, usually, the epigraph taken from a meditation by John Donne. Ordinarily, we remember best the lines that give the book its title: "And therefore never send to know for whom the *bell* tolls; it tolls for *thee*." Hemingway uses the epigraph as a statement of the theme of brotherhood, of human solidarity, of the involvement of all men in a common humanity. The statement, however, is not separable from the imagery of the passage:

No man is an *Iland* intire of it selfe; every man is a peece of the *Continent,* a part of the *maine*: if a *Clod* bee washed away by the *Sea, Europe* is the lesse. . . .

The images of the earth, of island, continent, the maine, a clod are not accidental and not unimportant. Nathaniel Hawthorne, in his story "Ethan Brand," described all men as linked in a "magnetic chain of humanity" and Herman Melville, in Chapter LXXII of *Moby-Dick,* used a rope tied between Queequeg and Ishmael to symbolize the "precise situation of every mortal that breathes," the "Siamese connexion with a plurality of other mortals." Hemingway's use of Donne's metaphor of the earth, rather than the more obvious metaphors of chain or rope, would be scant grounds on which to base a thesis if it were not for the accumulation of such seemingly trivial bits of evidence. Consider, for instance, Hemingway's elegy for "The American Dead in Spain."

The dead sleep cold in Spain tonight and they will sleep cold all this winter as the earth sleeps with them. But in the spring the rain will come. . . . This spring the dead will feel the earth beginning to live again. For our dead are a part of the earth of Spain now and the earth of Spain can never die. Each winter it will seem to die and each spring it will come alive again. Our dead will live with it forever. . . . The dead do not need to rise. They are a part of the earth now and the earth can never be conquered. For the earth endureth forever.

One need only to finish the quotation from Ecclesiastes, "And the sun also riseth," to feel the unity of Hemingway's best writing.[3]

Robert Jordan, a "peece of the *Continent,* a part of the *maine,*" does *not* join the International Brigades. Two British soldiers described fighting in the wreckage of Madrid's University City, beneath busts of "Plato, Spinoza, Aristotle and Voltaire," behind the bullet-proof barricades "of Indian metaphysics and early nineteenth-century German philosophy," but Robert Jordan joins a guerrilla band in the mountains—a band that fights on horseback, a band whose previous accomplishments include chiefly the destruction of a troop-train. Robert Jordan fights side by side with Anselmo, a man of natural wisdom. The two trust each other by instinct, but Pablo, the leader of the band, is suspicious and grants the American a tentative approval only after witnessing his knowledge of horses, the same horses that subsequently bring out what little kindness is left in Pablo. (Hemingway's portrayal of Pablo indicates that the book is not a naive affirmation of the Noble Savage.) Later, the horses play a vital role in the climax of Chapter XXVI, in the terrifying conflict between El Sordo's band, sprawled behind the dead bodies of their mounts, and the Fascist patrol. El Sordo's men hold out until the dive-bombers come. Then all is determined. On a hillside, where men are naturally accustomed to survey their dominions, the band is uncovered and helpless. They are all killed.[4]

Those less grim sections of the novel, the episodes concerning the affair with Maria, have been condemned as extraneous, but, looking specifically at the theme of the earth and the machine, one notes that Maria, Roberto's beloved "rabbit," is somehow identified with the Spanish earth that was then violated figuratively as Maria was violated literally. Maria's shaved head is so realistic a detail that one is surprised to see an obvious symbolism as well. The *least* one can say is that the story of Maria, taken prisoner, raped, rescued from a troop-train, and, finally, saved by Roberto from the approaching tanks of the enemy, parallels certain aspects of Spanish history from 1936 to 1939. Paired with Maria is Pilar—whom I have already called a kind of Iberian Earth-Mother—who is proud that the world itself moved during her love-making, who had lived nine years with three of the worst-paid matadors in the world, who reminds us again and again of the love-making and bullfighting that represent Spain as it should have been.

In symbolic opposition to the cluster of values represented by the two bands, their mounts, and the earth itself, we have the steel bridge, the bombers, and the approaching tanks. In the documentary film, the flow of water onto the hard, dry Spanish earth parallels the movement of mechanized equipment on the successfully defended Madrid-Valencia road. The bridge, in the film, is held by the Loyalists and preserved from capture by a counterattack of Loyalist tanks and troops. In *For Whom the Bell Tolls*, Hemingway exercises the greater freedom of the novelist and changes the values of bridge and tank. The Nationalists hold the bridge. It is their armor that must not cross.

Just as the lighthouse dominates the action of Virginia Woolf's novel, so the bridge controls and unifies the action of Hemingway's. In one sense it is the center of a series of concentric circles; in another it is the point toward which the elements of the plot converge. No matter what geometric metaphor is used to plot the book upon a plane surface, it is certain that the bridge is central. Robert Jordan thinks of it as "the point on which the future of the human race can turn." The character of each person is determined by his or her relation to the bridge. Pablo is, of course, against the demolition of the bridge. Pilar is for it, because she understands its significance: "I am for the Republic. . . . And the Republic is the bridge." Robert Jordan defines himself by the bridge: "You're a bridge-blower now. Not a thinker." At the end, he once more identifies himself with the emblem of technological civilization: "As Jordan goes, so goes the bloody bridge." The bridge *is* destroyed, but Robert Jordan, escaping on horseback, is hit by a shell fired from an enemy tank. Mortally wounded, he waits to confront the enemy.[5]

One need not, however, rely exclusively upon the action of the novel or upon the symbolic oppositions, for the characters speak out. Anselmo asserts bitterly, "We must take away their planes, their automatic weapons, their tanks, their artillery and teach them dignity." Pilar is completely explicit: "The sight of those machines does things to one. . . . We are nothing against such machines." Looking up at the Heinkels overhead, Robert Jordan thinks they are like "sharp-nosed sharks of the Gulf Stream," but only for a moment does he link the machine with the natural menace. As the tank was, in *The New Republic* dispatch, worse than the hurricane, so the bombers are worse than the worst of nature:

But these, wide-finned in silver, roaring, the light mist of their propellers in the sun, these do not move like sharks. They move like no thing there has ever been. They move like mechanized doom.[6]

Clearly then, for Hemingway, the Spanish Civil War was, among other things, a struggle waged by men close to the earth and to the values of a primitive society against men who had turned away from the earth, men who had turned to the machine and to the antithetical values of an aggressive and destructive mechanical order. When Hemingway addressed the American Writers Congress in 1937, he spoke of Spain and of the writer's responsibility to "write truly and having found what is true, to project it in such a way that it becomes a part of the experience of the person who reads it." Considering the facts both of Spanish history and of Hemingway's own career prior to 1936, *For Whom the Bell Tolls* seems the natural result of Hemingway's urge to write as truly as he could.[7]

The Machine as Menace

Ernest Hemingway was not the only writer to see the Spanish war as the opposition of man and machine. Waldo Frank's "organicism" led him to praise "the profoundly *whole* culture of Spain" and to glorify the land and the peasant who worked the land: "The peasant of Spain is real Spain. In no other country of Europe has culture and historic action sprung so directly from the humble human soil." At the same time, Frank shuddered to imagine "tens of thousands of bare breasts of simple men and women . . . there to confront the machine guns and bombing planes." Elliot Paul, John Dos Passos, and Josephine Herbst all emphasized the primitive village as the heart of Spain, the peasant or the fisherman as the truest Spaniard, as the victim of a mechanized enemy. In an early version, John Howard Lawson's film, *Blockade,* began with Marco, the peasant-hero, laboring in his vineyard. Norma, the soon-to-be-discovered Fascist, makes a destructive entry; she drives her motorcar through Marco's vines. But the car runs into a placid pair of oxen and expires with a smashed radiator. The scene was a preview of the triumph of the primitive over the mechanical order.[8]

Still other men and women, who did not necessarily share Hemingway's affirmation of the Spanish earth, shared this vision of the tank and the bomber as images of doom. Edwin Rolfe, poet and historian of the Lincoln Battalion, wrote that "there is something about an enemy tank approaching, its machine guns spitting uninterrupted death, which throws fear into the heart." *The New Republic,* which had printed Hemingway's dispatches from the front, presented in an editorial the image of the machine as menace:

Women and children torn to pieces by aerial bombs as they go to market, crowded buildings and boulevards . . . shattered by artillery, suburbs and outlying parks made into playgrounds for grinding tanks, men and women . . . sprayed to death . . . by machine guns in power-diving pursuit planes—this is Madrid today.

There is no sense of human agency behind the weapons of the Fascists; there is only the sense of impotent humanity beneath omnipotent machines. This sense of impotence and this image of conflict between men and machines run through a wide variety of writings and are found in the visual arts as well. For the sake of simplicity and clarity, I shall concentrate on the most nearly ubiquitous symbol of technological warfare—the bombing plane.[9]

Herbert Matthews of the *New York Times* described his own feelings of powerlessness beneath the then-experimental *Luftwaffe:* "It is a terrible moment when one can hear a bomber directly overhead, knowing its power of destruction

and feeling so helpless." Lester Ziffren, another correspondent, found air raids the most frightful aspect of the Spanish
war: "My dreams were of horrors." Irving Pflaum of United
Press admitted that his "one real fear" was that "methodical,
systematic, terroristic bombing . . . may be one of the decisive factors in future wars. With me it was decisive. It licked
me." Frank Pitcairn told the readers of *Travel* about the
fantastic risks taken in the

hopeless but still necessary effort to even out the difference between a German-manned Junker's plane with bombs and machine guns, and a peasant lad with eight days training, a rifle
and a few rounds of ammunition.

Similar observations were made by Jay Allen and Katherine
de Carreras in broadcasts over CBS, by Erskine Caldwell
in his contribution to *Salud!,* by Alvah Bessie in his account
of the last days of the Lincoln Battalion, and by Edwin
Rolfe in his history of that battalion.[10]

As names like Bessie, Caldwell, Dos Passos, and Herbst
suggest, bombing planes were symbolically present in novels
as well as in factual accounts of the war. The bomber
quickly became a part of the sound effects, of the backdrop,
for scenes of conflict. John Dos Passos uses this image of
terror in *Adventures of a Young Man* and Michael Blankfort
uses it in *The Brave and the Blind.* Upton Sinclair's *No
Pasaran!* comes to a dime-novel close in which two Americans, cousins who have volunteered for opposing sides, fight
it out. The quality of the novel is reflected faithfully in the
triumph of the foot soldier (Loyalist) who vanquishes his
air-borne relative (Fascist).[11]

The importance of this image as a metaphor for our
times becomes even more obvious when we see that the only
American novelist of any merit whatsoever to take General
Franco's side—the Baroness de Zglinitzki, *née* Helen Nicholson—also dramatized the opposition of man and machine. In

her account of the war in Andalusia, she refers to "Franco's army in overalls, fighting in the snow of the Guadarramas," and comments that they have shown "how far an intrepid spirit can triumph, even over the might and the machine-guns of Russia." The coming of the bombers ends her one-act play, *Shelter for the Night.* Her novel of the Spanish war, *The Painted Bed,* comes to a climax when an air raid brings death and a vision of Christ upon the cross.[12]

Numerous one-act plays make symbolic use of the bombing plane. Barrie Stavis wrote *Refuge,* a play set in a bomb shelter, and William Merrick's *Forgot in the Rains* (a Columbia Workshop play) concludes with the bombing of a village. Archibald MacLeish, who had joined Lillian Hellman is raising money for *The Spanish Earth,* wrote *Air Raid,* a verse-play broadcast by CBS, in which bombers are described by the narrator as a form of dehumanized menace:

> They swing like steel in a groove:
> They move like tools not men:
> You'd say there were no men:
> You'd say they had no will but the
> Will of motor on metal.

Implications of this vision become clearer as one recalls the visions of endangered primitivism that are found in Mac-Leish's earlier poem, *Conquistador.* Lacking this element of overt primitivism but quite as bitterly written, Norman Corwin's play, *They Fly through the Air with the Greatest of Ease,* was also broadcast by CBS. It was, like dozens of poems and hundreds of editorials, written as a response to the bombing of Guernica.[13]

When history contained horrors such as Guernica, it is hardly odd that bombing planes appeared in the poetry of the Spanish war. Norman Rosten's "Fragments for America" is a disquieting poem. He wrote of a

> peasant who tried to stop an enemy plane
> rising; ran cursing into the swift propeller
> to stop it with his hands; the plane rising
> . . . the sun shining on the stained steel.

Langston Hughes wrote, "A bombing plane's/The song of Spain," and added further poems to illustrate, poems in which he associates airplanes and death and undercuts the traditional connotations of moonlight: "Moonlight in Valencia: the moon meant planes./The planes meant death." Edwin Rolfe, in "A City in Anguish," described Madrid under bombardment:

> All night, all night
> flared in my city the bright
> cruel explosions of bombs.
> All night, all night,
> there, where the soil and stone
> spilled like brains from the sandbag's head,
> the bodiless head lay staring;
> while the anti-aircraft barked,
> barked at the droning plane. . . .

In "Casualty," Rolfe told how "one bomb, shrieking,/found the thin axis of his whirling fears,/the exact center." In an epitaph for an American volunteer, he used the imagery of the earth:

> This is the plot where the self-growing seed
> sends its fresh fingers to turn soil aside,
> over and under earth ceaselessly growing,
> over and under earth endlessly growing.

Another poet, Boris Todrin, wrote in a manner equally reminiscent of Hemingway's elegy on the American dead and the Spanish earth:

> Worn out fields where bomb and shell
> Scattered iron seeds of hell
> Grow their scarecrow crops. The torn
> Bones will keep the roots of corn.

John Berryman's more complex poem, "1938," contains bitter comments on the Spanish war and on the war that was still in preparation:

> Across the frontiers of the helpless world
> The great planes swarm, the carriers of death,
> Germs in the healthy body of the air,
> And blast our cities where we stand in talk
> By doomed and comfortable fires.

Randall Jarrell, who wrote several poems on the Spanish war, described in "The Winter's Tale" the collapsing world of the late thirties. His metaphor for fragmentation was the "disintegrating bomber" that had sown death "without hate or understanding."[14]

In this helpless world beneath the iron bombers, poets found a metaphor grounded in reality. They found a still more specific metaphor when the "necessities" of modern warfare sanctioned the bombing of cities, for then it became "necessary" that children die with their elders. Harold Rosenberg's eight-line "Spanish Epitaph" is representative:

> O tall men of Hades
> Have pity on this little one!
> His speech was not formed yet
> All he knew of life was laughing and growing
> Till the iron dropped on him out of the sky.
> O gaunt horses of Hades
> He has not even one weapon
> With which to defend himself.

Muriel Rukeyser had been in Spain and had written several poems on the Spanish Civil War (which she characterized as one of "humans against guns") when she wrote "M-Day's

William Gropper: "Air Raid." The second half of the opposition between man and machine is the vision of huddled and almost faceless people beneath the bombers. (Reproduced by permission of the painter.)

Anton Refregier: "Fascists over Spain." A surrealistic
vision of the bombing plane. (Reproduced by permission of *Masses and Mainstream*.)

A. Birnbaum: "Milk for Spanish Children." Another example of the political commitment of American artists. The commitment, in this case, seems to be one influenced by humanitarian considerations. (Reproduced by permission of *Masses and Mainstream*.)

"Mrs. Purvis is just back from Spain. She says they're wearing their skirts *quite* short." (Drawing by Helen E. Hokinson, copyright © The New Yorker Magazine, Inc.)

Child." This short poem contains the particular theme of the menaced child within a broader denunciation of military horror:

> M-Day's child is fair of face,
> Drill-day's child is full of grace,
> Gun-day's child is breastless and blind,
> Shell-day's child is out of its mind,
> Bomb-day's child will always be dumb,
> Cannon-day's child can never quite come,
> but the child that's born on the Battle-day
> is blithe and bonny and rotted away.

Poets like Charles Norman were infuriated by the defense of the raids on Spanish cities:

> . . . empty now the schoolhouse stands,
> And empty since the planes went by;
> Children in school in other lands
> Will mark this victory.

Langston Hughes, Aaron Kramer, and Norman Rosten are three poets of the many more who wrote of the bombers and the children.[15]

If bombing planes are almost ubiquitous in the written accounts, they are scarcely less so in the visual arts. Anton Refregier attempted a surrealist's vision of a bomber, a grotesque mixture of fiend and machine, but most American painters followed the lead of Luis Quintanilla, the Spanish artist whose drawings of the war expressed the simplicity of the slaughter. Quintanilla's drawings were exhibited and published in this country. In his Preface to Quintanilla's book, Ernest Hemingway refers to the artist's combat experiences in places "where men with rifles, hand grenades, and bundled sticks of dynamite faced tanks, artillery, and planes." We find the same stark opposition graphically transformed, in the book, into images of peasants fleeing in oxcarts from planes that hover over ruined villages and slaughtered animals. Louis Ribak's *Refugees*, Zoltan Hecht's

Air Raid, and Ione Robinson's sketches, *In a Refugio,*
Watching Enemy Planes, and *After Bombardment,* represent
scores of American paintings, drawings, cartoons. In an era
when reading "morals" into paintings is suspect, it is useful
to have Ernest Brace's comment on William Gropper's *Air*
Raid:

One senses . . . the terror of implacable, blind force, the sense-
less and indiscriminate destruction of human beings by other
human beings too remote, too mechanically indifferent to
wonder who or why.[16]

Just as the contrast between men and bombers becomes
in literature most striking when the child is opposed to the
Heinkel or Caproni, so in the iconography of the Spanish
war, the contrast is most awful when represented in these
images. Photographs of the dead children of Madrid appeared as "photomontages," as covers of pamphlets denouncing the bombing of cities, as frontispieces for poems, and,
paired with a picture of Cardinal Hayes flanking General
Franco, as an indictment of the Church.[17]

Paintings and drawings embody the same theme of conflict. Aldous Huxley, editing Oxford University Press' edi-
tion of drawings *by* Spanish children, noted the following:

To the little boys and girls of Spain, the symbol of contemporary
civilization, the one overwhelmingly significant fact in the world
today is the military plane. . . . For hundreds of thousands of
children . . . the . . . plane, with its bombs and its machine
guns, is the thing that . . . is significant and important above all
others. This is the dreadful fact to which the drawings in our
collection bear unmistakable witness.

The briefest examination of the pictures convinces us that
the children did indeed live in dread of the air raids. In
drawing after drawing, we see ruined cities, the little figures of
fleeing people, and the disproportionately enlarged bombers.

The Spanish children did not, of course, trail clouds of Words-worthian glory or understand international relations better than the diplomats, but children do often see certain things in a more immediate and less prejudiced way than adults do. It was the tough-minded Romans and not the Romantics who noted that *verba sapienta* came often *ex oribus in-fantum.*[18]

Coming to America to speak for Spain, André Malraux told an anecdote about the distribution of toys to the chil-dren of Madrid:

When it was all over, there remained in the immense empty space one little heap, untouched. . . . It was a pile of toy air-planes. It lay there in the deserted bull ring, where any child could have helped himself. The little boys had preferred any-thing, even dolls, and had kept away from that pile of toy air-planes . . . with a sort of mysterious horror.

Pablo Picasso's *Guernica* is no more pertinent to our theme, no more disturbing a revelation of *la condition humaine* in the twentieth century of the Christian era.[19]

America and Europe

These quotations are only a few instances of the theme of conflict between men and machines, and of the image of the machine as the appropriate symbol for the terrible reali-ties of the Spanish war. If we stop now to compare Heming-way's work with that of several European novelists, we can, perhaps, observe certain differences of emphasis between the American and the European imaginations. It must be said, of course, that the American and the European imaginations are very similar. From the point of view of someone *outside* the western tradition, the similarities are undoubtedly more obvious and more important than the dissimilarities, but we are *within* the western tradition and can profitably look for the subtler distinctions.

Gustav Regler's work is representative of the European radical tradition. His novel, *The Great Crusade,* is a novel of the International Brigades. Specifically, it is a novel of the Twelfth International Brigade (made up of Germans, Frenchmen, and Italians of the Thaelmann, Marty, and Garibaldi Battalions). Paul, the commander of the brigade, is an authoritarian determined to make Madrid the "tomb of Fascism." Werner, the doctor is charge of the brigade's medical detachment, represents the more humane aspects of the radical tradition. Albert, modeled on Regler himself (as the other two are drawn from General Lucasz and from Werner Heilbrunn), is the brigade's commissar and the novel's central character. Albert observes and learns from Paul, Werner, and the other men and women of the brigade. The characters are international but quite unlike the allegorical polyglots of William Rollins' *Wall of Men.* These exiles from Germany or Poland are real exiles. Regler himself was one of them. Unlike American fiction, *The Great Crusade* is riveted with allusions to European radicalism, to Bukharin, Dimitroff, Kamenev, Radek, Trotsky, Zinoviev. And the book is shadowed by the noonday darkness of the Moscow Trials. The most sophisticated of the Internationals knew that Stalin had betrayed their cause. Nevertheless, they fought Fascism and accepted the discipline that made the fight possible. In C. Day Lewis's phrase, they "defended the bad against the worse."[20]

The novel is episodic. It moves from the struggle in the lecture rooms of the University of Madrid (where the Fascist advance was finally halted) to the Jarama Front and thence to the Battle of Guadalajara. The conflict between men and machines is present here as in Hemingway's fiction, but the terms of the conflict are reversed. Now it is the Internationals who represent the future, the Fascists who represent the past. At the Jarama River, the French are attacked by General Franco's Moors. Werner watches the Moors advance and thinks of "the forest primeval." He thinks of "bestial Africans with the knife between their teeth. In reserve [for the French were] Italian proletarians. If the boys succeed in driving back that herd of beasts today, they must be sent home. To Lyons, to Ville-Juif, to Brussels, to Dunkirk." Not to Montana, not to the wilderness. But the Moors are not turned back. They swarm like animals over the overwhelmed French. They press forward then toward the positions held by the Dombrowski Battalion (Poles who had replaced the Germans of the Thaelmann Battalion). In a scene that seems to reverse the end of *For Whom the Bell Tolls,* the Loyalist armor arrives. The Moorish cavalry is stopped.

Now the tanks came wobbling in from both sides of the ravine in front of the line of Poles. Their guns felt out their targets for a moment, then as the machines rumbled slowly forward, the blue explosion burst.

The African invasion fails.[21]

Regler's novel, to which Ernest Hemingway wrote an introduction, is quite unlike *For Whom the Bell Tolls* or any other American novel of the Spanish Civil War. There was, however, one European of note who seemed to share something of Hemingway's vision. Ralph Bates, who lived in Spain as Hemingway had done, wrote—as Hemingway had —of Spanish life before the civil war. His novel, *The Olive Field,* describes the tumult of the years preceding the actual outbreak of the war. It is set, for the most part, in the agricultural south. The peasants are pitted against the effete landowners who collect ancient manuscripts; the peasants receive no help from the ascetic priests who do not understand that "the olive [trees are] the very spirit of the land." The action leads to the Left revolution of 1934, where the spontaneous action of the workers is overmatched by tanks and planes.[22]

When, in 1936, the Right tried *its* hand at revolution, Bates joined the Republican side and fought through what he later called "the legendary time" of the hastily organized militias. The struggle was one of man against machine. In the preface to one book on Spain, Bates wrote of a "docker who had charged through rifle, machine-gun and *artillery* fire, with a broken plank through which he had hammered nails as his sole weapon." In *The New Republic* he wrote of "Unarmed men [who] leap on the gunners, wrestle with them, strangle them, drag them to the ground and stab them with knives. Men dive at the machine guns . . . and upset them with their hands." The article ends with the plea of the Spanish peasant: "Compañero Americano, will you *sell* us rifles? Italian aircraft . . . roar overhead." In "Spanish Improvisation," he wrote of a plowman who sang folksongs. Bates speculated, "I suppose he is dead now, because he would certainly have tried to defend the Republic, with a shotgun, against those Caproni and Junkers which nightly raid us."[23]

Of all the writings on the Spanish Civil War, Bates' short stories, collected in *Sirocco and Other Stories,* are closest to Hemingway's in tone, theme, and diction. The protagonists are usually close to the land; their antagonists are associated with mechanized authoritarianism. In "The 43rd Division" (also published in two issues of *Harper's*), Pere, the undisciplined peasant-hero, insists on fighting the war on his own very individualistic terms. He fights alone and is in constant trouble with his commanding officer. Moreover, he condemns the newer modes of warfare:

The mechanical aid to the rebels was violating the nature of the Spaniard, he felt. Man to man, valor against valor; that was the

Spanish way of fighting. Not factory against factory, bald-head engineer against peasant.

The crucial episode of the story embodies this theme. An izard (a type of chamois) gives birth and a Fascist equipped with a panoply of technical inplements—Luger, Mannlicher-Cacano, Zeis range-finder, Leitz binoculars—kills the animal. Pere realizes that Fascism means the destruction of the natural order, that undisciplined battalions cannot hope to withstand the enemy offensive. Returning to his unit, he is first reprimanded and then given command of a guerrilla force. Asked if he wants a political commissar, Pere replies, "Yes . . . it won't be necessary, but I'd like one." He chooses the commissar who had reprimanded him. Through undiscipline, Pere learns, paradoxically, to accept discipline. In "The 43rd Division," as in other stories by Ralph Bates, we catch a glimpse of the promised land, a socialist Spain in which the machine and the olive tree will be forever reconciled.[24]

Excellent as many of these stories are, André Malraux's *L'Espoir* is the only piece of writing that compares well with *For Whom the Bell Tolls* or with George Orwell's *Homage to Catalonia*. No other European novel (of dozens) contains so much of the complexity of the Spanish Civil War. No other novel so well suggests the differences between the European and the American interpretations of the Spanish Civil War.

In *L'Espoir,* Hemingway's theme of primitivism—the affirmation of the natural man in the natural landscape—is sounded with a marvelous sense of the ambiguous overtones and then subordinated to another theme. The subtle distinction that is apparent in Bates' work and obvious in Regler's becomes, in Malraux, the theme. True to the European revolutionary tradition, Malraux debates and finally decides against the values of a primitive society. As

Joseph Warren Beach noted, "The most inspiring moments
in the book are those in which . . . individualists discover
their community of feeling and prove themselves as efficient
in action as the mechanized units of fascist violence. This
theme is . . . underscored . . . in the critical struggle between
men and property, men and machines." But, this affirmation
of the primitive community does not persist throughout the
novel. The conflict between man and machine becomes less
important as Russian equipment arrives. Scenes of heroic
struggle against a mechanical enemy give way to descriptions
of victory won by those who turn from the land to fight steel
with steel. The somehow humanized "crates" of the circus-
like volunteer air force are replaced by modern aircraft. The
pilots learn the necessity of strict obedience. As Malraux's
spokesman argues, "Our modest function . . . is to organize
the Apocalypse." Realizing the hopeless situation of the unarmed human being, Malraux finds in this realization a call
to action. The *milicianos* must be mechanized. Russian
chatos climb the air over Malraux's Madrid as they did over
the Madrid of historical fact. It is true that the theme of
discipline and the dramatic victory of the International Brigades at Guadalajara are interwoven with another strand,
with the theme of primitivism and the uncoerced action of
the peasants who, late in the novel, carry down from the
mountains, in ritual procession, the survivors of a wrecked
airplane. Nevertheless, despite this extraordinary episode,
Malraux's explicit approval is with the organizers of the
Apocalypse, with the Stalinists whose ultimate goal was the
socialization and industrialization of a "Progressive" Spain.[25]

In taking this position, Malraux was anticipating historical developments. As the war continued, discipline *was* imposed upon militiamen and modern weapons *were* placed
in the hands of the peasants. The *Volunteer for Liberty* replaced pictures of "half-armed militiamen" firing from the

earth at aircraft, with pictures and charts of Soviet industrialization. Ludwig Renn, German novelist and commander
of the Thaelmann Battalion, told *Esquire* readers, "Today
we have a modern army, well equipped, with planes, tanks
and the latest anti-tank guns. Today, with the disappearance
of the last of the party troops, we have a unified command,
discipline, and up-to-date training." James Hawthorne of
New Masses praised the "brand-new beauty" of the Loyalists' airplanes, and Louis Fischer of *The Nation* began a
statement by announcing that the war was one of "flesh
against steel" only to continue by boasting that the "Loyalist army is better equipped than ever; airplanes have been
imported." Poets wrote elegies for Ben Leider, an American
killed while flying in Spanish combat: "O Icarus, welcome
him,/wingless now and a wanderer," and

> No hawk, no eagle dies
> But broken lies—
> Ashes will stir,
> The phoenix shall arise.

And even Ralph Bates sounded the harsh call to discipline.
He insisted that the "legendary time" of undisciplined hero-
ism was over. A realistic attitude was needed. Changes had
been made and the army had become a "cleanly machine."[26]

In taking this position, however grudgingly, men like
Regler, Bates, and Malraux are representative of the mainstream of European radicalism, a tradition that has, for the
most part, rejected the strong element of primitivistic anarchism found in American *and* in Spanish radicalism. The
leading student of Spanish political history has this to say
of Spanish anarchism:

Spanish anarchism . . . is . . . dominated by that nostalgia for
the past that is so characteristic of Spain. . . . It voices more
clearly and intelligently than any other Iberian movement the

resistance offered by the whole Spanish people to the tyranny and soullessness of the modern machine-serving age.

Voiced by the Spanish, this resistance to mechanization was listened to by Europeans and by Americans. Europeans then shut their ears, but a few Americans—men like Hemingway—continued to listen, to remember the virgin land of the American past, and to hope. Although Karl Marx characterized modern man in industrial society as living in a state of alienation, Marxian socialism looks *forward*, to a classless society in which technology is used for the benefit of mankind and not as the instrument of exploitation, and *not* backward, to a vision of primitivistic anarchism. At the end of his chapter on "The Pond in Winter," Henry David Thoreau created a symbol that suggests the distinction between the two traditions. Thoreau described the voyage of the ice cut from Walden Pond.

The pure Walden water is mingled with the sacred water of the Ganges. With favoring winds it is wafted past the site of the fabulous islands of Atlantis and the Hesperides, makes the periplus of Hanno, and, floating by Ternate and Tidore and the mouth of the Persian Gulf, melts in the tropic gales of the Indian seas, and is landed in ports of which Alexander only heard the names.

The movement of this passage is toward Asiatic shores, and the flow of metaphors carries us backward in time. It is, perhaps, an oddity of the history of ideas that the influence of *Walden* was felt in Asia and in eastern Europe by anarchists distrustful of industrialism (such as Mahatma Gandhi and Leo Tolstoy), and far less strongly in industrialized western Europe; Friedrich Engels and Karl Marx dreamed not of the past but of the future, and never saw the "pure Walden water" mingle with the waters of the Thames.[27]

Primitivism versus Progress

Considering this theme of conflict between men and machines, it seems reasonable to suggest that at least *part* of the extraordinary fascination of the Spanish Civil War is related to a widespread, if barely articulated (or even unarticulated), fear of the implications and the actualities of technological society. We can ask two questions:

1. Does this theme of opposition represent a fear of machines *as such* or only the fears of those for whom the machines were not yet available, or were novel, or were in the hands of an enemy?

2. Does this fear have a counterpart in the affirmation of man in a natural, organic relationship to the land, in a tendency toward that stream of primitivism that has run, underground for the most part, through western civilization since the time of Montaigne's essay on the cannibals?

Any answers to these questions are, of course, extremely inconclusive, but the evidence indicates that most men, for one reason or another and *despite* their fears of a mechanized enemy, were quite willing to equip themselves with modern weapons and to use them to the utmost. When the Spanish war ended and World War II began, most of those who condemned the *Luftwaffe* became enthusiastic over the R.A.F. and, eventually, the United States Air Force. Hiroshima caused less of a stir than Guernica.

Nevertheless, to say that most men were willing to mechanize or to condone mechanization (which is, of course, to say that most men were not primitivists) is *not* to say that they were untouched by the fear of mechanization or by the values of primitivism, by a desire for the spontaneity and the freedom from repression that we associate with an organic relationship to the natural landscape.

What Ernest Hemingway has done in *For Whom the Bell Tolls* and in *The Spanish Earth* has been to orchestrate and make central a theme that runs through the work of scores of other writers and artists. He has, to change the figure, turned the various images of value into the characters of a drama, his version of the Spanish tragedy. Although the greatest caution must be exercised, we can surely study Hemingway's ordering of the historical events and speculate whether or not there is, within a vast complex of other and often contradictory values, an association of freedom with the earth, of tyranny with machines; on the one hand, fertility and spontaneity, and, on the other, sterility and repression.

The specter of an urbanized, industrialized, mechanized and regimented world—a specter that has haunted the Romantic imagination since Blake's dark Satanic mills and Melville's Tartarus of Maids—seemed, to Hemingway, Dos Passos, Frank, MacLeish, and a few men like them, to have materialized, to have become the bombing planes over Madrid and Barcelona. Perhaps this is but the symbol-maker's way of saying that capitalism was, in some countries, becoming Fascism. The problem is that the Marxists' vision of a Spain dotted with Magnitogorsks and Pittsburghs is not easily harmonized with the primitivists' vision of the Spain of Don Quixote, Sancho Panza, and Rosinante.

Looking back on the Spanish war, we can see now that Hemingway's primitivistic Spain was doomed the minute that the British Foreign Office warned Léon Blum that his siding with the Republic endangered the Franco-British alliance. Faced then by the mechanized armies of Germany and Italy, the Loyalists had either to secure modern weapons or go down to defeat. The failure of the Spanish Republic to arm itself and to achieve political unity meant the coming of a Spanish version of Fascism. *And*, had the Loyalists succeeded in their efforts, the Spanish peasants would have been forced in the process to accept limitations on their famous individualism; to adopt the mechanized weapons of modern war; to surrender their archaic relationship with the hard, dry Spanish earth; to become members of a technologically-based mass-society that might or might not have evolved eventually into the Marxist utopia. In either case, the result would have been a curtailment of freedom and an increase in repression.

In other words, there was in Spain as in nineteenth-century America the dilemma and the paradox of primitivism and progress that Henry Nash Smith has assayed in *Virgin Land*. Just as the dream of America as an industrial Titan contradicted the dream of America as a new Garden of Eden, so the attempt to discipline and organize and mechanize "feudal" Spain contradicted the desire to preserve a spontaneous, organic, archaic relationship of man and nature. Joy Davidman wrote bravely about the unarmed men in the Republican armies:

> We have only the bodies of men to put together,
> the wincing flesh, the peeled white forking stick,
> easily broken, easily made sick,
> frightened of pain and spoiled by evil weather;
> we have only the most brittle of all things the man
> and the heart the most iron admirable thing of all,
> and putting these together we make a wall.[28]

But Hemingway's interpretation seems closer to the truth when Robert Jordan is left, crippled and alone, waiting for the onslaught of the newest *conquistadores*. Perhaps the novel is closer to historical fact *because The Spanish Earth* failed to move Americans, *because* there were too many time-serving diplomats and too few volunteers for liberty, *because* the western democracies abandoned Spain to a choice between two forms of totalitarianism. Confronted by the mechanized enemy, Hemingway's primitivism became an impossible vision, but that is not to say that the values associated with primitivism are not still valid ones; one need not be a primitivist today to feel that technological mass-society is both repressive and frighteningly unstable. Perhaps we can thank the "practical" men of the 1930's that, in an era of abiding tension, in a time of ballistic missiles and atomic warheads, we are all as helpless as the children beneath the bombing planes.

At any rate, the extraordinary thing about the Spanish war is that the historical facts seemed almost of themselves to dramatize the conflicts of the age. The material facts did, as in nineteenth-century America, correspond to the spiritual facts, or, to continue in Emerson's language, the situation was such that the poet could attach the word to the thing. Within the labyrinth of events that historians have agreed to call the "Spanish Civil War," there was once again, on foreign soil as so often before in our literature, that opposition of the "two kingdoms of force," seen by Leo Marx as central to our experience: "For the contrast between the two cardinal images of value, the machine and the native landscape, dramatizes the great issue of our culture. It is the germ, as Henry James put it, of the most final of all questions about America."

In other words, Hemingway's vision of the Spanish war has its roots in a very *American* tradition of thought and feeling. The Spanish war was, among other things, a fight against the desecration of that relationship between man and nature that Natty Bumppo sought in forest and prairie, that Thoreau found while floating quietly on Walden Pond, that Herman Melville pursued in his quest for an "authentic Eden in a pagan sea," that Walt Whitman contemplated in a blade of summer grass, that Huck and Jim discovered while drifting down the Mississippi on a raft, that William Faulkner finds in the mule-powered and horse-swapping South, that John Dos Passos envisioned when he wrote that the "villages are the heart of Spain," that Ernest Hemingway located in upper Michigan and in an African Spain. Here, as elsewhere, we found in the Spanish war a mirror reflecting the image of our own unquiet desperation.

EPILOGUE

AND

CONCLUSIONS

On April 1, 1939, Generalissimo Francisco Franco issued, from his headquarters at Burgos, a communiqué announcing the end of the Spanish Civil War: "Today, after having made prisoner and disarmed the Red army, the Nationalist troops have reached their final military objective. The war is ended." Although it was true that the Nationalist troops had achieved a military victory, the war was not ended. Eighteen years later, the *New York Times,* still concerned, denounced President Eisenhower for interrupting his summer activities to congratulate General Franco on the happy anniversary of his rebellion. When President Eisenhower visited the *Caudillo* in 1959, Salvador de Madariaga—no more noted for radical tendencies than the *Times* itself— lamented that we had sunk to this presidential homage. When President Kennedy's secretary of state paid *his* tribute to the Spanish dictator, Samuel Guy Inman fired off a hot rebuke in the form of a letter to the *Times*. John Davis Lodge, recent ambassador to Madrid, replied with a lengthy defense of Spain as "a nation which . . . understands the implacable nature of the Communist threat." The arguments blaze in the letter columns almost as fiercely as they did a quarter century ago.[1]

There are other indications of the permanence of the passions aroused by the war: the fight to exclude Spain from the United Nations, the angry debate over American economic support and over American bases, the dismay of many at repeated gestures of friendship. The number of titles on the Spanish war, which passed 600 by 1940, now includes more than 2,000 books and pamphlets, and each year adds more histories, biographies, memoirs, polemics, novels. Interest in 1961 was keen enough to put Hugh Thomas's history on the bestseller lists and to keep it there for months. The heritage of bitterness is a rich one: a historian of Jacksonian America pauses in his narrative to chastise one of Theodore Sedgwick's twentieth-century descendants for having supported General Franco; Jack Levine and Robert Motherwell, two leading American painters, exhibit works entitled *Spanish Prison;* Eleanor Roosevelt and Winston Churchill exchange sharp words over policies adopted during the Spanish war; the hero of *Casablanca* loses his idealism while running guns for the Republic. Samuel Lubell comments that the

antagonism left over from the Spanish Civil War . . . remains one of the more important political dividers in the country. Both Catholics and non-Catholics . . . are fighting to vindicate the positions they took in that struggle.[2]

A further indication of the permanence of the concern is the yearly publication of novels in which the Spanish Civil War is first the scene of the conflict and then the symbol for a whole generation's attitudes. If we set aside American plays from Maxwell Anderson's *Key Largo* to Edward Albee's *Death of Bessie Smith*, if we consider only American novels and ignore translations from other languages and republication of British fiction, the list is still an impressive one. In 1940, Hemingway published *For Whom the Bell Tolls*, the most popular of all his writings. That same year, Michael Blankfort's *The Brave and the Blind* dramatized the siege of Toledo's Alcázar. The hero of Frederick Prokosch's overwritten novel, *The Skies of Europe*, becomes involved in the Spanish Civil War, as did the simpler hero of Frances Parkinson Keyes' *The Great Tradition*. The following year, 1942, Arthur McGratty braved public opinion and critical contempt with *Face to the Sun*, a long book intended—I hope—for Catholic children. (Until the Faithful stop them, "seedy-looking" Communists "sneer" and "smirk" and ·rape and desecrate and misbehave.)

Supporters of General Franco did not, however, monopolize literary ineptitude. In 1943, Upton Sinclair's Lanny Budd whirled off to Spain to find the meaning of the war: "What we have to do is to judge which side stands for freedom and enlightenment and which for medievalism and superstition." (It did not take Lanny Budd long to find an answer.) In 1944, Allan Chase, who had already written one monitory study of espionage in Latin America, wrote *Five Arrows*, in which Matthew Hall, a correspondent modeled from the *New York Times'* Herbert Matthews, moves prophetically from the Spanish Civil War to the troubles of the Caribbean. (Matthews, the *Times'* top man in Spain, was the first American to interview Fidel Castro.) In Lionel Trilling's *The Middle of the Journey* (1947), Gifford Maxim is tortured by the things he had seen in Spain:

My . . . heart is full of hatred and pity. . . . I have been in Spain, and I have seen Kermit Simpson shot and worse, and Nancy

Croom shot and worse, and John Laskell and Arthur Croom. And myself. And I have helped. I have done it. . . . And even if I had not been there to see, I would know that I was involved. I am involved in the cruelties I have never seen and never will see.

Gifford Maxim's anguished disillusionment was shared, in a sense, by McLeod, the mysterious hero of Norman Mailer's *Barbary Shore* (1951), but McLeod is lucky. He finds someone to whom he can bequeath whatever is left of his ideals. Piers Hungerford, the hero of Anne Fremantle's novel, *By Grace of Love* (1957), serves as a stretcher-bearer for the Fifteenth International Brigade. His journey to Spain is one step on the road to his discovery that "nothing mattered except that the Incarnation had happened."[3]

We are not surprised to find political themes in novels by Lionel Trilling and Norman Mailer. We should be surprised *not* to find the Spanish Civil War a major concern of Alvah Bessie's novel, *The Un-Americans*. But even William Faulkner, the idol of those who worship the nonpolitical novel, sends Linda Snopes off to drive an ambulance for the Loyalists. For Meyer Levin, Joseph Freeman, Ellen Glasgow, May Sarton, Charles Wertenbaker, Howard Nemerov, Alan Kapelner, Herbert Gold, and Daniel Cort, the Spanish war is a symbolic event whose meaning the reader is expected to understand from the most parenthetical reference. In an autobiographical novel of childhood and adolescence in the 1930's, Herbert Gold writes of "those strange suburban days in which Shirley Temple was the most passionate partisan of the Spanish loyalists" and reminds the middle-aged of the Dies Committee and its strenuous efforts to track down juvenile contributors of money to the Spanish Republic. The Spanish Civil War has become, in Daniel Aaron's phrase, the last great cause.[4]

For these reasons we can say to General Franco that the

Spanish Civil War is not yet ended. But this study has reached the point where some kind of summary is called for. When biographers complain that insurmountable difficulties prevent us from understanding another person, when psychoanalysts add that we can never really know ourselves, it is clear that an endeavor to analyze a nation's response to a war is a very risky enterprise. Nevertheless, certain conclusions are well supported.

Excepting only the Great Depression and the hostilities that began in September of 1939, no public event of the 1930's mattered so much to so many Americans as did the Spanish Civil War. Articulate Americans, many of whom had rarely before displayed interest in political affairs, were greatly concerned about the fate of the Spanish republic, and they still are.

For many Americans on the Right, the Spanish Civil War was an event that raised great (and often quite unfounded) hopes. These hopes were of many different kinds. A handful of frenzied American Fascists published periodicals such as *The American Bulletin* and *The New Liberation*. These predecessors of George Lincoln Rockwell applauded the *Movimiento Nacional* because it was part of an international repudiation of liberal democracy, of "Judaism," of other aspects of the modern world. These Americans did not speak for a large segment of the population.

Another group of Americans—men like Lawrence Dennis, Ralph Adams Cram, George Santayana, and Ezra Pound —hoped that the death of the Republic would be followed by the rebirth of a nationalistic and an aristocratic social order. The enthusiasm of these men for General Franco was never as intense as that of the American Fascists and never as uninformed. Often, the rigor and the individuality (if not the eccentricity) of their thought kept their following small.

Still another group of Americans supported the *Caudillo* because he seemed to promise a Christian society in which the menace of Communism would permanently be forestalled. Although a few Protestants sympathized with General Franco as a defender of the rights of property and the prerogatives of institutional religion, American Catholics rather than American Protestants supplied most of the articulate ardor for the "Holy War" in Spain. Ardent and avowedly Protestant support for the *Movimiento* was limited, for the most part, to one magazine, *The National Republic* (Washington, D.C.); ardent Catholic support, on the other hand, pervaded the pages of *America, Catholic Action, The Catholic Mind, Catholic Digest, Catholic World, Columbia, The Sign,* and even *The Catholic Historical Review.* Diocesan newspapers were usually more intensely partisan than were the magazines of orders and organizations. Catholic publishers—Sheed and Ward, the America Press, Bruce, the Paulist Press—issued a great number of pro-Franco books and pamphlets. Presses associated with Protestant denominations—the Westminster Press, etc.—published (to my knowldege) no books or pamphlets in which the pro-Franco argument was set forth. Public opinion polls reinforce such data and provide additional evidence of a sectarian split on this issue. While 39 per cent of the Catholic sample sympathized with the Spanish Nationalists, the American Institute of Public Opinion discovered that only 9 per cent of its Protestant sample did so.[5]

The curious thing about Catholic support for General Franco, as discussed in Chapter 3, is that relatively few American Catholics supported Franco as the man who would put into practice the principles enunciated in the social encyclicals of Leo XIII and Pius XI. Most of the Catholic backing for General Franco came, apparently, from men and women who felt that the Spanish insurgents were fighting against Communism and for a kind of Catholicism perfectly consonant with the ideals loosely referred to as "the American Way of Life." Since it is clear that General Franco was *not* fighting for this kind of Catholicism compatible with liberal democratic ideals, I am encouraged to see that 30 per cent of the Catholics polled answered that *their* sympathies were—despite the stand taken by the hierarchy—with the Republic. This remarkably high percentage of Loyalist sympathy, when considered along with the sometimes desperate attempts on the part of the hierarchy to portray General Franco as a Christian and a democrat, suggests that American Catholicism was neither "monolithic" nor without internal crisis. It seems clear that the laity remained largely unconvinced by the pronouncements of the clergy and that the clergy themselves were unable to endorse General Franco except as a kind of Hispanic George Washington. Isaac Hecker might well have been pleased by this. On the other hand, Hecker might have been distressed to see that, of periodicals read primarily by Catholics, only *Commonweal* and *The Catholic Worker* failed to support the Spanish Nationalists and that the circulation of *Commonweal* suffered greatly because of this editorial neutrality. No American Catholic magazine supported the Republic.

Americans on the Left were also stirred by the Spanish Civil War. Some Americans—men like Van Wyck Brooks, Waldo Frank, and Lewis Mumford—were greatly excited by the possibility that Spain was about to blossom forth into an organic society of complete men in a purposeful community. The Spanish Civil War seemed to promise the beginning of Spain's Golden Day. The dawn for American anarchists, for the writers who published in *Man!* and *Vanguard* and read Vernon Richards' *Spain and the World*, was that of the libertarian era dreamed of by Emma Goldman. As Stalinist repression ended the social revolution, anarchists realized

The Guggenheim money allowed Goldman and Berkman to live on the French Riviera during the 1930s. They were terrorists and murderers.

that they had thrilled to a false dawn, but the bitterness of betrayal served only to invest the lost cause with a still brighter aura. For still other Americans, the dream was of a return to a simpler life understood instinctively by peasants and by gypsies and, at least in Hemingway's world, by college teachers from Montana.

It is extremely difficult to say how many people were stirred by such hopes. Certainly, few Americans called themselves "organicists" or "primitivists," and not many more were willing to be identified as "anarchists," but it was possible for many men to share feelings that a few men felt with the utmost intensity. Some men who longed for wholeness or cherished the Spain celebrated in *The Sun Also Rises* worked within the North American Committee to Aid Spanish Democracy with men who abhorred bullfighting as a brutal vestige from Spain's "feudal" past, who wished to metamorphose "Man Thinking" into "Commissar Agitating." But even the Stalinists—such as Earl Browder and Louis Fischer—found in the end that their estimation of what was valuable differed from Stalin's. It is not impossible that men like Browder welcomed the Popular Front because their deepest and most enduring commitments were, after all, to something we may call (if the phrase has not become debased) the American heritage.

The socialists—both those who had "splintered" from the Communist Party and those who placed themselves in the older traditions of Daniel De Leon and Eugene Debs—agreed among themselves in their hope that the Spanish Civil War would result in the final attainment of the classless society predicted by Marx and Engels. They disagreed, often violently, on the means by which the end was to be accomplished. They all faced the problem confronted also by the Soviet Union: how could socialism be "in" the world without being "of" the world? In other words, how could socialists, in a capitalistic world, effectively counteract the threat of Fascism without becoming hopelessly enmeshed and compromised? Dimitroff answered, "Through the Popular Front," but the answer was not one that satisfied everyone. Of those who swallowed their distaste and joined the Popular Front, many found their hopes for the classless society quickly qualified by their fears that bourgeois democracy or, worse still, Stalinism, would be the only winner in Spain. Finally, there were some men who were, like Louis Fischer, about to break with Stalinism when the Spanish Civil War seemed to bring out the best in the Soviet system.

Whether or not the Stalinists themselves had faith in the eventual replacement of the bourgeois Republic by the Marxist utopia is a difficult question. The evidence seems to justify the distrust and the disbelief of those anti-Stalinists who wrote for *Workers Age* and for *The New International;* but, on the other hand, the disaffection and the renunciations of Stalinism that followed the Molotov-Ribbentrop Pact of 1939 (and continues to the present day) indicates that many sloganeers *believed* their slogans and left the Party when it became clear that the Party did not.

One thing at least can be said about *all* of these Americans who looked for a change in the Spanish "status quo ante bellum," whether by returning to happier times or by moving forward from liberalism. They were a minority of articulate opinion. In many instances, their analyses of the Spanish situation were far more informed and far more perceptive than those of the petition signers who envisioned Madrid as a kind of embattled Middletown. Certainly this study has relied heavily upon their information and their insights. Still, in many instances, the radicals (of both ends of the spectrum) were blinded by the fires of their hatred or by the brightness of their hopes.

The majority of articulate opinion, whether or not it

was rallied by the "front" organizations of the Communist Party, was concerned because the liberal democratic tradition seemed threatened by the retrogression of civilization toward a new Dark Age of irrationality, lawlessness, and barbarism. Although many expositions of liberal tenets seem to have been rhetorical screens covering a dislike of Catholicism or the cynical courtship of a frightened bourgeoisie, millions of Americans seem honestly to have believed in the ideal of a fundamentally decent and reasonable people making steady progress under representative institutions. For them, the Spanish Revolution of 1931 was, indeed, another 1641 or 1789 or—most commonly—1776. This belief in liberal democracy was a desperately precious (and precarious) one in the years when *Nationalsozialismus* practiced genocide and Italian fliers described the fun of bombing black men.

Committed to liberal democratic ideals, appalled by Fascism's spread from Italy and Germany into Spain, many private citizens, like Stuart Davis, repudiated the right to privacy and the ideal of the nonpolitical man. He, and others like him, joined exiles from Fascism, such as Thomas Mann, in protesting against the insanity that seemed to be sweeping Europe and in working for what Mann hopefully called "the coming victory of democracy."

The liberal view of Spain was often myopic. The newly "engaged" writer or artist or clergyman or lawyer or professor was often painfully naive and uninformed in his commitments. An illiberal and undemocratic Stalinist influence became dominant in Spain; such liberal leaders as President Manuel Azaña were deeply depressed by the bitter dissensions within the ranks of the Loyalists. Francisco Largo Caballero and Indalecio Prieto, the two socialists who fought hardest to counteract Stalinist influence in Spain, were both convinced Marxists. Neither was a liberal in the Jeffersonian tradition. Nevertheless, it can be maintained that the abandonment of the Republic by the western powers *assured* the Russian control so tirelessly exposed (often before it existed) by the Right. Furthermore, it seems very likely that, had the Republic been victorious, the Stalinists would have been ousted by anti-Stalinists dedicated to a more indigenous form of radicalism. If the Republic was not a liberal democratic Republic, it was, at least, moving in the direction of social democracy. It is, at any rate, hard to believe that a Spain in which the Republic had won would have equaled the wretchedness of contemporary Spanish society. In this sense, liberal democrats were wise to have supported the Republic.

To talk, however, of the "political spectrum" is to assume that all Americans were articulate, concerned, or "committed" vis-à-vis the Spanish Civil War. This is, of course, a simplification. Many Americans refused to take sides because they were divided in their loyalties or because they could not solve the dilemmas in which they found themselves. Other Americans were unwilling or unable to take sides because they were—bluntly speaking—quite unaware of the war that was being fought in Spain. Both of these groups—the undecided and the unaware—were, for the most part, inarticulate; both were classified by the American Institute of Public Opinion as having "No Opinion." The Gallup Polls showed that from 24 per cent to 34 per cent of the people fell into this category, but the polls did not subdivide these unresponsive citizens into further categories. The pollsters did, however, gather enough evidence for us to speculate on this question.

In the four polls taken during the course of the war, the highest percentage of "No Opinion" responses came from those groups that have, generally speaking, the least education and the least awareness of events abroad: the unskilled workers, the unemployed, and, to shift to a geographical rather than a vocational category, Southerners. (In one poll, for instance, 44 per cent of the Southerners and only 20 per cent of those from the Middle Atlantic States failed to respond.) This strongly suggests that the Spanish Civil War never occurred for the least conscious stratum of the American people. There were probably a number of people who ignored newspapers, magazines, radios, newsreels, and documentary films—and even the charms of Loretta Young, Dorothy Lamour, and Madeleine Carroll (who starred in *Love under Fire, The Last Train from Madrid,* and *Blockade*). It seems likely that a slightly less uninformed stratum of American society had only the most superficial interest in the Spanish Civil War as a series of sanguine and often perverse events under the general heading of "human interest." For this audience, *The American Magazine, Liberty,* and *True* published the adventures of Americans who flew in the Loyalist air force; for this audience, *Adventure Novels, Collier's, Cosmopolitan, Liberty, Scribner's,* and the publishers of "mysteries" provided popular fiction with the Spanish Civil War as hastily constructed backdrop. It is likely that many who had no opinion to give the pollsters were either totally unaware of the Spanish war or were alert only to the spectacle of naked nuns and Amazons or to the sentimentality and horror of "A Kiss in Spain" and "Witch of the Alcazar." It is probable that, for these people, the Spanish Civil War never was what William James called a "live option." They never *had* to choose between two meaningful alternatives.[6]

When, however, 23 per cent of those listed as "Professional" and 26 per cent of those listed as "Business" declined to comment on the Spanish war, when nearly a third of those responding refused to take sides, it seems quite likely that *some* of those who declined did so because they could not make up their minds. In other words, the process of coming to a decision was complicated by contradictory evidence and by conflicting loyalties. Since many of these contradictions are the very ones that anguished and often intensified the commitments of those who *had* chosen one side or the other, it is necessary to turn to the contradictions and dilemmas confronted by those Americans who attempted to take sides on the Spanish war.

Many groups, especially the Catholics who had made political and economic gains under the New Deal, found their status threatened by what happened in Spain and by American responses to Spanish events. Joseph Kennedy was at the Court of St. James, but his dream of the presidency must have seemed more and more distant as angry Protestants listened to Father Coughlin and concluded—too hastily —that all American Catholics were a tightly knit and a very alien minority. Some Catholics, like George Shuster, tried to explain their dilemma, but such explanations did little to lessen the ill will between religious groups. On the other hand, many Anglo-Saxon Protestants must have felt, as they had felt on the eve of World War I, that support for the liberal democratic element abroad was almost an act of public piety, a duty dictated by a tradition that Irish Catholics could never wholly understand. After all, they reasoned, were not those who threatened liberty in Spain the very ones who threatened Beacon Hill itself?

American concern was made more intense and more anxious by other dilemmas than those of status. How, for instance, could a Catholic claim allegiance to American traditions and, at the same time, support a dictator driving inhumanely to power behind the *Luftwaffe* and the veterans of the Ethiopian campaign? How could liberal democrats aid Spanish democracy without incurring the risk of another world war? How could Spanish democracy be aided without alienating those very Catholic voters who had helped to send a liberal to the White House? How could dedicated anarchists justify their Spanish brethren's participation in the institutions of political government? How could Marxists possibly suport a government that included liberals, anarchists, conservative businessmen, and Basque Catholics? How, on the other hand, could club ladies consort so with dedicated revolutionaries? On another level of generalization, how could one achieve peace by waging war? And how could one preserve the land of Don Quixote and of Carmen by developing the Hispanic equivalent of the *Wehrmacht?*

There were further complicating factors. In a time when governments neither rallied populations with bond sales nor exhorted citizens to do their "patriotic duty," individuals were left with something like freedom of choice. This freedom meant a certain excitement not always shared by the unhappy citizen conscripted into enormous armies dedicated by a mysterious Pentagon or Kremlin to fearsome and official, but not always specified, purposes. An individual, during the Spanish Civil War, could choose to work for a committee or even to go to Spain as a volunteer. But the freedom meant responsibility. No one could escape from what Jean-Paul Sartre moodily calls the "dreadful freedom" of individual choice. And, to realize the full difficulty of making up one's mind, we have to remember that the failure to take sides was, in a sense, taking sides. Franklin Roosevelt's decision to remain "neutral" helped to send the Spanish Republic—for better or for worse—to its doom. Hitler and Mussolini had already opted.

Finally, it can be argued that the very *success* of the liberal tradition in America is in itself paradoxically responsible for much of the frustration of the undecided, for much of the ingenuousness of the committed, and, more specifically, for the inability of Roosevelt's triumphantly re-elected liberal administration to take any action more effective than the "neutrality" legislation that pleased only the least liberal segments of the population. The liberal consensus in the United States, the consensus that Daniel Boorstin applauds, has led, in a sense, to the ideological equivalent of the one-party system and to the emotional and intellectual stagnation of a tradition that does not constantly define itself against an opposing tradition. Accustomed to government more or less by consensus, Roger Shaw, editor of the *Review of Reviews,* thought it was "a pity that conservatives and liberals [in Spain] cannot debate in parliament in the British or American way, uniting to smack hard the savage extremists of both lunatic fringes." Few liberal democrats seemed to realize that Spain was a deeply divided nation, that the "savage extremists" in Spain were far more numerous than the Christian Silvershirts or the IWW. The "extremists" in Spain were the largest and most powerful groups, the dominant elements of Spanish life. Acclimated to this nation's milder climate of opinion, we had no way of mapping the winds of doctrine that swept Spain and no satisfactory way of dealing with them. Confronted by the American embargo, liberals denounced the State Department as "Fascist." This was not an adequate response.[7]

It might be argued that radical voices, like conservative voices, are relatively few and *ought* to be ignored, but, while these voices grow shrill and even hysterical, while decisions are evaded and responsibilities ignored, conditions worsen until the guns fire on Fort Sumter, until the unquarantined aggressors appear in the sky over Pearl Harbor.

This is, of course, the thesis of Lionel Trilling's book, *The Liberal Imagination*:

In the United States . . . liberalism is not only the dominant but even the sole intellectual tradition. For it is the plain fact that nowadays there are no conservative or reactionary ideas in general circulation.

Conservative impulses, says Trilling, express themselves

not in ideas but in "irritable mental gestures which seek to resemble ideas." It is, moreover, "not conducive to the real strength of liberalism that it should occupy the intellectual field alone." Alone, liberalism becomes complacent and finally effete.[8]

One need not defend Trilling's thesis *in toto* in order to see that the various responses to and interpretations of the Spanish Civil War can be ordered and better understood by using the concepts of the liberal democratic tradition and that, in turn, the Spanish war enables one to see more clearly the strengths and the weaknesses of the liberal imagination.

Despite General Franco's communiqué of April 1, 1939, the Spanish Civil War is not yet over. And, as if the intensity of feeling had not been extreme enough already, there has been added the guilt of those who felt that they had chosen wrongly or that they had done too little to implement their choice. (The most famous example of futile regret is that of Sumner Welles: "Of all our blind isolationist policies, the most disastrous was our attitude on the Spanish civil war.") And then, to all of this, has been added the exasperation of those puzzled at the failure of others to accept the newest "status quo post bellum" and the frustration of those who have watched the mistakes of the neutrality policy compounded by early diplomatic recognition and then by American aid and friendship.[9]

Because the war was, in part, a conflict among the rival ideologies of the twentieth century, it will probably continue to be fought in the hearts of those who lived through it and, as this limited study suggests, by those who know it only as a historical event. Civil wars are difficult to judge, but it seems appropriate to say, in concluding, that, despite all the shortcomings of Comrade Browder, Manuel Azaña's Republic was worth defending. Most of the Americans who supported the Republic seem more American than the officials who have questioned their loyalty. One sometimes feels that the men who named their volunteer unit "The Lincoln Battalion" were closer to the traditions of liberal democracy than are those public men who persistently include General Franco's *Nuevo Estado* within the limits of that oddly gerrymandered jurisdiction, "The Free World."

ABBREVIATIONS

In footnotes and in bibliography, the following abbreviations
are used:

America	A
Among Friends	AF
The Atlantic Monthly	AM
The Catholic World	CW
The Nation	N
New Masses	NM
The New Republic	NR
The New Yorker	NY
The Saturday Evening Post	SEP
The Sign	S

NOTES

INTRODUCTION

1. Coughlin, "Democrats and Dubinsky," *Social Justice*, II (September 21, 1936), 4; Hinkel, *The Communistic Network* (New York, 1939); Kelly, "Foresworn Americans Serve Red Cause in Spain," *A*, LVIII (October 23, 1937), 55-56; Dies, *The Trojan Horse in America* (New York, 1940), pp. 293, 297; Hoover, *Masters of Deceit* (New York, 1958), pp. 71-72, 109.

2. Hayes, *The United States and Spain* (New York, 1951), p. 87; Bessie, *The Heart of Spain* (New York, 1952), pp. vi-vii; Nelson, *The Volunteers* (New York, 1953), p. 192; Voros, *American Commissar* (Philadelphia, 1961); Gates, *The Story of an American Communist* (New York, 1958).

3. Beach's comment is in *Writers Take Sides* (New York, 1938), p. 4.

CHAPTER 1

1. *Spain: World Ideas in Conflict* (Los Angeles, 1938), p. 29.

2. "On the Screen of Time," *Theosophical Quarterly*, XXXIV (October, 1937), 330-31.

3. For the British publications, see Francis Yeats-Brown, *European Jungle* (Philadelphia, 1939), p. 281; Robert Sencourt, "How Spain's War Ended," *Contemporary Review*, CLV (April, 1939), 398; Nigel Tangye, *Red, White and Spain* (London, 1937), p. 47. For American publications, see H. C. Plummer, "Barcelona Seized by Anarcho-Syndicalists," *A*, LVI (November 21, 1936), 149); Federico de Echeverria, *Spain in Flames* (New York, 1938), pp. 37-38. Komroff, "Spanish Episode," *Coronet*, V (January, 1939), 110.

4. Woolsey, *Death's Other Kingdom* (London, 1939), pp. 59, 66, 126.

5. "Hell in Spain as I Saw It," *Liberty*, XIII (October 3, 1936), 7.

6. Frank C. Hanighen, "Hell-Cats in the Spanish War," *Liberty*, XIII (October 31, 1936), 30-31; Berenice E. Noar, "The '76 of Spain," *Fight*, III (October, 1936), 6; "In the Ranks of Spain's Republican Army," *Travel*, LXVIII (November, 1936), 34-35; Frank Pitcairn, "On the Firing Line in Defense of Madrid," *Travel*, LXIII (February, 1937), 18-22. For Ishigaki's painting, see Bibliography.

7. H. E. Knoblaugh, *Correspondent in Spain* (London, 1937), p. 38; Sylvia T. Warner, "I Saw Spain," *Fight*, IV (February, 1937), 5; William Foss and Cecil Gerahty, *The Spanish Arena* (London, 1938), pp. 410-28; Terry Brennan, *Death Squads in Morocco* (London, 1937).

8. *For Whom the Bell Tolls* (New York, 1940), pp. 125-26. Quotations from this book by permission of Charles Scribner's Sons, Inc.

CHAPTER 2

1. Quotations are from Francisco Guillén Salaya, *Anecdotario de las JONS* (San Sebastian, 1938), p. 20; Stanley G. Payne, *Falange: A History of Spanish Fascism* (Stanford, 1961), p. 39; José Pemartín Sanjuan, *Los Origenes del Movimiento* (Burgos, 1938), p. 22; and Francisco Franco, *Palabras del Caudillo* ([No place given], 1938), pp. 59-62, 198.

2. For Hitler's speeches, see *New York Times*, September 10, 1936, and September 14, 1937. Goebbels, *The Truth about Spain* (Berlin, 1937), p. 32.

3. "Patriotic Rebellion in Spain," *American Bulletin*, II (July 21, 1936), 2; "Spanish-Soviet War," *American Gentile*, II (November, 1936), 1; "Did the American People Give a Mandate to This?" *New Liberation*, VII (January, 1937), 5; "Facts You Should Know about Europe's Blood-Drench," *New Liberation*, VII (May, 1937), 5-6.

4. Carlson, *Under Cover* (New York, 1943), p. 458 (Carlson's real name is Arthur Derounian). Hart, *America, Look at Spain* (New York, 1939), pp. 41, 72, 221-28, 102, 183.

5. Kuehnelt-Leddihn, "The Anatomy of the Leftist," *Examiner*, II (Spring, 1939), 149; Fitzgerald, "Manfred's Fate," *Examiner*, II (Spring, 1939), 184-90; Corliss, "Thunder on the Right," *Examiner*, II (Winter, 1939), 33-34.

6. Jerrold, "Red Propaganda from Spain," *American Review*, IX (May, 1937), 141; "The Issues in Spain," *American Review*, IX (April, 1937), 3, 23; *Georgian Adventure* (New York, 1938), p. 380; Yeats-Brown, *European Jungle* (Philadelphia, 1939), p. 281.

7. "Russia's Private War in Spain," *American Mercury*, XI (February, 1937), 158.

8. *The End of Democracy* (Boston, 1937), p. 62.

9. *The Letters of George Santayana,* ed. Daniel Cory (New York, 1955), pp. 314-15.

10. Maurras. *Vers l'Espagne de Franco* (Paris, 1943), p. 150; Lewis, *Count Your Dead: They Are Alive!* (London, 1937); Campbell, "'Flowering Rifles,'" *New Statesman and Nation,* XVII (April 8, 1939), 541; Eliot and Pound, *Authors Take Sides* (London, 1937).

CHAPTER 3

1. Kennedy is quoted in James M. Burns, *John Kennedy* (New York, 1960), p. 32.

2. See *The Papal Encyclicals,* ed. Anne Fremantle (New York, 1956), pp. 143-52, 229.

3. *Encyclical on Spain* . . . (New York, 1937), pp. 3-4.

4. Thomas, *The Spanish Civil War* (New York, 1961), p. 173. For address to Spanish refugees, see *Encyclical on Spain, op. cit.;* for *Divini Redemptoris, Catholic Mind,* XXXV (April 22, 1937); for the Pastoral Letter, *The Spanish Situation: A Survey* (Washington, D.C., 1937).

5. Parsons, "Tailor-Made Lies," *Catholic Digest,* I (September, 1937), 33-34; Masse, "Christian Liberals—To Whom Are They Allied?" *A,* LIX (June 11, 1938), 227.

6. See Bibliography for a sample of Carney's work.

7. "Clarifying the Issues in the Spanish Civil War," *A,* LVIII (October 23, 1937), 52.

8. The *Labor Charter* was published by General Franco's Peninsula News Service in 1938. See Bibliography for other articles by Connolly. Thorning, "Franco Speaks for Himself," *Columbia,* XVII (November, 1937), 17. Carney's article appeared December 26, 1937. Montavon's book was published by the National Catholic Welfare Conference in 1937.

9. McGuire, "The New Spain," *Commonweal,* XXVII (October 29, 1937), 5.

10. O'Brien, "Navarre: Salt of the Earth," *S,* XVII (March, 1938), 462-65, and "Soldier of Spain," *S,* XVIII (January, 1939), 350; Wall, *Spain of the Spaniards* (New York, 1938), pp. xxi-xxiii; McGuire, "After the Storm," *Columbia,* XVII (May, 1938), 16; De Hueck, "The Spirit of New Spain," *S,* XVII (October, 1937), 153-57; Belmonte, "Life in Nationalist Spain," *Commonweal,* XXVI (October 15, 1937), 567-68. European Catholics publishing abroad were more extreme yet. Florence Farmborough, for instance, felt Franco's battle to be a crusade for "Christianity, Civilization and Culture." The *Falange Española* was "all comprehension, all compassion," all mercy and justice. (*Life and People in National Spain* [London, 1938], pp. 68,

177.) Eleanora Tennant, often quoted in American journals, denounced Communists ("To stand well with the Reds a Communist must be able to claim that he has put at least one priest or nun in his game-bag") but praised "Republican" Franco ("In Nationalist Spain there is no fear, nor is anyone oppressed."). (*Spanish Journey* [London, 1936], pp. 86, 103, 114.) Arthur F. Loveday, head of the British Chamber of Commerce in Spain, condemned oriental Freemasonry, Judaism, and the Comintern for disturbances in Spain. He also noted that prewar bookstores were loaded with pornography as part of the "published Marxian programme" of destroying religion and the family by the "establishment of unbridled sexual license." (*World War in Spain* [London, 1939], p. 58.) None of these books gives an adequate summary of the Nationalists' ideology or institutions.

11. *Spain in Chains,* trans. Carmen de Arango (New York, 1937).

12. Pemartín Sanjuan's book was excerpted as *Franco's Mein Kampf: The Fascist State in Rebel Spain* (New York, 1939).

13. The phrase is Cardinal Hayes's, *New York Times,* November 2, 1936.

14. Eoin O'Duffy, *Crusade in Spain* (London, 1938), p. 34.

15. Paul McGuire, "In the Name of the Father," *S,* XVII (February, 1938), 409-11; Philip John, "The Troubled City," *CW,* CXLVI (December, 1937), 276-81; Mary Hutchison, "Los Molinos," *CW,* CXLIX (April, 1939), 19-23.

16. W. J. Randall, "Maria's Grand Finale," *S,* XVII (August, 1937), 23-26; Nancy Scoggins, "The Nun Who Met the Rebels," *Liberty,* XIII (October 24, 1936), 32-35; Pérez Olivarez, "Incident in a Spanish Camp," *Catholic Digest,* I (April, 1937), 75; Maher, " 'Unimpeachable Sources,' " *Columbia,* XVII (August, 1937), 5, 24-25; T. W. C. Curd, "Popular Front," *Catholic Digest,* I (August, 1937), 19-22.

17. David Gordon, "Threnos," *A,* LX (December 3, 1938), 212; Blacam, "For the Spanish Martyrs," *S,* XVI (December, 1936), 284; Benedict, "Song for Spain," *CW,* CXLVI (February, 1938), 549; Feeney, "The Spanish 'Loyalists,' " *A,* LVIII (November 27, 1937), 188.

18. Claudel, "To the Spanish Martyrs," *Spain,* I (October 12, 1937), 6-7; Mary St. Virginia, "Christ Returns to Barcelona," *A,* LX (February 25, 1939), 500, reprinted from *America,* The National Catholic Weekly Review, 920 Broadway, New York 10, New York.

19. Forrest, *Christian Civilization versus Bolshevist Barbarism* (Huntington, Ind., 1937), pp. 8, 18; Grimley, *The Spanish Conflict* (Paterson, N.J., 1937), p. 13; Kelly, "After Barcelona," *S,* XVIII (March, 1939), 480; Walsh, "Speaking of Spanish Democracy," *Spain,* I (December 1, 1937), 8; *Catholics Reply to "Open Letter" on Spain* (New York, 1937), p. 14.

20. *The Spanish War and Lying Propaganda* (New York, 1937), pp. 42, 48. (My italics.)

21. Sheen, "Spain through Red-Tinted Glasses," *Irish Monthly,* LXVII (March, 1939), 179; Oliveri, *Democracy! Which Brand, Stalin's or Jefferson's?* (San Francisco, 1937), p. 15; Curran, *Spain in Arms* (Brooklyn, 1936), p. 4, and *Franco: Who Is He? What Does He Fight For?* (Brooklyn, 1937), pp. 6, 40, 7; Coughlin, " 'It Can't Happen Here,' " *Social Justice,* II (August 10, 1936), 4; John P. Delaney, "Call Not These Men Rebels," *A,* LV (August 22, 1936), 460; Augustine C. Murray, "Behind the Scenes in Spain," *Catholic Digest,* I (February, 1937), 5-7; Thorning, "Neutrality versus Intervention," *Spain,* III (February 1, 1939), 21.

22. Rogers, *Spain: A Tragic Journey* (New York, 1937), pp. 64, 68, 88; Altabás Yus, *The Struggles of Spain* (New Orleans, 1938), pp. 1-2.

23. Parsons, "No Masses in Madrid," *Columbia,* XVI (September, 1936), 25; "True History: Past and Present," *CW,* CXLIV (March, 1937), 649; "The Real Problem in Spain," *CW,* CXLV (June, 1937), 258-59; "A Few Jottings on 'Propaganda,' " *CW,* CXLV (August, 1937), 521-23; Sencourt, "How Spain Has Reacted," *CW,* CXLVII (May, 1938), 138-42; Godden, "How Communism Attacked Spain," *CW,* CXLIV (January, 1937), 403-7; McSorley, *"A Diary of My Times,"* *CW,* CXLVIII (January, 1939), 503-4, and *"The Martyrdom of Spain,"* *CW,* CXLVIII (October, 1938), 113-16.

24. Shuster, "Some Reflections on Spain," *Commonweal,* XXV (April 2, 1937), 625-27; "Civil War in Spain and the United States," *Commonweal,* XXVIII (June 24, 1938), 229; Williams, "Views and Reviews," *Commonweal,* XXVIII (June 24, 1938), 241.

25. Talbot, "Further Reflections on the Spanish Situation," *A,* LVII (May 1, 1937), 76; *"The Commonweal and the Spanish War,"* *A,* LIX (July 2, 1938), 293; La Farge, "While Spain Burns They Strum Impartially," *A,* LIX (August 20, 1938), 462-63. For the outraged letter, see issue of July 15, 1938. For the review of Bernanos, see Charles P. Bruehl, "A Censor of his Age," *Commonweal,* XXIX (March 3, 1939), 515-18.

26. O'Connell, *New York Times,* March 19, 1938; Hayes, *New York Times,* March 24, 1938; Keating, "The Ethics of Bombing," *Catholic Mind,* XXXVI (July 22, 1938), 281; Maritain, Preface to Alfred Mendizábal, *The Martyrdom of Spain,* trans. C. H. Lumley (New York, 1938), p. 25; Day, "Explains *CW* [*sic*] Stand on Use of Force," *Catholic Worker,* VI (September, 1938), 4.

27. Fremantle, "Davos-Parsenn," *New Statesman and Nation,* XVII (March 4, 1939), 321-22; O'Sheel, "Spanish Rebellion and Catholic Doctrine," *NR,* XCIII (February 2, 1938), 368; Norris, *Letters from Spain* (San Francisco, 1937); Pegler, *Wilkes-Barre Leader,* April 27, 1938.

28. For Dulles' involvement, see John Morton Blum, *From the Morgenthau Diaries: Years of Crisis, 1928-1938* (Boston, 1959), pp. 506-8.

CHAPTER 4

1. *New York Journal*, July 29, and August 22, 1936. This and a number of other quotations from newspapers are either taken from or found with the help of James F. O'Brien's "American Press Opinion of the Spanish Civil War" (Unpublished thesis, Georgetown University 1950). Brisbane, "Today in Europe," *Cosmopolitan*, CI (October, 1936), 32-33.

2. Belmonte, "Introducing General Franco," *Today*, VI (September 5, 1936), 21, 27; Knickerbocker, "The Thing Called Civil War," *Today*, VII (December 5, 1936), 10-12, 24-25; Moley, "Perspective: The World Watches Spain," *Today*, VI (August 8, 1936), 17; Waldeck, "Civil War in Spain," *Today*, VI (August 22, 1936), 8-9, 28-29.

3. Steele, "Watch 'The Popular Front,'" *The National Republic*, XXIV (October, 1936), 3; McWilliams, "Barcelona in Scarlet," *The National Republic*, XXVI (June, 1938), 4, 29.

4. See Bibliography for articles by Pratt, Castellano, Bell, and Gellhorn.

5. *Time*'s elegy, "Fall of the City," appeared in the April 3, 1939 issue—in the later, but not in the first, printing.

6. "The Patron Saint of Andalusia," *AM*, CLXI (June, 1938), 784.

7. The Editors of *Fortune*, *The Background of War* (New York, 1937), pp. 56-58, 105.

8. All data on public opinion polls are taken from Hugh Jones Parry's "The Spanish Civil War: A Study in American Public Opinion, Propaganda, and Pressure Groups" (Unpublished thesis, University of Southern California, 1949), pp. 367-70. Samples include those who answered "Neither" but exclude those who answered "No Opinion."

9. For AFL, see *Report of Proceedings of the 56th Annual Convention* (Washington, D.C., 1936), pp. 578-80; Broun, "How Do You Sleep, Franco?" *New York World-Telegram*, March 21, 1938; ILGWU, "I.L.G.W.U. Asks $50,000 for Labor's Red Cross in Spain," *Justice*, XVIII (August 15, 1936), 2. Lewis and Murray are discussed in Matthew Josephson, *Sidney Hillman* (Garden City, N.Y., 1952), pp. 463-64, and Saul Alinsky, *John L. Lewis* (New York, 1949), pp. 200-202. For campus opinion, see Theodore Newcomb, "The Influence of Attitude Climate upon Some Determinants of Information," *Journal of Abnormal and Social Psychology*, XLI (July, 1946), 291-302. For DAR, see Mark Sullivan, "The Attack on Democracy," *National Defense News*, II (September, 1937), 11.

10. On Texaco, see Herbert Feis, *The Spanish Story* (New York, 1948), pp. 269-70. For the Du Pont connection, see *Business Week* for April 8, 1939. For Baruch, see Department of State's *Foreign Relations of the United States: Diplomatic Papers,* 1938, I (Washington, D.C., 1955), 317. For Ford's essay, see Keith Sward, *The Legend of Henry Ford* (New York, 1948), pp. 146, 451. The best account of foreign investments in Spain is Frank Jellinek, *The Civil War in Spain* (London, 1938), esp. pp. 49, 72, 278.

11. Code, *The Spanish War and Lying Propaganda* (New York, 1938), pp. 43-44; Hayes, *New York Times,* March 24, 1938; Clifford, "Editor, What of Your Bias?" *Columbia,* XVII (May, 1938), 2; Maguire, "Blind Leaders," *S,* XVII (November, 1937), 195; "Monsignor Ready Refutes Attack on Spanish Bishops," *Catholic Action,* XIX (October, 1937), 5-6; "Something to Live Down," *Columbia,* XVII (November, 1937), 3.

12. "Spain," *Consolation,* XIX (November 17, 1937; July 27, 1938; and August 24, 1938), 12-13; 13; and 25; "The Pope and General Franco," *The Christian Evangelist,* LXXIV (August 6, 1936), 1011; John Sommerlatte, "The Spanish Terror," *The Messenger . . .,* I (November 19, 1936), 5; William G. Wirth, "Spain and the Vatican," *Signs . . .,* (October 6, 1936), pp. 4-5.

13. "A Nation Torn by Class Hatred," *Lutheran Companion,* XLIV (September 5, 1936), 1123; Herring, "Spain's Bitter Days," *Advance,* CXXVIII (October, 1936), 593; "A Spanish Protestant on Spain," *Advance,* CXXXIX (July, 1937), 310; Eliot, " 'A Military Maneuver,' " *The Christian Register,* CXVII (March 31, 1938), 207; Hapgood, "Spain," *The Christian Register,* CXVI (September 10, 1936), 526; Holmes, "The Spanish Revolt," *Unity,* CXVII (August 17, 1936), 225; Priestly, "Spain—Yesterday and Tomorrow," *Christian Leader,* CXX (May 14, 1938), 616.

14. "Spain and the Catholic Church," *Radical Religion,* IV (Winter, 1938), 4; Niebuhr, "Arrogance in the Name of Christ," *Christian Century,* LIII (September 2, 1936), 1157; "Keep Out of Spain!" *Christian Century,* LIV (January 27, 1937), 104-6; Luccock, "Through the Novelist's Window," *Christendom,* IV (Winter, 1939), 154-58; "For the Record in Spain," *Protestant Digest,* I (December, 1938), 84; Davin, "Patent Blasphemy," *Protestant Digest,* I (March, 1939), 13-16.

15. Marlin, "Unhappy Spain," *United Presbyterian,* XCIV (July 30, 1936), 7; "The Spanish Civil War," *The Presbyterian Tribune,* LII (October 29, 1936), 5; "Roman Catholicism and Fascism," *The Presbyterian Tribune,* LIII (August 18, 1938), 5-6; "The Murder of Democracy," *Presbyterian Tribune,* LIV (March 16, 1939), 5.

16. Mecklenburg, "Three Tragedies of Europe," *Christian Advocate,* CXIV (March 30, 1939), 298.

17. Bradbury, "The Tragedy of Spain," *Watchman-Examiner,* CXVIII (December 10, 1936), 1386.

18. "Religion in Spain," *The Churchman,* CLIII (February 1, 1939), 8; Inman, "Religious Liberty in Spain," *The Churchman,* CL (November 15, 1936), 11; "The Roman Church in Spain," *The Chronicle,* XXXVII (November, 1936), 28-29; "Spain and Germany," *The Living Church,* XCV (September 5, 1936), 230.

19. Hawthorne, "Three Spanish Catholics," *NM,* XX (September 22, 1936), 3-4; "Mass in Madrid," *NM,* XXIV (August 24, 1937), 9; "Catholics and Spain," *NM,* XXVIII (July 12, 1938), 11-12.

20. Roger Abbott, "Who Backed the Spanish Revolt?" *NM,* XX (August 11, 1936), 13; Fearing, "The Program," *NM,* XXVIII (September 6, 1938), 20, reprinted by permission of *Masses and Mainstream;* Rosten, *The Fourth Decade and Other Poems* (New York, 1943), p. 52, reprinted by permission of Holt, Rinehart & Winston; *Kaltenborn Edits the News* (New York, 1937), pp. 7-8.

21. "The Church's Opportunity in Spain," *The Presbyterian Tribune,* LIII (March 3, 1938), 5-6.

22. *Days of Our Years* (New York, 1939), p. 425.

CHAPTER 5

1. For names cited, see these anonymous pamphlets: *The Crime of Guernica* (New York, 1937); *Bombs Over Barcelona* (New York, 1938); *An Open Letter of Culture and Democracy* (New York, 1938); *American Democracy versus the Spanish Hierarchy* (New York, 1938).

2. Elliott, "With the Rebels," *AM,* CLVIII (November, 1936), 541; Manuel, *The Politics of Modern Spain* (New York, 1938), pp. 188-89; Jones, in *From Spanish Trenches,* ed. Marcel Acier (New York, 1937), p. 146; Freeman, *Never Call Retreat* (New York, 1943), p. 312.

3. Black, "Ethical Values in Crisis," *Standard,* XXIII (December, 1936), 76; Amidon, "Ambassador of Spain: Fernando de los Ríos," *Survey Graphic,* XXVI (February, 1937), 87; Dewey, "Aid for the Spanish Government," *Christian Century,* LIV (March 3, 1937), 292; Reich, "Quaker Relief Workers in Spain," *Christian Register,* CXVI (September 30, 1937), 564; Herring, "Spain: Battleground of Democracy," *Social Action,* III (January 1, 1937), 7; Schuman, "The 'Little World War,'" *Events,* II (July, 1937), 17-18; Krich, "Single to Spain," *New Mexico Quarterly,* VII (November, 1937), 301.

4. Minifie, "A Battle Against Ignorance," *Journal of Adult Education,* IX (June, 1937), 258-60; "Schools in Spanish Trenches," *School and Society,* XLV (January 23, 1937), 111; De los Ríos, "The Republic Brings Education to Spain," *The American Teacher,* XXII (September-October, 1937), 15-17; Dilla, "On the Spanish Yesterday and Today," *Educational Forum,* II (March, 1938), 281-90; Harold W.

Allison, "The Classroom Democracy and the Spanish Civil War," *Clearing House*, XII (October, 1937), 99-102; "Spain Crystallizes an Issue," *The Social Frontier*, III (December, 1936), 70; Nicholson B. Adams, "Some Recent Novels of Revolutionary Spain," *Hispania*, XX (February, 1937), 81-84; Squires, *What of Spain?* (Los Angeles, 1939). For biased materials in texts and readers, see Anne Merriman Peck and E. A. Méras, *Spain in Europe and in America* (New York, 1937), pp. 252-64; Jay Allen, "City of Horrors: Badajoz," *Scholastic*, XXIX (November 7, 1936), 10-11; "German and Italian Bombs," *World Youth*, III (March 26, 1938), 5. For petition-signers, see *These Americans Say: "Lift the Embargo against Republican Spain"* (New York, 1939).

5. Capa and Taro, *Death in the Making* (New York, 1938); Sommerfield, "Volunteer in Spain," *NR*, XCI (July 21, 1937), 302; Cannon, *Spain Today* (New York, 1937), p. 12.

6. Gunther, *Inside Europe* (New York, 1938), pp. 165-67, 169; Bowers, *My Mission to Spain* (New York, 1954), p. vi, and Preface to F. Jay Taylor, *The United States and the Spanish Civil War* (New York, 1956), p. 19.

7. A good summary of the embargo legislation is found in Taylor, *op. cit.*, pp. 51-100.

8. Charles and Mary Beard, *America in Midpassage*, I (New York, 1939), p. 478; for Buell and Dean, see Bibliography; Raushenbush, *The Final Choice* (New York, 1937), p. 22; Garner, "The United States Neutrality Act of 1937," *American Journal of International Law*, XXXI (July, 1937), 395-96; for Padelford, see Bibliography; Dulles and Armstrong, *Can America Stay Neutral?* (New York, 1939), pp. 82, 96, 101; Borchard and Lage, *Neutrality for the United States* (New Haven, 1937), p. 336.

9. This controversy has been frequently reprinted. It is most easily found in Taylor, *op. cit.*, pp. 213-36.

10. *Congressional Record*, January 6, 1937, and May 2, 1938.

11. For Shipler and Spofford, see *Spain* (New York, n.d.), pp. 23-24; Dunham, "Neutrality: America-Spain, 1938," *The Presbyterian Tribune*, LIV (January 5, 1939), 7; Thompson, *Let the Record Speak* (Boston, 1939), p. 72.

12. For Bingham, Moley, and Wright, see Bibliography. Most newspapers urged retention of the embargo, but the *Christian Science Monitor*, the *New York Times*, and the *Washington Post* were, as so often, exceptional—they urged abolition. For Mumford, see *Men Must Act* (New York, 1939), p. 48.

13. *Spain* (New York, n.d.), p. 24; "Scientists' Plea Is Move to Save World from Fascism," *Science News Letter*, XXXIII (May 7, 1938), 298.

14. Spender, *Poems for Spain* (London, 1939), p. 7; Hemingway,

"The Writer and War," in *The Writer In a Changing World,* ed. Henry Hart (New York, 1937), p. 69.

15. Benét, "Singing Spain," *Saturday Review of Literature,* XVI (October 2, 1937), 18; Williams, "Federico Garcia Lorca," *Kenyon Review,* I (Spring, 1939), 148-58.

16. Warner, "Spain's Living Daughters," *Fight,* V (March, 1938), 8-9, 26; "Spain Accords Women Absolute Equality," *Equal Rights,* XXIII (April 1, 1937), 44; "The World Watches Spain," *Independent Woman,* XV (September, 1936), 275, 304; McCulloch, "Spain," *The Woman's Press,* XXX (December, 1936), 526-27. For Roosevelt and Catt, see *New York Times,* August 14, 1937, and January 31, 1939.

17. Mendelson's letter is printed in Jack Leeds, *Let My People Know* (New York, 1942), pp. 57-58; Franklin Gordon, "Is Spain Doomed to 'Non-Aryan' War?" *The American Hebrew,* CXXXIX (August 28, 1936), 227, 238; "Chronicles: Spain," *The Contemporary Jewish Record,* I (September, 1938), 82; Levin, *In Search* (New York, 1950), pp. 9, 108-9; Hirschbein, *Writers Take Sides,* p. 30; Mayteson, "Round and About the Jewish World: The International Brigades," *The American Hebrew,* CXLII (May 6, 1938), 8; "The New War in Spain," *Life,* IV (March 28, 1938), 57.

18. Thyra Edwards, "Moors and the Spanish War," *Opportunity,* XVI (March, 1938), 84-85; Strong, "I Visited Spain," *Crisis,* XLIII (December, 1936), 358; Pickens, "What I Saw in Spain," *Crisis,* XLV (October, 1938), 321; for Cullen *et al.,* see *Writers Take Sides;* Hughes, "Negroes in Spain," *Volunteer for Liberty,* September 13, 1937, and "Post Card from Spain," *Volunteer for Liberty,* April 9, 1938; for Robeson, see Eslanda Goode Robeson, "Journey into Spain," in Alvah Bessie, *The Heart of Spain,* p. 247.

19. Joseph North, *Men in the Ranks* (New York, 1939), p. 37; Hunter, "700 Calendar Days," in *The Heart of Spain,* p. 299; Baldwin, *Notes of a Native Son* (Boston, 1955), p. 3.

20. Ford, *The Negro and the Democratic Front* (New York, 1938), p. 93; Garland, "An Answer to Lynching," *AF,* I (Winter, 1938), 10; Todrin, *Seven Men* (New York, 1938), p. 18, reprinted by permission of G. P. Putnam's Sons. Copyright 1938 by G. P. Putnam's Sons; Hughes, "October 16th," *Volunteer for Liberty,* October 11, 1937.

21. Strong, *op. cit.,* 358.

22. Bessie, *Men in Battle* (New York, 1939), p. 33.

23. Weinert, *Camaradas: Ein Spanienbuch* (Berlin, 1951), pp. 15, 61; Rollins, *The Wall of Men* (New York, 1938), p. 155; Levin, "The Candid Cameraman," *Esquire,* IX (April, 1938), 94.

24. Lerner, *It Is Later than You Think* (New York, 1938), p. 260; Freeman, "Arnold Reid," *NM,* XXIX (September 13, 1938), 21; Rolland, *"Humanité Appelle à Toi," Unité,* III (April, 1938), 1.

25. Campbell, *Flowering Rifle* (London, 1939), p. 55. Quoted by permission of Curtis Brown, Ltd.

26. Tinker, *Some Still Live* (New York, 1938), p 1; *New York Times,* March 1, 1937.

27. *New York Times,* April 29, 1937; *Christian Science Monitor,* May 7, 1937; *New York Daily News,* May 7, 1937; *Wheeling Intelligencer,* May 7, 1937; Nye, *Congressional Record,* May 20, 1937; Coffee, *Congressional Record, Appendix,* June 8, 1937; Borah, *Congressional Record,* May 6, 1937.

28. *Ciano's Hidden Diary,* trans. Andreas Mayor (New York, 1953), p. 72; Hull, *New York Times,* May 22, 1938; Welles, *New York Times,* June 4, 1938; mayors, *New York Times,* July 26, 1938; bishops, *New York Times,* March 21, 1938; *Indianapolis News,* March 31, 1938; *Pittsburgh Post-Gazette,* April 1, 1938; *Washington Post,* May 27, 1938; Hearst, February 8, 1938. Quoted phrases from *Richmond Times-Dispatch,* March 19, 1938; *New York Times,* March 19, 1938; *Louisville Courier-Journal,* March 20, 1938; *Dallas News,* June 6, 1938; *New York World-Telegram,* March 18, 1938; and *New York Herald Tribune,* March 15, 1938. General Douhet advocated bombing cities to demoralize populations.

29. *Bombs over Barcelona* (New York, 1938).

30. Wolfe, *Letters,* ed. Elizabeth Nowell (New York, 1956), pp. 353-54; Hellman, "Day in Spain," *NR,* XCIV (April 13, 1938), 298; Parker, "Incredible, Fantastic . . . and True," *NM,* XXV (November 23, 1937), 16.

31. Joad, "What Is Happening in the Peace Movement?" *New Statesman and Nation,* XIII (May 15, 1937), 802-4; De Ligt, *The Conquest of Violence,* trans. Honor Tracy (London, 1937), pp. 191-202; Nehru, *Spain! Why?* (London, n.d.); Romilly, *Boadilla* (London, 1937).

32. Muste, "Tragedy of Spain," *The Presbyterian Tribune,* LIV (March 30, 1939), 10-11; Fisk, "Written in Blood Across Spain," *Fellowship,* II (October, 1936), 1-2; Brown, "Spain—A Challenge to Pacifism," *Unity,* CXVIII (December 21, 1936), 152-54; Hughan, *What about Spain?* (New York, 1937), p. 5; Holmes, *Spain—And the Next War* (New York, 1937); and "'Expeditionary Force' Scheme Censured . . .," *New Leader,* XX (January 2, 1937), 8.

33. Floyd, "Civil War in Spain," *The Arbitrator,* XVIII (September, 1936), 1-2, and "Arnica for Guernica," *The Arbitrator,* XIX (June, 1937), 1.

34. Jones, "A Quaker in an Anarchist Meeting," *Protestant Digest,* I (January, 1939), 91, and "An Eyewitness in Spain," *Christian Century,* LIV (April 7, 1937), 454; "It Happens Again in Spain," *The Messenger of Peace,* LXI (October, 1936), 4; Kershner, *Quaker Service in Modern War* (New York, 1950), p. 24.

35. Robert Moats Miller, *American Protestantism and Social Issues* (Chapel Hill, N.C., 1958), p. 333.

36. Orwell, *Homage to Catalonia* (New York, 1952), p. 48. See also Stephen Spender, *World within World* (London, 1951), p. 187.

37. The degree of Roosevelt's sympathy is difficult to establish, but he *was* pro-Loyalist. Claude Bowers quotes him as saying, after the war, "We have made a mistake; you have been right all along" (*My Mission to Spain*, p. 418); see also Eleanor Roosevelt, *This I Remember* (New York, 1949), p. 161; Harold L. Ickes, *Secret Diary*, II (New York, 1954), p. 569; John Morton Blum, *From the Morgenthau Diaries*, pp. 506-8.

38. My judgments are supported by F. Jay Taylor, *op. cit.*, pp. 124 ff.

39. *Memoirs of Cordell Hull* (New York, 1948), pp. 481-82 (my italics); see also the official papers, *Foreign Relations of the United States: Diplomatic Papers, 1936-1938* (Washington, D.C., 1953-55).

40. Roosevelt, *Public Papers and Addresses*, V-VI (New York, 1938, 1941), pp. 288, 406-11. Information on newspapers and on polls taken from studies by James F. O'Brien and Hugh Jones Parry, cited above.

41. Ickes, *op. cit.*, II p. 390; Tugwell, *The Democratic Roosevelt* (Garden City, N.Y., 1957), p. 618; Divine, *The Illusion of Neutrality* (Chicago, 1962), p. 227; Parry, *op. cit.*, p. 376.

CHAPTER 6

1. Frank, "Refugee from Palencia, Old Castile," in Jo Davidson, *Spanish Portraits* (New York, 1938), and "Spain in War," *NR*, XCV (July 27, 1938), 327.

2. De los Ríos, *What Is Happening In Spain?* (London, 1937), p. 17; Rexroth, "Two Poems," in *Salud!* ed. Alan Calmer (New York, 1938), p. 30.

3. Lewis, "Glorious Dirt," *Newsweek*, X (October 18, 1937), 34; Perkins, *Editor to Author* (New York, 1950), p. 118; Flanner, "Letter from Paris," *NY*, XII (September 19, 1936), 73; and "Letter from Perpignan," *NY*, XV (March 11, 1939), 65-66.

4. For Browder, Hicks, Cowley, Gellhorn, and Magil, see *The Writer in a Changing World*, pp. 48, 188, 47, 67-68, 241; MacLeish, "The War Is Ours," *NM*, XXIII (June 22, 1937), 5-6; Gold, *Ralph Fox: A Writer in Arms*, ed. John Lehmann (New York, 1937), p. 10.

5. The following appeared in *Poetry*: Todrin, "Two Poems," LII (May, 1938), 64-67; Funaroff, "To Federico Garcia Lorca," LII (July, 1938), 185; Sachs, "Heard from Spain," LI (January, 1938), 200; Humphries, "On an Official Occasion," LI (November, 1937), 60; and "Songs by Federico García Lorca," L (April, 1937), 8-9; Wheelwright,

"The Poetry of Lorca," LI (December, 1937), 167-70; Roethke, "Facing the Guns," LII (April, 1938), 43-46.

6. Stein, *Everybody's Autobiography* (New York, 1937), pp. 70, 89, 108; Stevens, *Collected Poems* (New York, 1957), p. 186; Swallow, *The Nameless Spirit* (Iowa City, 1956), p. 15.

7. "On to Spain," *Art Front,* III (March, 1937), 3; "Paul Block," *Art Front,* III (October, 1937), 4-5. See Bibliography for a selected list of art on Spanish themes.

8. For Briggs, see "Judson Briggs Returns from War-Torn Spain," *Art Digest,* XII (May 15, 1938), 16; for Davidson, *Spanish Portraits* (New York, 1938); for Davis, "American Artists and Spain," *Art Front,* III (October, 1937), 11; for cartoonists, "Street Corner Poster Artists," *NM,* XXIX (September 27, 1938), 18; for Hokinson, see *NY,* September 26, 1936; May 1, 1937; and November 20, 1937.

9. Steinbeck, "A Primer [of] the 1930's," *Esquire,* LII (June, 1960), 91; "*Life* Goes to a Party: With the Children of Hollywood for the Children of Spain," *Life,* III (December 20, 1937), 70-72. For Cagney, see *Somebody Had to Do Something* (Los Angeles, 1939); for Enters, see John Martin, *New York Times,* December 13, 1936; for Soyer, Owen Burke, "Young Choreographers," *NM,* XXVI (January 25, 1938), 30-31; for Graham, Owen Burke, "Dances of Protest," *NM,* XXVI (January 11, 1938), 28-29; Riesenfeld, *Dancer in Madrid* (New York, 1938), p. 298; for music to *The Spanish Earth,* see Kathleen Hoover and John Cage, *Virgil Thomson* (New York, 1959), pp. 85-86; for showings of the film, see John T. McManus, *New York Times,* July 25, 1937; for benefits, see blurb in *NM,* XXIII (May 25, 1937), 26; and Leo Marx, "The Teacher," in *F. O. Matthiessen: A Collective Portrait,* eds. Paul Sweezy and Leo Huberman (New York, 1950), p. 41; for Robinson, *A Wall to Paint On* (New York, 1946), p. 349.

10. Mann, "I Stand with the Spanish People," *N,* CXLIV (April 17, 1937), 429; Auden, "Spain," *Saturday Review of Literature,* XVI (May 22, 1937), 10.

11. MacLeish, "In Challenge Not Defense," *Poetry,* LII (July, 1938), 218.

12. Trilling, "Hemingway and His Critics," *Partisan Review,* VI (Winter, 1939), 60.

13. Richard Drinnon, *Rebel in Paradise: A Biography of Emma Goldman* (Chicago, 1961), p. 310. Chapter XXXI, "Spain: The Very Top of the Mountain," is an excellent discussion of Emma Goldman and the Spanish Civil War.

14. Lawrence, "Nine Years Ago . . .," *Vanguard,* III (August-September, 1936), 6; Brooks, "Adelante, Companeros!" *Man!* IV (October-November, 1936), 1, and "We Are Cowards!" *Man!,* VI (February-March, 1937), 2; Graham, "The People of Spain Call to You," *Man!,* V (December, 1936-January, 1937), 2.

15. "Oil for Lisbon Goes to Franco," *Industrial Worker*, XIX (May 22, 1937), 1.

16. "Behind the Lines in Spain," *Man!*, IV (October-November, 1936), 1, 2; "Spanish Revolution from an Ivory Tower," *Vanguard*, III (December, 1936), 13.

17. Montseny, *Militant Anarchism and the Reality in Spain* (Glasgow, 1937), p. 4; "Conspiracy against Spain," *Man!*, V (June, 1937), 1, 3. For Richards, see *Lessons of the Spanish Revolution* (London, 1953).

18. "Senex," "Revolutionary Tactics in Spain," *Vanguard*, IV (February, 1939), 14; and "Anarchist Tactics in Spain," *Vanguard*, IV (February, 1938), 3-4, 13-15.

19. Gannes, *How the Soviet Union Helps Spain* (New York, 1936), pp. 4-5; Gannes and Repard, *Spain in Revolt* (New York, 1936); pp. 221-22; Browder, *Fighting for Peace* (New York, 1939), p. 66; "Review of the Month," *The Communist*, XV (September, 1936), 809; Hathaway, "Fighting for Democracy in Spain," *The Communist*, XV (September, 1936), 839-40.

20. Browder, Introduction to Dallet, *Letters from Spain* (New York, 1938), p. 5; William Z. Foster's comment, p. 4, that Dallet was helping to write the "epitaph of capitalism" was atypical. Fischer, "Franco Cannot Win," *N*, CXLV (August 7, 1937), 148-50; Sheean, *Not Peace But a Sword* (New York, 1939), p. 185; Lash, " 'Time Works for Us,'— Spain, 1937," *NM*, XXV (October 19, 1937), 6. The last quotations are from "M. Ercoli" (Togliatti), "Specific Features of the Spanish Revolution," *The Communist*, XV (December, 1936), 1170-71.

21. Cornford, "Full Moon at Thierz," *NR*, XCI (July 21, 1937), 305.

22. Quin, *On the Drumhead* (San Francisco, 1948), p. 71; North, "But—Catalonia Broke Napoleon," *NM*, XXVII (April 26, 1938), 9; Rolfe, *The Lincoln Battalion* (New York, 1939); "After One Year in Spain," *NM*, XXIV (July 20, 1937), 12; Rosten, "Fragments for America," *NM*, XXVIII (July 12, 1938), 154-56.

23. Fischer, *The War in Spain* (New York, 1937), p. 27, "Spain's 'Red' Foreign Legion," *N*, CXLIV (January 9, 1937), 36; and "The Drive Along the Ebro," *N*, CXLVII (September 3, 1938), 220; Strong, *Spain in Arms: 1937* (New York, 1937), p. ix; Joseph, *Shop Talk on Spain* (New York, 1938), p. 18; Michael O'Flanagan, "I Speak to Catholics," *NM*, XXVIII (August 2, 1938), 9; Rolfe, *The Lincoln Battalion*, p. 16; Mangold, "Betraying Spanish Democracy," *Fight*, IV (March, 1937), 9; Kline, "The Voice of Madrid," *NM*, XXIII (April 13, 1937), 7; and *New York Times*, April 18, 1937; North, "July 4th-July 19th," *Volunteer for Liberty*, July 19, 1938. For symbolism, see Browder and Lawrence, *Next Steps to Win the War in Spain* (New York, 1938); White and Hawthorne, *From These Honored Dead* (New

York, 1939); Gannes, *Spain Defends Democracy* (New York, 1936), p. 3.

24. Browder, *The People's Front* (New York, 1938), pp. 98, 285-86, 292.

25. Stowe, "Madrid—After Three Years," *Volunteer for Liberty*, September 6, 1937, and "Spain's Shirt-Sleeve Heroes," *N*, CXLVI (April 23, 1938), 467.

26. Sinclair, *No Pasaran!* (Pasadena, Calif., 1937), p. 72, "The Haves and the Have Nots," *American Guardian*, XIX (October 23, 1936), 1; and *No Pasaran!*, p. 44; Acier, "No Pasaran!" *Fight*, IV (January, 1937), 29.

27. Harrison, *Meet Me on the Barricades* (New York, 1938), p. 167.

28. Seldes, *The Catholic Crisis* (New York, 1939), p. 25; Acier, *From Spanish Trenches*, p. 192; Browder, *The Writer in a Changing World*, pp. 52, 54; Hawthorne, "Political 'Suppression' in Spain," *NM*, XXIV (September 21, 1937), 19.

29. Browder and Lawrence, p. 8, and *The People's Front*, 324; Ford, p. 168; Hawthorne, "Spain's Government Girds for War," *NM*, XXIII (June 22, 1937), 7; Minor, "The Change in Spain," *The Communist*, XVI (August, 1937), 697-98; Marty, *Heroic Spain* (New York, 1937), pp. 16-24; Dimitroff, "Communists and the United Front," *The Communist*, XVI (June, 1937), 513; Reeve, "Lovestoneism—Twin of Fascist-Trotskyism," *The Communist*, XVII (August, 1938), 737. For Soria, see *Trotskyism in the Service of Franco* (New York, 1938).

30. Gunther, *Inside Europe*, p. 169; " 'Spain in Flames,' " *N*, CXLIV (March 27, 1937), 340-41; Winchell Taylor, "Secret Movie Censors," *N*, CXLVII (July 9, 1938), 38-40; Leo Lehmann, "The Catholic Church in Politics," *NR*, XCVII (December 14, 1938), 64-66; "Spain Crystallizes an Issue," *Social Frontier*, III (December, 1936), 70.

31. *New York Daily News*, July 23, 1937; Ornitz, *Captured by Franco* (New York, 1939), p. 5; Bishop's comment is found in a letter from him to Rolfe Humphries. For Cohen, see *Writers Take Sides*, p. 14; for Brooks and Duffus, "An Attack on Democracy," *Commonweal*, XXV (April 9, 1937), 671-72; Lerner, "I Was in Spain," *Fight*, IV (November, 1936), 40-41; Green, "Spain at Gettysburg," *NM*, XXI (October 27, 1936), 7-8; Hemingway, Foreword to North, p. 4, and sketch of Milton Wolff in Jo Davidson, *Spanish Portraits* (New York, 1938).

32. *For Whom the Bell Tolls*, p. 336.

33. Sherman, "Moon over Spain," *Frontier and Midland*, XVIII (Spring, 1938), 174; Rolfe, "Entry," *First Love and Other Poems* (Los Angeles, 1951), pp. 9-12.

34. Trotsky, *Leçon d'Espagne* (Paris, 1946), pp. 62, 67.

35. Bell, "The Background and Development of Marxian Socialism in the United States," in *Socialism and American Life*, Donald Drew Egbert and Stow Persons eds. (Princeton, 1952), p. 387; Burnham, *The*

Peoples' Front: The New Betrayal (New York, 1937), p. 17; "P.O.U.M. and the Spanish Revolution," *Socialist Appeal* (Chicago), II (December, 1936), 6; Morrow, *Revolution and Counter-Revolution in Spain* (New York, 1938), pp. 4, 9; and "The War in Spain," *New International,* IV (February, 1938), 60.

36. Wolfe, *Civil War in Spain* (New York, 1937), 31; Herberg, "Civil War in Spain," *Worker's Age,* V (August 15, 1936), 4.

37. Lovestone, *The People's Front Illusion* (New York, 1937), p. 50; Oehler, *Barricades in Barcelona* (New York, 1937), p. 9. For one of Oehler's followers, see E. H. Oliver, *6th Anniversary . . .* (Chicago, 1937), p. 7; Mienov, "Declaration of the Editorial Board," *Spark,* I (February, 1938), i-ii, and "The Imperialist War in Spain," *Spark,* I (February, 1938), 1-10. For the last split, see Bell, *op. cit.,* p. 368.

38. "Spain," *In Defense of Bolshevism,* I (May, 1938), 19; Keracher, "The Civil War in Spain and Its Lessons," *Proletarian News,* VIII (April 1, 1939), 4-5; "Whither Spain?" *Bulletin of the Proletarian Group,* October, 1936, pp. 2-3; Abraham Ziegler, "The Crisis in Spain," *Industrial Unionist,* V (September, 1936), 5-6, 12. For Workers Socialist Party, see "The Loyalist Program," *Socialist,* II (July, 1938), 6.

39. Calverton, "Beyond Franco and Stalin," *Modern Monthly,* X (September, 1937), 2; and "Will England Give Spain to Franco?" *Modern Monthly,* X (August, 1937), 7.

40. Rahv, "Twilight of the Thirties," *Partisan Review,* V (Summer, 1939), 7; "Leon Trotsky to André Breton," *Partisan Review,* VI (Winter, 1939), 126-27; Dupee, "André Malraux," *Partisan Review,* IV (March, 1938), 35; Hook, "The Anatomy of the Popular Front," *Partisan Review,* VI (Spring, 1939), 29-45.

41. Bell, *op cit.,* p. 221.

42. Thomas, "At the Front: Civil War in Spain," *The Socialist Call,* II (August 8, 1936), 1, and *Socialism on the Defensive* (New York, 1938), pp. 66, 202-3. For the other socialists, see Bibliography.

43. For the Debs Column, see Amicus Most, "Men to Spain—The Eugene V. Debs Column," *American Socialist Monthly,* V (February, 1937), 21-24; for Thomas's response to criticism, see *The Socialist Call,* February, 13, 1937.

44. Last two quotations are from "The Church and Spain," *The New Leader,* XXI (July 9, 1938), 8; and "It Is Not Safe to 'Play Safe' With World's Peace at Stake," *The New Leader,* XX (June 5, 1937), 8.

45. "Spanish Win-the-War Cabinet Is Formed to Open Great Offensive," *The American Guardian,* XIX (May 21, 1937), 1; E. Haldeman-Julius, "Questions and Answers," *The American Freeman,* June, 1937, pp. 1-4; Chamberlain, "Was It a Congress of American Writers?" *Common Sense,* VI (August, 1937), 16; Dos Passos, "The Communist Party and the War Spirit," *Common Sense,* VI (December, 1937), 14; for Franklin Folsom's unkind remark, see Daniel Aaron, *Writers on*

the Left (New York, 1961), p. 361; "The 'Military Objectives' in the Barcelona Bombings," *The Progressive,* II (April 2, 1938), 8; Will Lissner, "Why Spain Is Torn Asunder," *The Freeman,* I (November, 1937), 13; "Dr. . . . Alonso, Tarragona, Spain," *The Freeman,* II (March, 1939), 8.

46. *New York Times,* July 18, 1937, and July 20, 1937.

CHAPTER 7

1. *The Spanish Earth* (Cleveland, 1938), p. 19. The published text of Hemingway's narration. My interpretation is seconded by Joris Ivens, the film's director, who told John McManus, "It is . . . a war for melons, tomatoes, onions—not . . . for broad principles of ideology." McManus added, "Mr Ivens' picture is, to use his words, a document of a people, a drama of the soil." *New York Times,* July 25, 1937.

2. "Hemingway Reports Spain," *NR,* XC (May 5, 1937), 377. For the other titles, see Bibliography.

3. *NM,* XXX (February 14, 1939), 3.

4. British comments by Keith Scott Watson, *Single to Spain* (New York, 1937), p. 142; and John Sommerfield, *Volunteer in Spain* (New York, 1937), p. 146.

5. Quotations from pp. 43, 17, 438, 328.

6. Quotations from pp. 328, 89, 87.

7. *The Writer in a Changing World,* p. 69.

8. Frank, "Refugee from Palencia, Old Castile," in Jo Davidson, *Spanish Portraits* (New York, 1938), and "Viva España Libre!" *NM,* XX (August 18, 1936), 13; Paul, *The Life and Death of a Spanish Town* (New York, 1937); Dos Passos, "The Villages are the Heart of Spain," *Esquire,* IX (February, 1938), 32-33, 151-53; Herbst, "Night Comes to the Valley," *Direction,* I (April, 1938), 18-20. The typescript for Lawson's film is in the New York Public Library.

9. Rolfe, "Spain's Shirt-Sleeve General," *NM,* XXV (December 7, 1937), 13; "Britain's Responsibility for Spain," *NR,* LXXXIX (November 25, 1936), 95.

10. Matthews, *Two Wars and More to Come* (New York, 1938), p. 206; Ziffren, "I Lived in Madrid," *Current History,* XLVI (April, 1937), 41; Pflaum, "Death from the Skies," in *Nothing But Danger,* ed. Frank C. Hanighen (New York, 1939), p. 220; Pitcairn, "On the Firing Line in Defense of Madrid," *Travel,* LXVIII (February, 1937), 54; Allen, "Death from the Air," *Talks,* II (July, 1937), 4-5; Carreras, "Death from the Air," *Talks,* II (July, 1937), 6-7; Caldwell, "In Barcelona," *Salud!,* ed. Alan Calmer (New York, 1938), pp. 38-39; Bessie, *Men in Battle, passim;* Rolfe, *The Lincoln Battalion, passim.*

11. Blankfort's novel is not to be confused with his play of the same title.

12. *Death in the Morning* (London, 1937), p. 102.

13. *Air Raid* (New York, 1938), pp. 33-34. Copyright 1938 by Harcourt, Brace and Co. Quoted by permission of Archibald MacLeish.

14. Rosten, "Fragments for America," *NM*, XXVIII (July 12, 1938), 155, reprinted by permission of *Masses and Mainstream;* Hughes, "Song of Spain," in *Romancero de los Voluntarios de la Libertad* (Madrid, 1937), p. 14, and "Moonlight in Valencia," in *Seven Poets in Search of an Answer*, ed. Thomas Yoseloff (New York, 1944), p. 51; Rolfe, *First Love*, pp. 16, 26, 28; Todrin, "Spanish Sowing." Reprinted by permission of G. P. Putnam's Sons from *Seven Men*, p. 21. Copyright, 1938 by G. P. Putnam's Sons. Berryman, "1938," *Kenyon Review*, I (Summer, 1939), 258-59 Quoted by permission of the author and *The Kenyon Review;* Jarrell, "The Winter's Tale," *Kenyon Review*, I, (Winter, 1938-39), 59.

15. Rosenberg, *Trance above the Street* (New York, 1942), quoted by permission of the author. Rukeyser, *A Turning Wind* (New York, 1939), p. 84, quoted by permission of the author. Norman, "Triumphal Entry," *The Savage Century* (Prairie City, Ill., 1942), p. 19, quoted by permission of the author; Hughes, "Air Raid: Barcelona," *Esquire*, X (October, 1938), 40; Kramer and Rosten, *Seven Poets in Search of an Answer*, pp. 56, 103.

16. Hemingway, Preface to Luis Quintanilla, *All the Brave* (New York, 1939), p. 7; Brace, "William Gropper," *Magazine of Art*, XXX (August, 1937), 467-68. For reproductions of art, see Bibliography.

17. See John Heartfield, "Greetings," *NM*, XXIX (October 25, 1938), 8; *Madrid: The "Military" Atrocities of the Rebels* (London, 1937); George Barker, *Elegy on Spain* (Manchester, 1939); Hemingway, "The Cardinal Picks a Winner," *Ken*, I (May 5, 1938), 38.

18. Huxley, *They Still Draw Pictures* (New York, 1939), p. 9.

19. Malraux, "Forging Man's Fate in Spain," *N*, CXLIV (March 20, 1937), 316.

20. Lewis, *Collected Poems* (London, 1954), p. 228.

21. *The Great Crusade*, trans. Whittaker Chambers and Barrows Mussey (New York, 1940), pp. 256-57, 271.

22 *The Olive Field* (London, 1936), p. 58.

23. "Of Legendary Time," *Virginia Quarterly Review*, XV (January, 1939), 21-36; Preface to Frank Pitcairn, *Reporter in Spain* (London, 1936), p. 8; "Compañero Sagasta Burns a Church," *NR*, LXXXVIII (October 14, 1936), 275-76; "Spanish Improvisation," *NR*, LXXXIX (November 11, 1936), 37.

24. *Sirocco and Other Stories* (New York, 1939), pp. 362-63, 387.

25. Beach, "The Quality of Man," *Kenyon Review*, I (Spring, 1939), 217; Malraux, *L'Espoir* (Paris, 1937), p. 90.

26. Renn, "Who Will Win the War in Spain?" *Esquire*, IX (April, 1938), 41; Hawthorne, "American Fliers in Spain," *NM*, XXIII (June

8, 1937), 18; Fischer, "The Drive Along the Ebro," *N.* CXLVII (September 3, 1938), 220. The first lines of poetry are from Norman Rosten, *The Fourth Decade,* p. 49, quoted by permission of Holt, Rinehart and Winston; the second poem is Boris Todrin, "The Flight," Reprinted by permission of G. P. Putnam's Sons from *Seven Men,* p. 16. Copyright 1938 by G. P. Putnam's Sons. Bates, "International Fighters for Spanish Democracy," *AF,* I (Winter, 1938), 8-9, 23; and "Castilian Drama: An Army Is Born," *NR, XCII* (October 20, 1937), 290.

27. Gerald Brenan, *The Spanish Labyrinth* (2nd ed.; Cambridge, 1950), p. 196. Not all took a mechanized position grudgingly. Joseph Dallet, an American killed in Spain, wrote, "Man, what a feeling of power you have when entrenched behind a heavy machine gun! You know how I always enjoyed gangster movies for the mere sound of the machine guns. Then you can imagine my joy at finally being on the business end of one." *Letters from Spain* (New York, 1938), p. 45. My suspicions about Dallet were corroborated by Sandor Voros, *American Commissar,* pp. 336-43.

28. Davidman, "Near Catalonia," *Letter to a Comrade* (New Haven, 1938), p. 67. Quoted by permission of Yale University Press.

EPILOGUE AND CONCLUSIONS

1. Communiqué quoted in P. A. M. van der Esch, *Prelude to War* (The Hague, 1951), p. 159; *New York Times,* July 21, 1957; Dec. 20, 1959; Dec. 24, 1961; Jan. 4, 1962

2. Arthur Schlesinger, Jr., *The Age of Jackson* (Boston, 1945), p. 503; for reproductions of Levine and Motherwell, see the Whitney Museum's catalogue, *Contemporary American Painting* (New York, 1961); and Sidney Janis, *Abstract and Surrealist Art in America* (New York, 1944), p. 65; Roosevelt, *This I Remember,* p. 275; Lubell, *The Future of American Politics* (New York, 1952), p. 224.

3. Quotations are from Sinclair, *Wide Is the Gate* (New York, 1943), p. 611; Trilling, *The Middle of the Journey* (New York, 1947), p. 220; Fremantlle, *By Grace of Love* (New York, 1957), p. 161.

4. Levin, *Citizens!* (New York, 1940); Glasgow, *In This Our Life* (New York, 1941); Freeman, *Never Call Retreat* (New York, 1943); Sarton, *Faithful Are the Wounds* (New York, 1955); Wertenbaker, *The Death of Kings* (New York, 1954); Nemerov, *The Homecoming Game* (New York, 1957); Kapelner, *All the Naked Heroes* (New York, 1960); Gold, *Therefore Be Bold* (New York, 1960); Cort, *The Minstrel Boy* (New York, 1961). Quotation is from Gold, *op. cit,* p. 83.

5. Information on polls taken from Hugh Jones Parry, cited above.

6. Orrin Dwight Bell and George W. Campbell, "I've Stopped Killing for Money," *American Magazine,* CXXV (June, 1938), 35, 80, 82, 84; and Orrin Dwight Bell as told to Frederick C. Painton, "I Fly

in the Spanish War," *Liberty*, XIV (December 18, 1937), 6-11 (first of three parts); Bert Acosta, "America's Ace Pilot Tells of His Air Adventures," *True*, I (June, 1937), 42-47, 108-9; Burnham Carter, "Tomorrow Will be Fair," *Collier's*, XCIX (April 17, 1937), 9-10, 76, 78-82; Walter Duranty, "Witch of the Alcazar," *Collier's*, XCVIII (December 5, 1936), 7-9, 59; Edward Hope, "Spanish Omelette," *Cosmopolitan*, CII (April, 1937), 28-31, 130-54, 158-63; Borden Chase, "A Kiss in Spain," *Liberty*, XIII (October 10, 1936), 26-29; Rion Bercovici, "Beleaguered," *Scribner's*, CI (March, 1937), 39-41; Charles Yates, *The Body Came by Post* (New York, 1937). For *Adventure Novels*, see H. B. Ucello, "Propaganda in the Pulps," *NM*, XXII (March 2, 1937), 8.

7. Shaw, "Hell over Spain," *Review of Reviews*, XCIV (September, 1936), 57.

8. *The Liberal Imagination* (New York, 1951), pp. ix-x.

9. *The Time for Decision* (New York, 1944), p. 57.

A SELECTED

BIBLIOGRAPHY

This bibliography includes primary sources only. In this case, "primary" sources are American materials from the years 1936 through 1939. Entries have publication dates as recent as 1962, but the materials themselves date from the years of the Spanish Civil War. If Europeans appear in this bibliography, they appear by error.

Many writers wrote a great number of articles and dispatches for the daily or periodical press. For such writers, I give one or two representative titles. For the same reason—to avoid a bloated bibliography—no anonymous articles or dispatches are listed. The magazines from which anonymous *and* signed articles are taken are listed in the second section, entitled "American Periodicals: 1936-1939." I have read, with whatever closeness seemed appropriate, all the pertinent editorials and articles in the magazines listed.

The third section is a list of newspapers used. Most of this material is taken from a secondary source. (See note, page 269, for my source.)

The fourth section is devoted to novels, plays, stories, and poems. The fifth section is devoted to the graphic arts, the sixth to films shown in the United States (American and foreign, features and documentaries), and the seventh to music and the dance.

BOOKS, PAMPHLETS, AND ARTICLES

Abbott, Roger. "How the Spanish Intellectuals Reached the Masses," *NM,* XX (August 25, 1936), 25-26.

————. "Who Backed the Spanish Revolt?" *NM,* XX (August 11, 1936), 13-14.

Abel, Hilde. "Notes from a Spanish Diary," *Midwest,* I (November, 1936), 8-9, 25.

Acier, Marcel (ed.). *From Spanish Trenches.* New York, 1937.

————. "No Pasaran!" *Fight,* IV (January, 1937), 7, 26, 29-30.

Acosta, Bert. "America's Ace Pilot Tells of His Air Adventures," *True,* I (June, 1937), 42-47, 108-9.

Adams, Mildred. "The 'Day of the Dead' in Madrid," *New York Times Magazine,* July 25, 1937, pp. 4-5, 18.

Allen, Jay. "Blood Flows at Badajoz," in Alvah Bessie (ed.), *The Heart of Spain.* New York, 1952, pp. 83-89.

————. "Death from the Air," *Talks,* II (July, 1937), 4-5.

————. "General José Miaja," in Jo Davidson's *Spanish Portraits.* New York, 1938.

Allen, Jay, and Paul, Elliot. Text to Luis Quintanilla's *All the Brave.* New York, 1939.

Allinson, Brent Dow. "The Importance of Being Neutral Toward Spain," *Unity,* CXIX (March 1, 1937), 6-8.

Allison, Harold W. "The Classroom Democracy and the Spanish Civil War," *Clearing House,* XII (October, 1937), 99-102.

American Democracy versus the Spanish Hierarchy. New York, 1937.

Amidon, Beulah. "Ambassador of Spain: Fernando de los Ríos," *Survey Graphic,* XXVI (February, 1937), 86-87.

Background of War. New York, 1937.

Barnes, Harry Elmer. "Spain versus Fascism," *Champion of Youth,* I (September, 1936), 9, 15.

Baron, H. "Exhibition in Support of Democracy in Spain," *Art Front,* II (November, 1936), 14.

Baron, Sam. "Open Letter to Louis Fischer," *Socialist Review,* VI (September-October, 1938), 11-12, 18.

Barone, C. "The World Today" [Monthly column], *Proletarian News,* VI (November 1, 1937), 1.

Barry, Dick. "Soldier of Misfortune," *SEP*, CCIX (May 1, 1937), 20-21, 81, 82, 84.

Beach, Joseph Warren. "The Quality of Man," *Kenyon Review*, I (Spring, 1939), 215-17.

Beals, Carleton. "The Spanish War of Words," *NR*, XCI (June 2, 1937), 94-96.

Beard, Charles A. "Will Roosevelt Keep Us Out of War?" *Events*, II (July, 1937), 1-6.

Bedford-Jones, Nancy. *Students under Arms*. New York, 1938.

Bell, Orrin Dwight, with Campbell, George W. "I've Stopped Killing for Money," *American Magazine*, CXXV (June, 1938), 35, 80, 82, 84.

————, as told to Painton, Frederick C. "I Fly in the Spanish War" [1st of three parts], *Liberty*, XIV (December 18, 1937), 6-11.

Ben Leider: American Hero. New York, n.d.

Benardete, M. J. "Why Did They Kill Garcia Lorca?" *NR*, XCIII (November 10, 1937), 25-26.

Benét, James. "Return from Spain," *NR* XCVI (November 2, 1938), 356-57.

Benét, William Rose. "Singing Spain," *Saturday Review of Literature*, XVI (October 2, 1937), 18.

Benn, William J. "Further Processes in Spanish Sovietization," *A*, LVII (September 25, 1937), 585-86.

Bennett, Milly. " 'Refugio! Refugio!' " *AF*, I (Spring, 1938), 13, 20-21.

Bernard, John T. "Treasure Trove in a Sardine Can," *AF*, I (Winter, 1938), 6, 22-23.

Bessie, Alvah. "An American Flier in Spain," *Fight*, IV (July, 1937), 8-9.

———— (ed.). *The Heart of Spain*. New York, 1952.

————. *Men in Battle*. New York, 1939.

Bissell, Eleanor. "Spain Then and Now," *Christian Leader*, XXXIX (October 24, 1936), 1356.

Black, Algernon D. "Ethical Values in Crisis," *Standard*, XXIII (December, 1936), 76-77.

Bliven, Bruce. "The Second World War Is Here," *NR*, XCII (October 6, 1937), 231-33.

Bombs over Barcelona. New York, 1937.

Borchard, Edwin. " 'Neutrality' and Civil Wars," *American Journal of International Law*, XXXI (April, 1937), 304-6.

Bowers, Wayne H. "A Story from Spain," *Protestant Digest*, I (January, 1939), 34-35.

Brace, Ernest. "William Gropper," *Magazine of Art*, XXX (August, 1937), 467-71.

Bradbury, John W. "The Tragedy of Spain," *Watchman-Examiner*, CXVIII (December 10, 1936), 1385-87.

Briggs, Judson. "Painted in Spain," *Direction,* I (September-October, 1938), 18-19.

Briggs, Marion (ed.). *Youth Letters from Spain.* New York, 1939.

Brisbane, Arthur. "Today in Europe," *Cosmopolitan,* CI (October, 1936), 32-33, 132-34.

Brodsky, Joseph R. "An Embargo on Democracy," *NM,* XXII (January 26, 1937), 13-14

Brooks, Van Wyck, and Duffus, R. L. "An Attack on Democracy," *Commonweal,* XXV (April 9, 1937), 671-72.

Brooks, Walter. "Adelante, Companeros!" *Man!,* IV (October-November, 1936), 1.

————. "We Are Cowards!" *Man!,* VI (February-March, 1937), 2.

Browder, Earl. *Fighting for Peace.* New York, 1939.

————. *Lenin and Spain.* New York, 1937.

————. *The People's Front.* New York, 1938.

————. *Trotskyism against World Peace.* New York, 1937.

Browder, Earl, and Lawrence, Bill. *Next Steps to Win the War in Spain.* New York, 1938.

Brown, Carlton. "Fifty-Two Weeks of War," *Fight,* IV (August, 1937), 22-23, 30.

Brown, H. Runham. "Spain—A Challenge to Pacificism," *Unity,* CXVIII (December 21, 1936), 152-54.

Browne, Richard. "In Franco's Prison," *Fight,* VI (December, 1938), 5-6, 26.

Buell, Raymond Leslie. "Faults in Our Neutrality Policy: Letter to the Editor," *New York Times,* April 17, 1938.

————. "The Neutrality Act of 1937," *Foreign Policy Reports,* XIII (October 1, 1937), 166-80.

————. "United States Neutrality in the Spanish Conflict," *Foreign Policy Reports,* XIII (November 15, 1937), 206-16.

Burgum, Edwin Berry. "Hemingway's Development," *NM,* XXIX (November 22, 1938), 21-23.

Burke, Owen. "Dances of Protest," *NM,* XXVI (January 11, 1938), 28-29.

————. "Young Choreographers," *NM,* XXVI (January 25, 1938), 30-31.

Burke, Philip. "The Claws of the Bear," *S,* XVI (December, 1936), 265-67.

Burnett, Whit. "Writers Smell Gunpowder," *Story,* XI (August, 1937), 2-8, 104-10.

Burnham, James. *The People's Front: The New Betrayal.* New York, 1937.

————. "Spain and the Coming World War," *Socialist Appeal* [New York], I (October 2, 1937), 6.

Cadden, Joseph. *Spain: 1936.* New York, 1936.

————. "With the Spanish Youth Alliance," *Direction,* I (January, 1938), 21.

Callender, Harold. "Can Spain Rise above Her Ruins?" *New York Times Magazine,* July 10, 1938, pp. 6-7, 13.

Calverton, V. F. "Beyond Franco and Stalin," *Modern Monthly,* X (September, 1937), 2, 27.

————. "Bolshevism in Spain," *Modern Monthly,* X (May, 1937), 2.

————. "Will England Give Spain to Franco?" *Modern Monthly,* X (August, 1937), 5-8.

Cannon, Walter B. *Spain Today.* New York, 1937.

Carney, William P. "Franco Tells What He Plans to Do for Spain," *New York Times Magazine,* December 26, 1937, pp. 5, 17.

————. "No Democratic Government in Spain," *Catholic Mind,* XXXV (January 8, 1937), 1-8.

————. "Two Funerals," *S,* XVII (September, 1937), 83-85.

Carreras, Katherine de. "Death from the Air," *Talks,* II (July, 1937), 6-7.

Carsley, C. F. "Democracy in Spain under the Hammer and Sickle," *A,* LX (January 28, 1939), 388-90.

Carter, Barbara Barclay. "European Catholics and Spain," *Commonweal,* XXV (March 5, 1937), 516-17.

Catholic Evidence on Spain. New York, 1939.

Catholics Reply to "Open Letter" on Spain. New York, 1937.

Catholics Speak for Spain. New York, 1937.

Cebrian, Katherine Crofton. "The Wall of the Virgin," *Catholic Digest,* II (February, 1938), 67-69.

Chamberlain, John. "Was It a Congress of American Writers?" *Common Sense,* VI (August, 1937), 14-16.

Chase, Gilbert. "The Ireland of Spain," *New York Times Magazine,* March 26, 1939, pp. 16, 18.

Childs, Richard S. (ed.). *War in Spain* [photo-history]. New York, 1937.

Cienfuegos, Jane Anderson de. "Horror in Spain," *Catholic Digest,* I (August, 1937), 69-74.

Clifford, Anthony. "Editor, What of Your Bias?" *Columbia,* XVII (May, 1938), 2, 16.

Cocot, Paul, and Johnson, Stephen. "A Protest and an Answer on Spain," *Catholic Worker,* IV (February, 1937), 6.

Code, Joseph B. "Francisco Franco," *Catholic Historical Review,* XXIV (July, 1938), 203.

————. "The Recognition of Franco: An Office of Friendship," *Spain,* III (March 1, 1939), 5, 17, 22.

————. "Spanish Propaganda Floods the United States," *A,* LX (December 10, 1938), 220-21.

————. *The Spanish War and Lying Propaganda.* New York, 1938.

Cog, Harold. "A Socialist Murdered," *Socialist Call,* II (November 21, 1936), 5.

Cohen, Joe. "Youth Defends Spain," *Young Communist Review,* I (September, 1936), 8-9.

Colvin, Ian D. "The Case for Franco," *AM,* CLXI (March, 1938), 397-402.

Connolly, Francis X. "The Fascist State Is Not Emerging in Spain," *A,* LIX (September 24, 1938), 580-82.

————. "The Religious Question in the Two Spains," *Spain,* I (November 15, 1937), 4-5.

Corliss, A. D. "Thunder on the Right," *Examiner,* II (Winter, 1939), 17-37.

Coughlin, Charles E. "Democrats and Dubinsky," *Social Justice,* II (September 21, 1936), 4.

————. " 'It Can't Happen Here,' " *Social Justice,* II (August, 10, 1936), 4.

Courtney, W. B. "Rehearsal in Spain," *Collier's,* XCIX (January 23, 1937), 12-13, 34, 36, 37.

Cowles, Virginia. "Behind the Fighting Fronts in the Two Clashing Spains," *New York Times Magazine,* January 9, 1938, pp. 8-9, 13, 23.

Cowley, Malcolm. "Abyssinia and Spain," *NR,* XCIV (February 16, 1938), 50-51.

————. "Apocalypse," *NR,* XCIV (March 2, 1938), 106-7.

————. "A Congress in Madrid," *NM,* XXIV (August 10, 1937), 16.

————. "Hemingway in Madrid," *NR,* XCVI (November 2, 1938), 367-68.

————. "Hemingway: Work in Progress," *NR,* XCII (October 20, 1937), 305-6.

————. "To Madrid" [first of five parts], *NR,* XCII (August 25, 1937), 63-65.

————. "Spain in Revolt," *NR,* LXXXVIII (September 2, 1936), 107.

————. "Spanish War Posters," *NR,* XCII (September 8, 1937), 122-23.

Crabitès, Pierre. *Unhappy Spain.* Baton Rouge, 1937.

The Crime of Francisco Franco. New York, n.d.

The Crime of Guernica. New York, 1937.

Curran, Edward Lodge. *Franco: Who Is He? What Does He Fight For?* Brooklyn, 1937.

————. *Spain in Arms.* Brooklyn, 1936.

Curtiss, John S. "The Soviet Union and the Spanish Civil War," *American Quarterly on the Soviet Union,* I (January, 1939), 50-65.

Cuthbertson, Stuart. "Escaping from the Spanish Revolution," *Hispania,* XIX (December, 1936), 451-60.

Dallet, Joseph. *Letters from Spain*. New York, 1938.

Dalrymple, Gwynne. "Will Fascism or Communism Win in Europe?" *Signs of the Times,* October 6, 1936, pp. 2-3, 11.

Dana, Henry Wadsworth Longfellow. "Longfellow on Spain," *NM,* XXVII (April 12, 1938), 92-93, 95.

Daura, Louise Blair de. "The Soldier Returns," *AM,* CLXI (January, 1938), 28-34.

Davidson, Martha. "Art or Propaganda?" *Art News,* XXXVI (December 25, 1937), 14, 24.

Davin, Tom. "Patent Blasphemy," *Protestant Digest,* I (March, 1939), 13-16.

Davis, Frances. *My Shadow in the Sun*. New York, 1940.

Davis, Robert. "Franco, the Man," *Catholic Digest,* III (May, 1939), 85-87.

Davis, Stuart. " 'Viva España Libre! ...' " *NM,* XX (August 18, 1936), 11.

Day, Dorothy. "Explains CW [*sic*] Stand on Use of Force," *Catholic Worker,* VI (September, 1938), 1, 4, 7.

Dean, Vera Micheles. "European Diplomacy in the Spanish Crisis," *Foreign Policy Reports,* XII (December 1, 1936), 222-32.

Delaney, John P. "Call Not These Men Rebels," *A,* LV (August 22, 1936), 460.

————. "Catholic Spaniards Have Only One Choice," *A,* LV (September 12, 1936), 536.

Dennis, Lawrence. "Russia's Private War in Spain," *American Mercury,* XL (February, 1937), 158-66.

Demarest, Virginia Booth. "The Threat to Christianity," *National Defense News,* II (April-May, 1938), 6-9.

Dewey, John. "Aid for the Spanish Government," *Christian Century,* LIV (March 3, 1937), 292.

De Wilde, John C. "The Struggle over Spain," *Foreign Policy Reports,* XIV (April 1, 1938), 14-24.

Dilla, G. P. "On the Spanish Yesterday and Today," *Educational Forum,* II (March, 1938), 281-90.

Dorland, Norman E. "In Franco's Prison Camp," *NM,* XXIX (November 22, 1938), 16-19.

Dos Passos, John. "The Communist Party and the War Spirit," *Common Sense,* VI (December, 1937), 11-14.

————. "Farewell to Europe!" *Common Sense,* VI (July, 1937), 9-11.

————. *Journeys between Wars*. New York, 1938.

————. "The Road to Madrid," *Esquire,* VIII (December, 1937), 62, 238-40, 243.

————. "Room and Bath at the Hotel Florida," *Esquire,* IX (January, 1938), 35, 131-32, 134.

————. "Spanish Diary: Coast Road," *Esquire*, VIII (November, 1937), 47, 202, 204, 206.

————. *The Theme Is Freedom*. New York, 1956.

————. "The Villages Are the Heart of Spain," *Esquire*, IX (February, 1938), 32-33, 151-53.

Draper, Theodore. "Behind the Lines in Spain," *NM*, XXII (January 26, 1937), 15-17.

Dreiser, Theodore. "Barcelona in August," *Direction*, I (November-December, 1938), 4-5.

————. "Dreiser Recounts Loyalist Tension," *New York Times*, September 11, 1938, p. 30.

————. *Letters of Theodore Dreiser*, ed. Robert H. Elias. Philadelphia, 1959.

————. " 'Viva España Libre! . . .' " *NM*, XX (August 18, 1936), 11.

Dunn, Thomas. "Where Do Catholics Stand?" *Fight*, V (April, 1938), 41, 50, 54.

Dupee, F. W. "André Malraux," *Partisan Review*, IV (March, 1938), 24-35.

Dupuy, R. Ernest. "The Checkerboard of Mars," *Today*, VII (November 21, 1936), 12-13, 31.

Duranty, Walter. "Spanish Crazy Quilt," *Collier's*, XCVIII (December 12, 1936), 10-11, 28-31.

Duroc, Margaret. "Spain Speaks," *Fight*, IV (November, 1936), 5-7.

————. "With the Artists in Catalonia," *Art Front*, II (September-October, 1936), 12-13.

Eddy, Sherwood. "The Tragedy of Spain," *Christian Century*, LIV (September 22, 1937), 1163-65.

Edwards, James F. "Social Injustice the Real Cause of the War in Spain," *Social Justice*, IA (February 28, 1938), 5, 17.

Edwards, Thyra. "Moors and the Spanish War," *Opportunity*, XVI (March, 1938), 84-85.

Eloesser, Leo. "With the Spanish Army of Manoeuvre," *Direction*, I (July-August, 1938), 20-21.

Eliot, Frederick May. " 'A Military Maneuver,' " *Christian Register*, CXVII (March 31, 1938), 207.

Eliot, George Fielding. "Battle Lines in Spain," *Today*, VI (October 3, 1936), 16-17, 25.

————. "Foreign Fodder for Spanish Guns," *Today*, VII (January 30, 1937), 13-14, 22-23.

Ellard, Gerald. "The Spanish Revolt Enters the Liturgy," *Orate Fratres*, XI (January 24, 1937), 103-6.

Elliot, John. "With the Rebels," *AM*, CLVIII (November, 1936), 534-42.

Engelbrecht, H. C. "Hitler's Spies in Spain," *N*, CXLIV (June 5, 1937), 639-41.

Enters, Angna. "Ramon, Miguel and Dolores," *NR,* XCV (May 18, 1938), 47.

———. "Spain and the Artist," *NM,* XXII (January 5, 1937), 7-8.

———. "Spain Says 'Salud,'" *New Theatre,* III (September, 1936), 8-9, 28.

Erber, Ernest. "Spain: New Outpost of World Revolution," *American Socialist Monthly,* V (December, 1936), 17-20.

Eustace, C. J. "Maritain Looks at Franco," *Commonweal,* XXVII (February 4, 1938), 402-4.

Fadiman, Clifton. "In a Little Spanish Town," *NY,* XIII (August 7, 1937), 49-51.

Feeney, Thomas J. *The Church in Spain, Rich or Poor?* New York, 1937.

Ferger, Edward J. "A People Intent on Winning the War," *A,* LVII (July 24, 1937), 366-67.

Ferguson, Otis. "'And There Were Giants on the Earth,'" *NR,* XCII (September 1, 1937), 103-4.

Fernsworth, Lawrence. "Back of the Spanish Rebellion," *Foreign Affairs,* XV (October, 1936), 87-101.

———. "Foreign Aims in Spain," *Current History,* XLV (March, 1937), 52-58.

———. "Lt. Colonel Valentin Gonzalez," in Jo Davidson's *Spanish Portraits.* New York, 1938.

———. "Revolution on the Ramblas," in *Nothing But Danger,* ed. Frank C. Hanighen. New York, 1939, pp. 15-47.

Finch, George A. "The United States and the Spanish Civil War," *American Journal of International Law,* XXXI (January, 1937), 74-81.

Finick, Eugene. "Bombers Aloft," *True,* V (August, 1939), 73-97.

———. "I Fly for Spain," *Harper's,* CLXXVI (January, 1938), 138-48.

Fischer, Louis. "The Drive Along the Ebro," *N,* CXLVII (September 3, 1938), 219-21.

———. "The Road to Peace," *AF,* I (Spring, 1938), 3, 21-22.

———. "Spain's 'Red' Foreign Legion," *N,* CXLIV (January 9, 1937), 36-38.

———. *The War in Spain.* New York, 1937.

———. "We Must Lift the Embargo," *Fight,* III (March, 1939), 5.

Fisher, Dorothy Canfield. "In Defense of a Free Spain," *NM,* XX (September 8, 1936), 11.

Fisk, Alfred G. "Written in Blood across Spain," *Fellowship,* II (October, 1936), 1-2.

Fitts, Dudley. "What Spanish Children See," *Saturday Review of Literature,* XIX (November 19, 1938), 11.

Fitzgerald, William. "Manfred's Fate," *Examiner,* II (Spring, 1939), 184-90.

Flanner, Janet. "Letter from Paris," *NY,* XII (September 19, 1936), 73-74.

————. "Letter from Perpignan," *NY,* XV (March 11, 1939), 65-66.

Flores, Angel, and Ossa, Ben. "The Role of the Artist in Spain," *Art Front,* II (September-October, 1936), 9.

Floyd, William. "Arnica for Guernica," *Arbitrator,* XIX (June, 1937), 1.

————. "Civil War in Spain," *Arbitrator,* XVIII (September, 1936), 1-2.

Flye, James H. "American Neutrality, 1938," *Sewanee Review,* XLVI (April-June, 1938), 133-46.

Folsom, Franklin. "Insurgent Spain: Letter to the *New York Times,*" February 27, 1938.

Forbes, W. Cameron. "Lessons Learned from a Visit to Spain," *Spain,* II (July 18, 1938), 21.

Ford, James W. *The Negro and the Democratic Front.* New York, 1938.

Forrest, M. D. *Christian Civilization versus Bolshevist Barbarism.* Huntington, Ind., 1937.

Forsythe, Robert. "The Last Refuge," *NM,* XX (September 1, 1936), 7.

Fortesque, Granville. *Frontline and Deadline.* New York, 1937.

Foster, William Z. " 'Viva España Libre! . . .' " *NM,* XX (August 18, 1936), 13.

Frank, L. "The New Economy in Catalonia," *Vanguard,* III (February-March, 1937), 6.

Frank, Marc. "Committees," *NR,* XCIII (December 29, 1937), 221-22.

Frank, Waldo. "A Communication: A Letter to Léon Blum," *NR,* LXXXVIII (October 7, 1936), 254-55.

————. "Refugee from Palencia, Old Castile," in Jo Davidson's *Spanish Portraits.* New York, 1938.

————. "Spain in War" [1st of three parts], *NR,* XCV (July 13, 1938), 269-72.

————. " 'Viva España Libre! . . .' " *NM,* XX (August 18, 1936), 12-13.

Freed, Grace. "Do You Know My Brother?" *AF,* I (Spring, 1938), 9, 19-20.

Freeman, Joseph. "Arnold Reid," *NM,* XXIX (September 13, 1938), 21.

Freemasons and Spain. New York, 1938.

From a Hospital in Spain: Letters from American Nurses. New York, 1937.

Fuhr, Lini. "I Was a Nurse in Loyalist Spain," *AF,* I (Spring, 1938), 10, 18.

Gannes, Harry. *How the Soviet Union Helps Spain.* New York, 1936.

————. *Spain Defends Democracy.* New York, 1936.

————, and Repard, Theodore. *Spain in Revolt*. New York, 1936.

Gannon, John M. "Red Propaganda Is Vicious," *Catholic Mind*, XXXVI (November 22, 1938), 443-48.

Garcia, John. "Spanish Barricades," *Fight*, III (September, 1936), 5, 24, 29-30.

Garland, Walter. "An Answer to Lynching," *AF*, I (Winter, 1938), 10-11.

Garner, James W. "Questions of International Law in the Spanish Civil War," *American Journal of International Law*, XXXI (January, 1937), 66-73.

————. "Recognition of Belligerency," *American Journal of International Law*, XXXII (January, 1938), 106-13.

————. "The United States Neutrality Act of 1937," *American Journal of International Law*, XXXI (July, 1937), 385-97.

Gavit, John Palmer. "Toward the New Armageddon?" *Survey Graphic*, XXV (September, 1936), 531-32, 538.

Gellert, Hugo. " 'Viva España Libre! . . .' " *NM*, XX (August 18, 1936), 12.

Gellhorn, Martha. "City at War," *Collier's*, CI (April 2, 1938), 18-19, 59-60.

————. "Madrid to Morata," *NY*, XIII (July 24, 1937), 31, 34, 37-39.

————. "Men without Medals," *Collier's*, CI (January 15, 1938), 9-10, 49.

————. "Only the Shells Whine," *Collier's*, C (July 17, 1937), 12-13, 64-65.

————. "Writers Fighting in Spain," in *The Writer in a Changing World*, ed. Henry Hart. New York, 1937. Pp. 63-68.

Gershoy, Leo. "France 'Appeases' Franco," *Events*, V (April, 1939), 273-77.

Gittler, Louis F. "Barcelona: An Anarchist State," *N*, CXLIII (December 12, 1936), 701-2.

Good, Orville Brisbane. *The Truth on Spain*. Atascadero, Calif., 1939.

Gordon, Franklin. "Is Spain Doomed to 'Non-Aryan' War?" *American Hebrew*, CXXXIX (August 28, 1936), 227, 238.

Gorman, Francis J. "Spain—Pivot of Democracy," *AF*, I (Spring, 1938), 8, 19.

Goodman, Richard. "What Is Happening in Spain?" *NM*, XXXI (March 21, 1939), 9-11.

Gold, Michael. "Mr Dooley on Spain," *NM, XXV* (November 9, 1937), 6-7.

Goldman, Emma. "Enemy Within," *Man!, V* (December, 1936-January, 1937), 2.

————. "Naive Anarchists: Letter to *New York Times*," July 4, 1937.

————. "Political Persecution in Republican Spain," *Man!*, VI (January, 1938), 3, 6.

————. "P.O.U.M. Frame-Up Fails," *Vanguard,* IV (February, 1939), 15-16.

————. " 'Whom the Gods Would Destroy...,' " *Vanguard,* III (October-November, 1936), 2.

Graham, Marcus. "The People of Spain Call to You," *Man!,* V (December, 1936-January, 1937), 2.

Greene, E. P. "Forging Labor Unity," *Fight,* IV (August, 1937), 21, 26, 29.

Green, Gil. "Spain at Gettysburg," *NM,* XXI (October 27, 1936), 7-8.

Gunther, John. *Inside Europe.* New York, 1938.

————. "Manuel Azaña," in Jo Davidson's *Spanish Portraits.* New York, 1938.

Gwynn, Denis. "Spain and the Mediterranean," *S,* XVI (October, 1936), 171-73.

Hallgren, Mauritz A. "The U.S. Plays Ostrich," *Fight,* IV (August, 1937), 5-7.

Hanighen, Frank C. "Hell-Cats in the Spanish War," *Liberty,* XIII (October 31, 1936), 30-31.

————. (ed.). *Nothing But Danger.* New York, 1939.

————. "The Radio General," *Esquire,* IX (January, 1938), 39, 122.

————. "Spanish Volcano," *Review of Reviews,* XCIV (October, 1936), 40-43.

————. "The War for Raw Materials in Spain," *N,* CXLIV (April 24, 1937), 456-58.

Hapgood, Norman. "Freedom," *Christian Register,* CXVI (September 3, 1936), 510.

————. "Spain," *Christian Register,* CXVI (September 10, 1936), 526.

Harris, Thomas L. "Stop Aiding Aggression!" *Fight,* VI (April, 1939), 5.

Hart, Henry. (ed.). *The Writer in a Changing World.* New York, 1937.

Hart, Merwin K. *America, Look at Spain.* New York, 1939.

Hartzell, Arthur. "Why Spain Wages Civil War So Bitterly," *New York Times Magazine,* April 18, 1937, pp. 6-7, 22.

Hasbrouck, F. M. "Is Spain Done For?" *South Atlantic Quarterly,* XXXVII (July, 1938), 252-62.

Hathaway, Clarence A. "Fighting for Democracy in Spain," *Communist,* XV (September, 1936), 829-44.

Havel, Hippolyte. "United Front," *Man!,* IV (October-November, 1936), 4.

Hawthorne, James. "American Fliers in Spain," *NM,* XXIII (June 8, 1937), 17-18.

————. "Political 'Suppression' in Spain," *NM,* XXIV (September 21, 1937), 19-20.

————. "Spain's Government Girds for War," *NM*, XXIII (June 22, 1937), 7-8.

Hecht, George J. "Help Save the Children of Spain!" *Parents Magazine*, XII (October, 1937), 13.

Heline, Theodore. *Spain: World Ideas in Turmoil.* Los Angeles, 1938.

Hellman, Lillian. "Day in Spain," *NR*, XCIV (April 13, 1938), 297-98.

Hemingway, Ernest. "Call for Greatness," *Ken*, II (July 14, 1938), 23.

————. "The Cardinal Picks a Winner," *Ken*, I (May 5, 1938), 38.

————. "Dying, Well or Badly," *Ken*, I (April 21, 1938), 68.

————. "False News to the President," *Ken*, II (September 8, 1938), 17-18.

————. "Fascism Is a Lie," *NM*, XXIII (June 22, 1937), 4.

————. Foreword to Joseph North's *Men in the Ranks*. New York, 1939, pp. 3-4.

————. "Fresh Air on an Inside Story," *Ken*, II (September 22, 1938), 28.

————. "Good Generals Hug the Line," *Ken*, II (August 25, 1938), 28.

————. "The Heat and the Cold," *Verve*, I (Spring, 1938), 46.

————. "Hemingway Reports Spain," *NR*, XC (May 5, 1937), 376-79. [Other dispatches appeared in *NR* on January 12, 1938; April 27, 1938; June 8, 1938.]

————. "H.M's Loyal State Department," *Ken*, I (June 16, 1938), 36.

————. "Luis Quintanilla: Artist and Soldier," *AF*, I (Spring, 1938), 7.

————. "Major Milton Wolff," in Jo Davidson's *Spanish Portraits*. New York, 1938.

————. "The Next Outbreak of Peace," *Ken*, III (January 12, 1939), 12-13.

————. "On the American Dead in Spain," *NM*, XXX (February 14, 1939), 3.

————. Preface to Gustav Regler's *The Great Crusade*. New York, 1940, pp. vii-ix.

————. "A Program for U.S. Realism," *Ken*, II (August 11, 1938), 26.

————. *The Spanish War.* London, 1938.

————. Three Prefaces to Luis Quintanilla's *All the Brave*. New York, 1939, pp. 7-11.

————. "The Time Now, the Place Spain," *Ken*, I (April 7, 1938), 36-37.

————. "Treachery in Aragon," *Ken*, I (June 30, 1938), 26.

————. "The Writer and War," in *The Writer in a Changing World*, ed. Henry Hart, New York, 1937. Pp. 69-73. [Reprinted as "Fascism Is a Lie."]

_____. "The Writer as a Writer," *Direction*, II (May-June, 1939), 3.

Henle, R. J. "Spain Remembers Its Origins," *Catholic World*, CXLIX (April, 1939), 54-57.

Henson, Francis A. "An American in Spain," *Presbyterian Tribune*, LII (November 26, 1936), 7-8, 10.

Heras, Antonio. "The Present Spanish Conflict," *World Affairs Interpreter*, VII (Autumn, 1936), 230-42.

_____. "Some Aspects of the Spanish Conflict," *World Affairs Interpreter*, IX (Winter, 1939), 394-400.

Herberg, Will. "Civil War in Spain," *Workers Age*, V (August 15, 1936), 3-4.

Herbst, Josephine. "Evening in Spain," *Fight*, V (November, 1937), 13, 30.

_____. "Night Comes to the Valley," *Direction*, I (April, 1938), 18-20.

_____. "Spanish Village," *N*, CXLV (August 14, 1937), 169-70.

Herman, Ben. "Caballero at the Helm," *Socialist Appeal* [Chicago], II (October 1, 1936), 10-12.

Herring, Hubert C. "Spain: Battleground of Democracy," *Social Action*, III (January 1, 1937), 3-30.

_____. "Spain's Bitter Days," *Advance*, CXXVIII (October, 1936), 593-94.

Hicks, Granville. "A Writer in Arms," *Communist*, XVII (January, 1938), 92-93.

Hinkel, John V. *The Communistic Network*. New York, 1939.

_____. "Keep the Embargo on Munitions for Spain" [1st of three parts], *A*, LX (January 14, 1939), 340-42.

Holmes, John Haynes. " 'Expeditionary Force' Scheme Censured...," *New Leader*, XX (January 2, 1937), 8.

_____. *Spain—And the Next War*. New York, 1937.

Hook, Sidney. "The Anatomy of the Popular Front," *Partisan Review*, VI (Spring, 1939), 29-45.

House, Roy Temple. "Spain's 'Holy War,' " *Christian Century*, LIV (October 6, 1937), 1228-29.

_____. "Spain's Useful Reminder," *Christian Century*, LIV (July 7, 1937), 867-68.

Howe, Quincy. "Has the Second World War Begun?" *Cosmopolitan*, CIII (December, 1937), 26-27, 170.

_____. "Spain's Threat to American Peace," *Common Sense*, V (October, 1936), 11-14.

Huberman, Leo. "Review and Comment," *NM*, XXII (February 2, 1937), 23.

Hughan, Jessie Wallace. *What About Spain?* New York, 1937.

Hughes, Langston. "Laughter in Madrid," *N*, CXLVI (January 29, 1938), 123-24.

————. "Madrid's House of Culture," *Volunteer for Liberty*, (October 18, 1937), pp. 3, 6.

————. "Negroes in Spain," *Volunteer for Liberty*, (September 13, 1937, p. 4.

————. "Too Much of Race," *Crisis*, XLIV (September, 1937), 272.

Humphries, Rolfe. "Cultural Heritage," *Fight*, V (April, 1938), 46-47.

————. "The Life and Death of Garcia Lorca," *N*, CXLV (September 18, 1937), 293-94.

Hunter, Edward. "U.S. Press on Fascist Side in Spanish War," *New Leader*, XX (February 6, 1937), 5.

Hutner, Herb. "My Dear Mr. and Mrs. Wolman," *AF*, I (Spring, 1938), 11, 23.

Inman, Samuel Guy. "Religious Liberty in Spain," *Churchman*, CL (November 15, 1936), 10-11.

Italian Prisoners in Spain. New York, 1937.

It's Happening in Spain. New York, 1937.

Jackson, W. Elmore. "Intervention in Spain," *Friends Intelligencer*, XCIV (January 30, 1937), 73-74.

James, Stanley B. "Blasphemy," *Commonweal*, XXV (March 26, 1937), 602-4.

Janeway, Eliot. "The Capitalist International," *N*, CXLV (September 25, 1937), 312-15.

Jessup, Philip C. "The Spanish Rebellion and International Law," *Foreign Affairs*, XV (January, 1937), 260-79.

Jewell, Edward Alden. "Art under a Democracy," *New York Times*, May 8, 1938.

Jones, Alfred W., and Carter, Mary. *War Relief in Spain.* Philadelphia and Boston, 1938.

Jones, Dorsey D. "Modern Spanish Troubles," *Social Science*, XIII (January, 1938), 20-29.

Jones, Sylvester. *Through Loyalist and Insurgent Spain.* Philadelphia, 1937.

Joseph, Don. *Shop Talk on Spain.* New York, 1938.

Josephson, Matthew. "'Viva España Libre! . . .'" *NM*, XX (August 18, 1936), 13.

Kaltenborn, H. V. *Kaltenborn Edits the News.* New York, 1937.

————. "They All Want to 'Help' Spain," *Commentator*, II (August, 1937), 25-29.

Kazin, Alfred. "Modern Men on the Battlefield," *New York Herald Tribune Books*, November 13, 1938, p. 5.

Kell, Werner. "Stamp War," *SEP*, CCXI (March 11, 1939), 7, 41, 45.

Kellogg, Paul. "Between Going to War and Doing Nothing," *Survey Graphic*, XXVIII (March, 1939), 226-28.

Kelly, Fred C. "Ambassador as Democrat," *Esquire,* VII (April, 1937), 62, 219-20.

Kelly, John E. "After Barcelona," *S,* XVIII (March, 1939), 479-80.

_____. "Foresworn Americans Serve Red Cause in Spain," *A,* LVIII (October 23, 1937), 55-56.

_____. "Military Operations," *Spain,* II (May 1, 1938), 16-19.

_____. "Spanish Waifs," *A,* LVIII (January 15, 1938), 343-44.

Kennedy, John E. "If This Be Heresy," *NM,* XXVI (March 8, 1938), 15-16.

Kent, Rockwell. " 'Viva España Libre! . . .' " *NM,* XX (August 18, 1936), 12.

Keracher, John. "The Civil War in Spain and Its Lessons," *Proletarian News,* VIII (April 1, 1939), 4-5.

Khoran, Alva. "World a Red Battleground," *National Republic,* XX (November, 1936), 20-21, 31.

King, Gordon J. "Fascist Week-end in Montreal," *Christian Century,* LIII (November 25, 1936), 1560-62.

Kiniery, Paul. "The Catholic Answer to Communism," *CW,* CXLIV (March, 1937), 652-60.

Kirchwey, Freda. " 'Peace' in Spain," *N,* CXLVIII (April 8, 1939), 393-94.

Klein, Roger. "Adventures with Spain's Defenders," *Champion of Youth,* II (February, 1937), 12.

Kline, Herbert. "At a Hospital," *Fight,* VI (August, 1937), 16-17, 24, 26.

_____. "The Voice of Madrid," *NM,* XXIII (April 13, 1937), 7-8.

Knickerbocker, H. R. "The Cosmopolite of the Month: General Francisco Franco," *Cosmopolitan,* CIII (July, 1937), 8, 148.

_____. *The Siege of Alcazar.* Philadelphia, 1936.

_____. "The Thing Called Civil War," *Today,* VIII (December 5, 1936), 10-12, 24-25.

Knoblaugh, H. Edward. *Correspondent in Spain.* New York, 1937.

_____. "How the Loyalist Propaganda Machine Operates," *Spain,* I (December 15, 1937), 18, 20.

Koenig, Arthur E. "Candid Camera View of the Alleged Spanish War," *A,* LIX (August 13, 1938), 438-40.

Kohn, Hans. "The Twilight of Nationalism?" *American Scholar,* VI (Summer, 1937), 259-70.

Korsch, Karl. "Collectivization in Spain," *Living Marxism,* IV (April, 1939), 178-82.

Krehm, William. "Barricades in Barcelona!" *Labor Front,* IV (June-July, 1937), 1, 5.

Kronenberger, Louis, "Unromantic Spain," *N,* CXLVIII (February 25, 1939), 235, 237.

La Farge, John. "While Spain Burns They Strum Impartially," *A,* LIX (August 20, 1938), 462-63.

Laird, Megan. "A Diary of Revolution," *AM,* CLVIII (November, 1936), 513-33.

Lardner, James. "What Are the Duties of a Cabo?" *Volunteer for Liberty,* July 19, 1938, p. 11.

Lardner, Ring, Jr. "The Life and Death of James Lardner," in *Somebody Had to Do Something.* Los Angeles, 1939, pp. 8-14.

Lash, Joseph P. " 'Time Works for Us'—Spain, 1937," *NM,* XXV (October 19, 1937), 6-8.

Lee, Algernon. "Spanish Struggle Affects Future of Latin America," *New Leader,* XIX (November 28, 1936), 8.

Leeds, Jack. *Let My People Know.* New York, 1942.

Lehane, J. C. "Spain's First Soldier," *Catholic Digest,* II (January, 1938), 35-37.

Leider, Ben. "Last Letters from Spain," *Current History,* XLVI (April, 1937), 46.

Lerner, James. "I Was in Spain," *Fight,* IV (November, 1936), 40-41.

Lerner, Max. "Behind Hull's Embargo," *N,* CXLVI (May 28, 1938), 607-10.

Letters from Spain. San Francisco, 1937.

Letters from the Trenches from Our Boys in Spain. New York, n.d.

Levin, Meyer. "The Candid Cameraman," *Esquire,* IX (April, 1938), 94, 197-202.

Levinger, Samuel. "Journey to Albacete," *AF,* I (Winter, 1938), 7, 22.

Lewis, Sinclair. "Glorious Dirt," *Newsweek,* X (October 18, 1937), 34.

Libby, Frederick J. "Open Letter to our Readers on Neutrality," *Peace Action,* III (March, 1937), 1.

Lingelbach, William E. "The Spanish Tragedy," *Events,* I (January, 1937), 29-38.

Lissner, Will. "Why Spain Is Torn Asunder," *Freeman,* I (November, 1937), 13.

Lloyd, Lola Maverick. "Mediation in Spain," *Unity,* CXIX (June 21, 1937), 150-52.

Loeb, James. "Spain's Tragedy," *Socialist Call,* V (March 25, 1939), 1.

Lord, Frederick I. "The Education of an Adventurer," *NM,* XXIV (August 10, 1937), 3-5.

Lore, Ludwig. "The Challenge of Catalonia," *Modern Monthly,* X (May, 1937), 5-7.

————. "Has Britain Betrayed Spain?" *NR,* XC (March 3, 1937), 99-100.

————. "The Score in Spain," *Current History,* XLV (November, 1936), 41-45.

Loth, David. "Juan March—Franco's Money Man," *NM,* XXV (September 28, 1937), 18-20.

Lothrop, Donald G. "A True American Policy toward Spain," *Unity,* CXIX (April 5, 1937), 53-54.

Lovestone, Jay. *The People's Front Illusion*. New York, n.d.

Luccock, Halford E. "Through the Novelist's Window," *Christendom*, IV (Winter, 1939), 154-58.

Lund, Harold. "Aid to the Children of Spain," *Social Work Today*, V (October, 1937), 18.

Lyndhurst, Henry. "The Shadow of Dictators over Europe," *New York Times Magazine*, August 23, 1936, pp. 3, 20.

Lyons, Eugene. "Where the News Ends," *New Leader*, XXII (January, 7, 1939), 8.

Macauley, Thurston. "Spain: When Peace Explodes," *Survey Graphic*, XXVIII (March, 1939), 212-13, 253-54.

McBride, Robert H. "It Happened in Spain," *American Foreign Service Journal*, XIV (January, 1937), 7-10, 46-47.

McCabe, Joseph. *The Causes of the Civil War in Spain*. Girard, Kan., 1937.

McConnell, Dorothy. "As to Women," *Fight*, V (April, 1938), 50.

McConnell, Francis J. "Letter to the President on Spain," *Protestant Digest*, I (January, 1939), 76-77.

McCormick, Anne O'Hare. "Right versus Left: A Great Struggle," *New York Times Magazine*, August 30, 1936, pp. 1-2, 14.

McCulloch, Rhoda E. "Spain," *Womans Press*, XXX (December, 1936), 526-27.

Macdonald, Dwight. "Reading from Left to Right," *New International*, V (February, 1939), 55-56.

McGuire, Owen B. "The Basque Nationalists," *Thought*, XII (June, 1937), 283-300.

————. "Legal and Democratic," *S*, XVI (April, 1937), 523-26.

————. "The New Spain," *Commonweal*, XXVII (October 29, 1937), 5-8.

McKay, Virginia. "The Spanish Tragedy," *Social Justice*, IIA (October 17, 1938), 15, 18.

McKenney, Ruth. "Ben Leider: In Memoriam," *NM*, XXXI (March 21, 1939), 8.

MacLeish, Archibald. "The War Is Ours," *NM*, XXIII (June 22, 1937), 5-6.

McManus, John T. "Down to Earth in Spain," *New York Times*, July 25, 1937.

McManus, Paul G. "What's Happening on the Embargo," *NM*, XXXI (February 14, 1939), 14-15.

McMillen, Wayne. *This Is Our Concern*. New York, 1937.

McSorley, Joseph, *"The Martyrdom of Spain . . .,"* *CW*, CXLVIII (October, 1938), 113-16.

McWilliams, Raymond J. "Barcelona in Scarlet," *National Republic*, XXVI (June, 1938), 4, 29.

Magner, James A. "Alternatives in Spain," *Commonweal,* XXVI (June 11, 1937), 173-75.

————. "The Catholic Church in Modern Europe," *Catholic Historical Review,* XXIII (April, 1937), 1-16.

Maguire, Theophane. "Blind Leaders," *S,* XVII (November, 1937), 195.

Mangold, William P. "Betraying Spanish Democracy," *Fight,* IV (March, 1937), 8-9, 24-25.

Manuel, Frank E. *The Politics of Modern Spain.* New York, 1938.

Marlin, H. H. "Unhappy Spain," *United Presbyterian,* XCIV (July 30, 1936), 7.

Marvin, Henry A. "The Truth about Spain" [1st of two parts], *National Republic,* XXV (February, 1938), 7-8, 23, 30.

Masse, Benjamin L. "Christian Liberals—To Whom Are They Allied?" *A,* LIX (June 11, 1938), 226-27.

Matthews, Herbert L. "Colonel Juan Modesto," in Jo Davidson's *Spanish Portraits.* New York, 1938.

————. *Two Wars and More to Come.* New York, 1938.

Mecklenburg, George. "Three Tragedies of Europe," *Christian Advocate,* CXIV (March 30, 1939), 298.

Memoria del Congreso Nacional. Brooklyn, 1937.

Merriman, Robert. "The Work of the Americans in Spain," *Our Fight,* December, 1937-January, 1938, 14.

Mienov, Karl. "The Imperialist War in Spain," *Spark,* I (February, 1938), 1-10.

Miller, Webb. "The Little World War in Spain," in *We Cover the World,* ed. Eugene Lyons. New York, 1937, pp. 413-41.

Milton, Harry. "Aragon Front Veteran Tells of Sabotage...," *Socialist Appeal* [New York], I October 16, 1937), 4.

Minifie, James M. "A Battle against Ignorance," *Journal of Adult Education,* IX (June, 1937), 258-60.

Minor, Robert. "The Change in Spain," *Communist,* XVI (August, 1937), 697-708.

Minton, Bruce, and Stuart, John. "Franco Aims at the Mines," *NM,* XXV (November 9, 1937), 8-9.

Mitchell, Jonathan. "Death Rides the Wind," *NR,* XCI (May 26, 1937), 63-64.

Mitchison, Naomi. "Waifs of the Storm," *NM,* XXIV (July 6, 1937), 15.

Moley, Raymond. "Perspective: The Duty to Be Neutral," *Newsweek,* X (October 4, 1937), 44.

————. "Perspective: The World Watches Spain," *Today,* VI (August 8, 1936), 17.

Monica, Sister M. *And Then the Storm.* New York, 1937.

Monks, Bernard J. "Franco of Spain," *CW*, CXLVII (September, 1938), 667-74.

Montavon, William F. *Insurrection in Spain*. Washington, D.C., 1937.

———. "Is There Hope for Spain?" *Columbia*, XVI (February, 1937), 8, 22.

Moody, V. Alton. "Spain in Revolt," *Social Forces*, XV (May, 1937), 563-69.

Morgan, William Thomas. "Mr. Neville Chamberlain and the Dictators," *South Atlantic Quarterly*, XXXVIII (January, 1939), 1-22.

Morris, George L. K. "Miro and the Spanish Civil War," *Partisan Review*, IV (February, 1938), 32-33.

Morrison, S. "Betrayal in Spain," *Vanguard*, III (June, 1937), 3-4.

Morrow, Felix. "Anarchism in Spain," *New International*, IV (January, 1938), 6-7.

———. "The G.P.U. Orders a Novel," *New International*, V (March, 1939), 94.

———. "How the Workers Can Win in Spain," *Socialist Appeal* [Chicago], II (October 1, 1936), 6-8.

———. *Revolution and Counter-Revolution in Spain*. New York, 1938.

———. "The War in Spain," *New International*, IV (February, 1938), 59-61.

Most, Amicus. "Men to Spain—The Eugene V. Debs Column," *American Socialist Monthly*, V (February, 1937), 21-24.

Mowrer, Edgar Ansel. "Julio Alvarez del Vayo," in Jo Davidson's *Spanish Portraits*. New York, 1938.

———. "The Spanish Conflict: Its International Repercussions," in *Geneva and the Drift to War, Problems of Peace: 12th Series*. London, 1938.

Mumford, Lewis. "Good Will Must Act," *Fight*, VI (February, 1939), 22-23, 26.

Murphy, James Q. "Anti-Religion in Spain," *S*, XVI (March, 1937), 457-60.

Murray, Augustine C. "Behind the Scenes in Spain," *Catholic Digest*, I (February, 1937), 5-7.

Murray, Helen G. "Jesu-Cristo in Spain," *Advance*, CXXVIII (October, 1936), 591-92.

Muste, A. J. "Another War to Save Democracy?" *Messenger of Peace*, LXII (April, 1937), 2-4.

———. "Tragedy of Spain," *Presbyterian Tribune*, LIV (March 30, 1939), 10-11.

Nall, T. Otto. "Behind Spain's Lurid Flames—A Menacing Shadow," *Christian Advocate*, CXI (August 6, 1936), 746.

A Negro Nurse in Republican Spain. New York, 1938.

Nelson, Steve. "In a Spanish Town," *Fight*, V (June, 1938), 22-23, 30.

Neugass, James. "Spanish Diary," *NM*, XXVII (June 14, 1938), 133-34.

Neville, Robert. "Spain: Church against Republic," *NR*, LXXXVIII (September 16, 1936), 145-47.

Nevins, Allan. "Fascist Setback in Spain," *Events*, I (May, 1937), 346-51.

Nicholson, Helen. *Death in the Morning*. London, 1937.

Niebuhr, Reinhold. "Arrogance in the Name of Christ," *Christian Century*, LIII (September 2, 1936), 1157-58.

Noar, Berenice E. "The '76 of Spain," *Fight*, III (October, 1936), 6.

North, Joseph. "Across the Ebro," *NM*, XXVII (May 3, 1938), 7.

————. "But—Catalonia Broke Napoleon," *NM*, XXVII (April 26, 1938), 9.

————. "Hero in Horn-Rimmed Glasses," in *Salud!*, ed. Alan Calmer. New York, 1938. pp. 42-45.

————. *Men in the Ranks*. New York, 1939.

————. *Why Spain Can Win*. New York, 1939.

Oak, Liston M. "Balance Sheet of the Spanish Revolution," *Socialist Review*, VI (September, 1937), 7-9, 26.

————. "Behind Barcelona Barricades," *New Statesman and Nation*, XIII (May 15, 1937), 801-2.

————. "What Happened in Barcelona," *Socialist Call*, III (June 5, 1937), 6.

O'Brien, John. "Fighting for Social Justice" [1st of three parts], *Commonweal*, XXVI (May 28, 1937), 117-19.

Oehler, Hugo. *Barricades in Barcelona*. New York, 1937.

————. "What Is Happening in Spain?" *Modern Monthly*, X (August, 1937), 11-12.

Oestreicher, J. C. "Getting the News Out of Spain," *Quill*, XXIV (August, 1936), 10-11.

O'Flanagan, Michael. "I Speak to Catholics," *NM*, XXVIII (August 2, 1938), 9, 11.

Oliver, Bryce. "Catholic Hierarchy Hurt by Franco Stand," *New Leader*, XXII (January 14, 1939), 5.

Oliver, Edward H. *Sixth Anniversary of the Spanish Republic in Barcelona*. Chicago, 1937.

One Year in Spain: The Story of American Doctors and Nurses. New York, 1937.

One Year of War, New York, 1937.

An Open Letter on Culture and Democracy in Spain. New York, 1938.

Ornitz, Lou. *Captured by Franco*. New York, 1939.

O'Rourke, Vernon A. "Recognition of Belligerency in the Spanish War," *American Journal of International Law*, XXXI (July, 1937), 398-413.

O'Sheel, Shaemas. "Spanish Rebellion and Catholic Doctrine," *NR*, XCIII (February 2, 1938), 367-68.

Ossa, Ben. "Artists in Arms," *Art Front*, II (November, 1936), 6-7.

Padelford, Norman J. "Foreign Shipping During the Spanish Civil War," *American Journal of International Law*, XXXII (April, 1938), 264-79.

_____. *International Law and Diplomacy in the Spanish Civil Strife.* New York, 1939.

_____. "International Law and the Spanish Civil War," *American Journal of International Law*, XXXI (April, 1937), 226-43.

_____. "The International Non-Intervention Agreement and the Spanish Civil War," *American Journal of International Law*, XXXI (October, 1937), 578-603.

Padelford, Norman J., and Seymour, Henry. "Some International Problems of the Spanish Civil War," *Political Science Quarterly*, LII (September, 1937), 364-80.

Palmer, Gretta. "Reds, Rebels and Reporters," *Today*, VII (January 16, 1937), 12-13, 26-27.

Palmer, Russell. "Return to Malaga," *Spain*, I (November 15, 1937), 8-10.

Parker, Dorothy. "Incredible, Fantastic . . . and True," *NM*, XXV (November 23, 1937), 15-16.

_____. "Not Enough," *NM*, XXXI (March 14, 1939), 3-4.

Parsons, Wilfrid. "Atrocities Made to Order," *Columbia*, XVI (July, 1937), 6, 21.

_____. "No Masses in Madrid," *Columbia*, XVI (September, 1936), 4, 25.

Partnow, Hyde. "Without Bands or Medals," *NM*, XXVI (March 1, 1938), 7.

Pasionaria: People's Tribune of Spain. New York, 1938.

Pass, Joseph. "Two Republics," *Fight*, IV (August, 1937), 35.

Patch, B. W. *Spain's Civil War and the Great Powers.* Washington, D.C., 1939.

Patterson, Laurence K. "Right and Left Battle for Spain," *A*, LV (August 8, 1936), 412-13.

Paul, Elliot. "Constancia de la Mora," in Jo Davidson's *Spanish Portraits.* New York, 1938.

_____. *The Life and Death of a Spanish Town.* New York, 1937.

_____. "Luis Quintanilla," *NM*, XXVIII (September 13, 1938), 14.

Peck, Anne Merriman, and Meras, E. A. *Spain in Europe and America.* New York, 1937.

Pegler, Westbrook. "Fair Enough," *NR*, XCV (May 11, 1938), 19-20.

Pennington, Leslie T. "Fascism and Democracy," *Christian Register*, CXVI (June 10, 1937), 382.

Pflaum, Irving. "Death from the Skies," in *Nothing But Danger*, ed. Frank C. Hanighen. New York, 1939. Pp. 203-23.

————. "Russia's Role in Spain," *American Mercury,* XLVII (May, 1939), 9-17.

Phillips, Thomas. "Preview of Armageddon," *SEP,* CCX (March 12, 1938), 12-13, 95, 98, 100.

Pickens, William. " 'It Is the War'—In Spain," *Unity,* CXXII (November 7, 1938), 75-77.

Pickens, William. "What I Saw in Spain," *Crisis,* XLV (October, 1938), 319-21, 330.

Pickett, Clarence E. "Succor Knows No Sides," *Survey Graphic,* XXVI (September, 1937), 463.

Pitkin, Rex. "An Explosion," *AF,* I (Winter, 1938), 16, 21-22.

Plummer, Harry C. "Barcelona Seized by Anarcho-Syndicalists," *A,* LVI (November 21, 1936), 148-49.

Polinow, S. "The Revolution Upside-Down," *Man!,* IV (August-September, 1936), 3.

Poole, Evelyn. "Harvest Time in Spain," *Fight,* IV (September, 1937), 22-23, 30.

Pratt, Fletcher. "Hot-Air Castles in Spain," *American Mercury,* XLIII (April, 1938), 450-61.

————. "Propaganda Captures the Newspapers," *American Mercury,* XLIV (August, 1938), 450-58.

Price, Clair. "Peace for the Little Basques," *New York Times Magazine,* June 20, 1937, pp. 18-19.

Priestly, S. E. Gerard. "Spain—Yesterday and Tomorrow," *Christian Leader,* CXX (May 14, 1938), 616-18.

Putnam, Mrs. George H. "Street Scene," *AM,* CLVIII (November, 1936), 636-39.

Ramus, Pierre. "Catalonia: Anarchism in Practice," *Man!,* VI (February, 1938), 2.

Randall, Ray. "Camillo Berneri—Murdered by Counter-Revolutionists in Spain," *Man!,* V (June, 1937), 5.

Rahv, Philip. "Twilight of the Thirties," *Partisan Review,* V (Summer, 1939), 3-15.

Ravage, M. E. "Hopeful Catalonia," *NR,* LXXXIX (December 9, 1936), 171-73.

Ready, Michael J. "Monsignor Ready Refutes Attack on Spanish Bishops," *Catholic Action,* XIX (October, 1937), 5-8.

————. "Monsignor Ready Scores Action of Congressmen Who Sent Congratulations to Spanish Leftists," *Catholic Action,* XX (February, 1938), 5.

Recht, Charles. "One-Armed Neutrality," *Fight,* VI (December, 1938), 7, 24, 26.

Reeve, Carl. "Lovestoneism—Twin of Fascist-Trotskyism," *Communist,* XVII (August, 1938), 732-42.

Reich, John F. "Quaker Relief Workers in Spain," *Christian Register*, CXVI (September 30, 1937), 563-64.

Reilly, H. J. "Factories Win Modern Wars," *Nation's Business*, XXVII (March, 1939), 17-19, 56-59.

Reinlieb, Harry. "More Piercing than Bombs," *NM*, XXXI (March 28, 1939), 12.

Reissig, Herman F. "Life in the Balance," *Fight*, V (April, 1938), 34-35, 62.

Rend, Gordon. "Germany Wins in Spain," *American Spectator*, IV (October, 1936), 1-3.

Resch, Peter A. "Corpus Christi in Red Bilbao," *CW*, CXLVII (June, 1938), 350-53.

Rhoads, Grace. "The Quakers in Spain," *Christian Century*, LV (August 24, 1938), 1012-14.

Rice, A. Hamilton. "The Spirit of Spain," *Spain*, II (July 18, 1938), 45.

Rice, Philip Blair. "The Spanish War," *N*, CXLVII (November 19, 1938), 541-42.

Rich, J. C. "Spanish Complications," *Justice*, XVIII (September 1, 1936), 7.

Riegel, O. W. "Press, Radio, and the Spanish Civil War," *Public Opinion Quarterly*, I (January, 1937), 131-36.

Riesenfeld, Janet. *Dancer in Madrid*. New York, 1938.

Riggs, Arthur Stanley. "No Surprise in Spain," *CW*, CXLIV (November, 1936), 156-59.

Roberts, Louis. "Bullets or Ballots," *Fighting Worker*, I (August 8, 1936), 2.

Robinson, Ione. *A Wall to Paint On*. New York, 1946.

Roethke, Theodore. "Facing the Guns," *Poetry*, LII (April, 1938), 43-46.

Rogers, F. Theo. *Spain: A Tragic Journey*. New York, 1937.

Rogers, Paul Patrick. "The Culture of Spain," *Fight*, IV (August, 1937), 25-26.

Rolfe, Edwin. *The Lincoln Battalion*. New York, 1939.

————. "Spain's Shirt-Sleeve General," *NM*, XXV (December 7, 1937), 13-14.

Romer, Sam. "Personal Notes from Spain," *Socialist Review*, VI (September-October, 1938), 4, 6.

Rorty, James. "Mobilizing the Innocents," *Forum and Century*, XCIX (January, 1938), 43-47.

Rosen, Herbert. "Friends of Democracy," *AF*, I (Winter, 1938), 17, 20-21.

Rukeyser, Muriel. "Barcelona, 1936," *Life and Letters Today*, XV Autumn, 1936), 26-33.

————. "Barcelona on the Barricades," *NM*, XX (September 1, 1936), 9-11.

Russell, Charles E. " 'Neutrality' Is Cloak for Aid to Fascists," *New Leader*, XX (January 16, 1937), 5.

Russell, Sam. "Offensive in Spain," *NM*, XXX (January 10, 1939), 7.

Ryan, William G. "Escape from Loyalist Spain," *American Mercury*, XLVI (April, 1939), 456-62.

Santayana, George. *The Letters of George Santayana*, ed. Daniel Cory. New York, 1955.

Saunders, Jane. "U.S. Press Joined Axis' Drive on Loyalists," *New Leader*, XXII (March 4, 1939), 5, 7.

Scarpa, Joseph. "We Make Shoes for Spain," *Fight*, IV (June, 1937), 22-23.

Schachner, Eugene. "Somosierra Charge," *NM*, XXI (November 3, 1936), 7.

Schechter, Rubin. "Four Letters from Spain," *NM*, XXV (October 5, 1937), 16-17.

Schiff, Isaac. "A Visit to the Spanish President," *New Leader*, XX (February 27, 1937), 5, 7.

Schiff, Victor. "A New Partnership Arises to Revitalize Spain's Government," *New Leader*, XX (June 5, 1937), 4.

Schubert, David. "Correspondence: The Congress of American Writers," *Poetry*, L (September, 1937), 357-58.

Schuman, Frederick L. "The 'Little World War,' " *Events*, II (July, 1937), 12-18.

Schwinn, Gretchen. "We Escape from Madrid," *National Geographic*, LXXI (February, 1937), 251-68.

Scott, George. "Radio," *Fight*, V (April, 1938), 36.

Sedgwick, Ellery. "One Man's Testimony," *Spain*, II (July 18, 1938), 3.

————. "The Patron Saint of Andalusia," *AM*, CLXI (June, 1938), 777-84.

Seldes, George. "Franco's Sixth Column," *Fight*, V (April, 1938), 5-7.

————. "On the Subject of Guernica: Letter to *New York Times*," January 13, 1938.

"Senex." "Anarchist Tactics in Spain," *Vanguard*, IV (February, 1938), 3-4, 13-15.

————. "Problems of Revolution in Spain," *Vanguard*, III (February-March, 1937), 3-6.

————. "Revolutionary Tactics in Spain" [1st of two parts], *Vanguard*, IV (November, 1938), 20-22.

Serge, Victor. "Crimes in Russia—Intrigue in Spain," *International Review*, II (January, 1937), 2-3.

Shaw, Roger. "Franco's Big Push," *Current History*, L (March, 1939), 15-16, 34.

_____. "Hell over Spain," *Review of Reviews*, XCIV (September, 1936), 56-58.

Sheean, Vincent. "Dolores Ibarruri," in Jo Davidson's *Spanish Portraits*. New York, 1938.

_____. *Not Peace But a Sword*. New York, 1939.

_____. "The War Which Is Not Yet Ended," *NM*, XXXI (March 7, 1939), 9-10.

Sheehan, J. Eastman. "Help for the Wounded," *Spain*, II (July 18, 1938), 24.

Sheen, Fulton J. "Spain through Red-Tinted Glasses," *Irish Monthly*, LXVII (March, 1939), 169-80.

Shields, Art. "The Misery in Perpignan," *NM*, XXXI (March 14, 1939), 7-8.

Shotwell, James T. "The Spanish Bishops' Letter: Letter to *New York Times*," September 7, 1937.

Shuster, George N. "A Catholic Defends His Church," *NR*, XCVII (January 4, 1939), 246-48.

_____. "Some Further Reflections," *Commonweal*, XXV (April 23, 1937), 716-17.

_____. "Some Reflections on Spain," *Commonweal*, XXV (April 2, 1937), 625-27.

Sinclair, Upton. "The Haves and the Have Nots," *American Guardian*, XIX (October 23, 1936), 1.

Solon, S. L. "Largo Caballero," *Modern Monthly*, X (December, 1936), 11-13.

Somebody Had to Do Something. Los Angeles, 1939.

Sommerlatte, John. "The Spanish Terror," *Messenger of the Evangelical and Reformed Church*, I (November 19, 1936), 5.

Soval, Justin. "Spain Blasts Alcazar . . . ," *Social Justice*, II (September 28, 1936), 3, 7.

Spain. New York, 1936.

Spain. New York, 1937.

Spofford, William B. "Bill Spofford Hails the United Front," *Protestant Digest*, I (December, 1938), 77-78.

Squires, Alma. *What of Spain?* Los Angeles, 1939.

Starobin, Joseph. *The Life and Death of an American Hero*. New York, 1938.

Stavis, Barrie. "Barcelona Horror," *NM*, XXVII (March 29, 1938), 7.

_____. "In Barcelona at Dusk," *NM*, XXVI (February 15, 1938), 17.

Stebbins, Robert, and Leyda, Jay. "Joris Ivens: Artist in Documentary," *Magazine of Art*, XXXI (July, 1938), 392-99, 436-38.

Steele, Walter S. "Watch 'the Popular Front,'" *National Republic*, XXIV (October, 1936), 3-5, 31-32.

Steffens, Lincoln. "'Viva España Libre! . . .'" *NM*, XX (August 18, 1936), 11.

Sterling John. "The Line-Up in Spain," *NM*, XX (September 15, 1936), 18-19.

Sterling, Max. "Revolutionary Spain," *Modern Monthly*, X (December, 1936), 5-7.

————. "Spanish Labor Fights for Liberty," *Socialist Call*, II (October 10, 1936), 8.

Stewart, Donald Ogden. " 'Viva España Libre! . . .' " *NM*, XX (August 18, 1936), 11.

Stewart, Maxwell S. "Catalonia in Revolution," *N*, CXLIII (August 15, 1936), 173-74.

————. "Inside Spain," *N*, CXLIII (August 29, 1936), 233-36.

Stimson, Henry L., *et al. American Foreign Policy and the Spanish Situation*. New York, 1939.

The Story of the Abraham Lincoln Brigade. New York, 1937.

Stowe, Leland. "Colonel Enrique Lister," in Jo Davidson's *Spanish Portraits*. New York, 1938.

————. "Evelyn the Truck-Driver," *Harper's*, CLXXVIII (February, 1939), 278-86.

————. "Madrid—After Three Years," *Volunteer for Liberty*, September 6, 1937, pp. 1, 4-6.

————. "Part of War Isn't News," *Ken*, I (June 30, 1938), 61-62.

————. "Spain's Shirt-Sleeve Heroes," *N*, CXLVI (April 23, 1938), 467-69.

Street, Walcott D. (ed.). "Should Our Neutrality Law Be Repealed or Revised?" *Bulletin of America's Town-Meeting of the Air*, IV (December 26, 1938), 5-16.

Strong, Anna Louise. "Children of the Spanish War," *Survey Graphic*, XXVI (September, 1937), 459-62.

————. "People of Spain," *NM*, XXII (January 26, 1937), 4-6.

————. *Spain in Arms: 1937*. New York, 1937.

Strong, Edward E. "I Visited Spain," *Crisis*, XLIII (December, 1936), 358-59.

Sullivan, Mark. "The Attack on Democracy," *National Defense News*, II (September, 1937), 11.

Swing, Raymond Gram. "Foreign Policies, Private and Public," *Ken*, II (August 11, 1938), 12-13.

Talbot, Francis X. "Clarifying the Issues in the Spanish Civil War," *A*, LVIII (October 23, 1937), 52.

————. "Further Reflections on the Spanish Situation," *A*, LVII (May 1, 1937), 76-77.

————. "In Answer to Some Reflections on the Spanish Situation," *A*, LVII (April 10, 1937), 9-10.

————. "May Franco Win in the United States . . . ," *Spain*, II (July 18, 1938), 18, 20, 39.

Temperley, A. C. "Military Lessons of the Spanish War," *Foreign Affairs*, XVI (October, 1937), 34-43.

These Americans Say: Lift the Embargo against Republican Spain. New York, 1939.

They Did Their Part: Let's Do Ours! New York, 1939.

Thomas, Norman. "At the Front...," *Socialist Call*, II (August 8, 1936), 1.

————. "In Defense of a Free Spain," *NM*, XX (September 8, 1936), 11.

————. "Spain: A Socialist View," *N*, CXLIV (June 19, 1937), 698-700.

————. "Thomas Protests," *Socialist Call*, II (September 5, 1936), 2.

Thomson, Charles A. *Spain: Civil War.* New York, 1937.

————. *Spain: Issues Behind the Conflict.* New York, 1937.

————. *The War in Spain.* New York, 1938.

Thorning, Joseph F. "Franco Speaks for Himself," *Columbia*, XVII (November, 1937), 6, 17.

————. "Franco's Spain," *CW*, CXLVIII (February, 1939), 568-73.

————. *Mercy and Justice!* New York, 1939.

————. "Neutrality versus Intervention," *Spain*, III (February 1, 1939), 5, 19, 21.

————. *Professor De Los Rios Refutes Himself.* New York, 1939.

————. "Up Spain!" *CW*, CXLVI (October, 1937), 55-57.

————. *Why the Press Failed on Spain.* Brooklyn, n.d.

Thurber, John Newton, "People's Front Tried and Found Wanting...," *American Socialist Monthly*, V (October, 1936), 19-23.

Tilson, John Q. *The Embargo on Spain.* New Haven, 1938.

Tinker, F. G., Jr. *Some Still Live.* New York, 1938.

Tisa, John. "Bidding the International Good-Bye," *Volunteer for Liberty*, November 7, 1938, p. 3.

Toomey, John A. "Press Propaganda Tinctures the News," *A*, LVIII (December 11, 1937), 225-26.

Towler, John. "Spain's Little Caesar," *Modern Monthly*, X (May, 1937), 7-8.

Train, Arthur, Jr. "Spanish Loot," *Today*, VII (January 2, 1937), 16-17, 28-29.

Trilling, Lionel. "Hemingway and His Critics," *Partisan Review*, VI (Winter, 1939), 52-60.

Tunis, John R. "Nazis in North Africa," *Today*, VII (January 23, 1937), 14-15, 30.

Untermeyer, Louis. " 'Viva España Libre!...' " *NM*, XX (August 18, 1936), 12.

Vanderbilt, Cornelius, Jr. "Hell in Spain as I Saw It," *Liberty*, XIII (October 3, 1936), 5-7.

Villard, Oswald Garrison. "Stage Set for Massacre," *N*, CXLVIII (April 1, 1939), 378.

Wadsworth, Julian S. "Spanish Refugees in Geneva," *Zion's Herald*, CXV (April 14, 1937), 463.

Walsh, Gerald B. "The European Crisis and the Spanish War," *Spain*, II (May 1, 1938), 10.

Walsh, William. "Speaking of Spanish Democracy," *Spain*, I (December 1, 1937), 8-10.

Walters, Walter. "The Hammer and Sickle at Work," *Spain*, I (November 15, 1937), 12-13.

Ward, Harry F. *The Fascist International*. New York, 1937.

————. "For Peace and Democracy," *Crisis*, XLV (March, 1938), 76-77.

————. "A Statement on Spain," *Fight*, IV (February, 1937), 30.

————, and MacLeod, A. A. *Spain's Democracy Talks to America*. New York, 1936.

Watson, Godwin. " 'When There Is No Peace,' " *Social Frontier*, III (May, 1937), 239-42.

Watts, Richard, Jr. "Madrid's Victory Complex," *Current History*, XLVII (October, 1937), 45-48.

Weber, Max. " 'Viva España Libre! . . .' " *NM*, XX (August 18, 1936), 11-12.

Weisbord, Albert. "Running the International Blockade," *N*, CXLV (July 17, 1937), 64-66.

Weller, George. "A Window on Spain," *NY*, XII (October 31, 1936), 55-57.

West, Dan. *Needy Spain*. Philadelphia, 1938.

Wheelwright, John. "The Poetry of Lorca," *Poetry*, LI (December, 1937), 167-70.

Whelan, Albert. "Church Services in Spain: Letter to *New York Times*," March 2, 1938.

————. "Flashes of Light on a Red Horizon," *A*, LVIII (December 25, 1937), 285.

Whelan, Edward J. "Spanish Nationalists After Two Years of Civil War," *A*, LIX (July 16, 1938), 340-41.

"Whiffin, Peter." "A Priest Warns the Church," *Forum and Century*, XCVII (April, 1937), 195-201.

White, David McKelvey. "Return of the Veterans," *Voice of Spain*, I (February, 1939), 50-51.

————. "Vanguard of Peace," *AF*, I (Winter, 1938), 4-5.

————. "We Will Not Forget," *AF*, I (Spring, 1938), 6.

————. "What America Can Do," *NM*, XXVIII (July 19, 1938), 17-18.

————. "With the Lincoln Volunteers," *Fight*, V (April, 1938), 44-45.

White, Leigh. "Barcelona Faces Front," *N*, CXLVI (March 5, 1938), 266-68.

————. "Hitch-Hiking behind the Front," *Globe*, II (April-May, 1938), 61-65, 91, 113.

————. "Rebellion in Rebel Spain," *N*, CXLV (December 11, 1937), 635-38.

Why the Embargo against the Spanish Republic Should Be Lifted Now. New York, 1939.

Wiegand, Karl H. von. "I Cover the Spanish Front," *Cosmopolitan*, CI (December, 1936), 26-27, 174-78.

Wilcox, Francis O. "The League of Nations and the Spanish Civil War," *Annals of the American Academy of Political and Social Science*, CXCVIII (July, 1938), 65-72.

————. "The Localization of the Spanish War," *American Political Science Review*, XXXII (April, 1938), 237-60.

Wiley, S. Ernest. "War in Old Toledo," *Columbia*, XVI (November, 1936), 9, 26.

Williams, Albert. "Spanish Masses Meeting New Needs of Struggle," *Workers Age*, VI (May 8, 1937), 1, 4, 6.

Williams, Michael. "The Church Warns Her Priest," *Forum and Century*, XCVII (June, 1937), 323-31.

————. "Degradation of Democracy," *Commonweal*, XXV (April 9, 1937), 655-58.

————. "How Many Slain?" *Current History*, XLV (December, 1936), 46-50.

————. "Open Letter to Leaders of the American Press" [1st of many], *Commonweal*, XXVI (May 7, 1937), 33-37.

————. "Views and Reviews," *Commonweal*, XXVIII (June 24, 1938), 241-42.

Williams, Walter E. "Strategy after Barcelona," *NM*, XXX (February 7, 1939), 5-6.

Williams, William Carlos. "Federico Garcia Lorca," *Kenyon Review*, I (Spring, 1939), 148-58.

Wilson, Edmund. "Hemingway and the Wars," *N*, CXLVII (December 10, 1938), 628, 630.

Wirth, William G. "Spain and the Vatican," *Signs of the Times*, October 6, 1936, pp. 4-5, 13.

Wise, James Waterman. "Tell Them the Truth!" *Fight*, V (April, 1938), 8-9, 52.

Wolfe, Bernard. "The Truth about Spain," *New International*, IV (June, 1938), 190.

Wolfe, Bertram D. "Background of Spain's Civil War," *Marxist Quarterly*, I (October-November-December, 1937), 345-55.

————. *Civil War in Spain*. New York, 1937.

————, and Fischer, Louis. "The Struggle in Catalonia," *N*, CXLIV

(June 5, 1937), 657-58, 660.

Wolfe, Thomas. *The Letters of Thomas Wolfe,* ed. Elizabeth Nowell. New York, 1956.

Woolsey, Gamel. *Death's Other Kingdom.* London, 1939.

WPA Teachers in Spain. New York, 1938.

Wright, Herbert. "Insurgency in International Law: Letter to *New York Times,*" April 10, 1938.

————. *Memorandum in Support of the Retention of the Spanish Embargo.* Washington, D.C., 1939.

Wright, Richard. "Adventure and Love in Loyalist Spain," *NM,* XXVI (March 8, 1938), 25-26.

Writers Take Sides. New York, 1938.

Yancey, P. H. "Spanish Church and the Workers," *S,* XVII (June, 1938), 664-66.

Ybarra, T. R. "Spain à la Franco," *Collier's,* C (August 7, 1937), 13, 29-30.

Young, Art. "In Defense of a Free Spain," *NM,* XX (September 8, 1936), 11.

Zam, Herbert. "May Day and International Labor," *Socialist Review,* VI (May-June, 1938), 1-3.

————. "What Next in Spain?" *Socialist Call,* II (August 1, 1936), 10.

Ziegler, Abraham. "The Crisis in Spain," *Industrial Unionist,* V (September, 1936), 5-6, 12.

————. "The Spanish Workers Betrayed," *Industrial Unionist,* VI (August-September, 1937), 7-8, 12.

Ziffren, Lester. "The Correspondent in Spain," *Public Opinion Quarterly,* I (July, 1937), 112-16.

————. "I Lived in Madrid," *Current History,* XLVI (April, 1937), 35-41.

SUPPLEMENT: UNITED STATES GOVERNMENT PUBLICATIONS

Congressional Record. LXXXI-LXXXIV, 75th Congress, 1st Session, to 76th Congress, 2nd Session. Washington, D.C., 1936-39.

United States Congress, House Committee on Foreign Affairs. *Hearings before Committee on Foreign Affairs: American Neutrality Policy, 1937.* H. J. Res. 147, 75th Congress, 1st Session. Washington, D.C., 1937.

United States Department of State. *Foreign Relations of the United States: 1936-1938.* Vols. I of 1936, 1937, 1938, and Vol. II of 1936. Washington, D.C., 1953-55.

United States Department of State. *Peace and War: United States Foreign Policy, 1931-1941.* Washington, D.C., 1943.

AMERICAN PERIODICALS: 1936-39

Advance
America
American Artist
American Bulletin, The
American Foreign Service Journal,
  The
American Friend, The
American Freeman, The
American Gentile, The
American Guardian, The
American Hebrew, The
American Historical Review, The
American Journal of
  International Law, The
American Legion Magazine
American Mercury, The
American Political Science Review
American Prefaces
American Quarterly on the Soviet
  Union, The
American Review, The
American Review of Reviews, The
American Scholar
American Socialist Monthly
American Spectator, The
American Teacher Magazine
Among Friends
Annals of the American Academy
  of Political and Social Science,
  The
Appeal to Reason, The
Arise
Arbitrator, The
Art Digest
Art Front
Art News
Arts and Decoration
Atlantic Monthly
Ave Maria

Barron's

Book Digest of Best Sellers
Bulletin of the Proletarian
  Group, The
Business Week

Catholic Action
Catholic Digest
Catholic Historical Review, The
Catholic Mind, The
Catholic Worker, The
Catholic World
Champion of Youth, The
Christendom
Christian Advocate
Christian Century, The
Christian Evangelist, The
Christian Front
Christian Leader, The
Christian Register, The
Chronicle, The
Churchman, The
Clearing House, The
Collier's
Columbia
Command and General Staff
  School Quarterly, The
Commentator, The
Commercial and Financial
  Chronicle, The
Common Sense
Commonweal
Communist, The
Communist International, The
Consolation
Contemporary Jewish Record, The
Coronet
Cosmopolitan
Crisis, The
Current History

Direction

Editor and Publisher
Educational Forum, The
Equal Rights
Esquire
Events
Examiner, The

Federal Council Bulletin, The
Fellowship
Fight, The
Fighting Worker, The
Foreign Affairs
Foreign Policy Reports
Fortune
Forum and Century, The
Freeman, The
Friends Intelligencer
Frontier and Midland, The

Globe

Harper's Magazine
Hispania
Hispanic American Historical
  Review, The
In Defense of Bolshevism
Independent Woman
Industrial Unionist, The
Industrial Worker, The
Infantry Journal, The
International Class Struggle
International Council
  Correspondence
International Review, The

Journalism Quarterly
Journal of Adult Education
Journal of Commerce, The
Justice

Ken
Kenyon Review

Labor Front, The

Liberty
Life
Literary Digest, The
Little Man, The
Living Age, The
Living Church, The
Living Marxism
Look
Lutheran Companion, The

Magazine of Art, The
Man!
Marxist Quarterly, The
Messenger of Peace, The
Messenger of the Evangelical and
  Reformed Church, The
Midwest
Missionary Herald, The
Missionary Review of the
  World, The
Modern Language Forum, The
Modern Monthly, The
Museum News

Nation, The
National Defense News
National Geographic Magazine
National Municipal Review
National Republic, The
Nation's Business
New Age, The
New Christianity, The
New International, The
New Leader, The
New Liberation, The
New Masses
New Mexico Quarterly
New Republic
New Theatre
New Yorker
Newsweek

Opportunity
Orate Fratres

Parents Magazine
Partisan Review
Peace Action
Photo History
Pictures on Exhibit
Plan Age
Plans and Results
Poetry
Political Science Quarterly
Presbyterian Tribune, The
Proceedings of the Academy of
    Political Science, The
Progressive, The
Proletarian News
Proletarian Outlook, The
Propaganda Analysis
Protestant Digest
Public Opinion Quarterly, The
Publisher's Weekly

Quill, The

Radical Religion
Reader's Digest
Religion in Life
Religious Digest, The
Review of Reviews
Rosicrucian Digest, The
Rotarian

Saturday Evening Post
Saturday Review of Literature
Scholastic
School and Society
Science and Society
Science News Letter
Scribner's
Sewanee Review
Sign, The
Signs of the Times
Social Action
Social Forces
Social Frontier, The
Social Justice

Social Science
Social Work Today
Socialist, The
Socialist Appeal, The (Chicago)
Socialist Appeal, The (New York)
Socialist Call, The
Socialist Review
South Atlantic Quarterly
Spain
Spark, The
Spirit
Standard, The
Story
Survey, The
Survey Graphic

Talks
Theosophical Quarterly
Thought
Time
Today
Travel
Twice a Year

United States News
Unity

Vanguard
Virginia Quarterly Review
Vital Speeches

Watchman-Examiner, The
Witness, The
Woman's Press, The
Workers Age
World Affairs
World Affairs Interpreter
World Events
World Youth

Yale Review
Young Communist Review, The

Zion's Herald

NEWSPAPERS USED*

Knickerbocker Press (Albany)
Albuquerque Journal
Atlanta Constitution
Augusta (Maine) Kennebec
    Journal
Birmingham News
Boston Evening Transcript
Boston Herald
Buffalo News
Chicago Daily News
Chicago Tribune
Cincinnati Enquirer
Christian Science Monitor
    (Boston)
Cleveland Plain-Dealer
Cleveland Press
Dallas News
Detroit Free Press
Hartford Courant
Houston Post
Idaho Statesman (Boise)
Indianapolis News
Indianapolis Star
Kansas City Journal Post
Kansas City Star
Los Angeles Times
Louisville Courier-Journal
Nashville Banner
New Orleans Times-Picayune

New York Daily Mirror
New York Daily News
Daily Worker (New York)
New York Herald Tribune
New York Journal
New York Post
New York Times
New York World-Telegram
Philadelphia Bulletin
Philadelphia Inquirer
Pittsburgh Post-Gazette
Pittsburgh Press
Pittsburgh Sun-Telegraph
Portland (Oregon) Oregonian
Richmond Times-Dispatch
Rochester (New York) Democrat-
    Chronicle
St. Louis Globe-Democrat
St. Louis Post-Dispatch
St. Paul Pioneer-Press
St. Paul Dispatch
San Francisco Chronicle
Seattle Times
Spokane Spokesman Review
Topeka Daily Capital
Wall Street Journal (New York)
Washington Herald
Washington Post
Washington Star

---

*This list is derived largely from an invaluable secondary source, James F. O'Brien's "American Press Opinion of the Spanish Civil War, 1936-1939" (unpublished thesis, Georgetown University, 1950). After testing this thorough and well-documented thesis for accuracy, I used it as guide and sourcebook. I supplemented O'Brien's work by looking at other newspapers, at studies of the British press, and at thirty-two months of the *New York Times*.

NOVELS, PLAYS, STORIES, AND POEMS

Anderson, Maxwell. *Key Largo* [play]. Washington, D.C., 1939.
Ap-Rhys, Llewellyn. "Madrid: Year Two" [poem], *Man!*, VI (February, 1938), 2.

Benardete, M. J., and Humphries, Rolfe (eds.). *And Spain Sings* [poems]. New York, 1937.

Benedict, Herman. "Song for Spain," *CW*, CXLVI (February, 1938), 549.

Benet, William Rose. "Catalonia" [poem], *NM*, XXVII (May 31, 1938), 19.

Bercovici, Rion. "Beleaguered" [story], *Scribner's*, CI (March, 1937), 39-41.

Berryman, John. "Two Poems," *Kenyon Review*, I (Summer, 1939), 257-59.

Bessie, Alvah (ed.). *The Heart of Spain* [anthology]. New York, 1952.

Blacam, Hugh de. "For the Spanish Martyrs" [poem], *S*, XVI (December, 1936), 284.

Blankfort, Michael. *The Brave and the Blind* [play]. New York, 1937.

_____. *The Brave and the Blind* [novel]. Indianapolis, 1940.

Brinnin, John Malcolm. "For a Young Poet Dead in Spain" [poem], in *Salud!*, ed. Alan Calmer. New York, 1938, pp. 39-40.

Burdin, Ruth. *Incident* [play]. New York, 1937.

Caldwell, Erskine. "In Barcelona" [story], in *Salud!*, ed. Alan Calmer. New York, 1938, pp. 38-39.

Caldwell, James. *Defense in University City* [story]. Cincinnati, 1939.

Calmer, Alan (ed.). *Salud!* [anthology]. New York, 1938.

Carter, Burnham. "Tomorrow Will Be Fair" [story], *Collier's*, XCIX (April 17, 1937), 9-10, 76, 78-82.

Chase, Borden. "A Kiss in Spain" [story], *Liberty*, XIII (October 10, 1936), 26-29.

Chittick, Conrad. "Spain" [poem], in *Negro Voices*, ed. Beatrice Murphy. New York, 1938, pp. 31-32.

Coblentz, Stanton A. "Spain—1938" [poem], *Unity*, CXXI (August 1, 1938), 174.

Cook, Harold Lewis. "In Time of Civil War" [poem] *NY*, XIV (May 7, 1938), 25.

_____. "1937" [poem], *NY*, XIII (December 4, 1937), 32.

Corwin, Norman. *They Fly through the Air . . .* [play], in *Thirteen by Corwin*. New York, 1942.

Davidman, Joy. *Letter to a Comrade* [poems]. New Haven, 1938.

Deacon, Ruth. *Spain: 1937* [play]. New York, 1937.

Dos Passos, John. *Adventures of a Young Man* [novel]. New York, 1938.

Douglas, Harold. "In Memoriam: John Cookson" [poem], *NM*, XXX (December 27, 1938), 9.

Dunham, Barrows. "Neutrality: America-Spain, 1938" [poem], *Presbyterian Tribune*, LIV (January 5, 1939), 7.

Duranty, Walter. "Witch of the Alcazar" [story], *Collier's*, XCVIII (December 5, 1936), 7-9, 59.

Earls, Michael. "Spain's Wintered Oak" [poem], *S*, XVI (March, 1937),

472.

Evanson, Norman. *Camaradas* [play]. New York, 1939.

Fearing, Kenneth. "The Program" [poem], *NM,* XXVIII (September 6, 1938), 20.

Feeney, Leonard. "The Spanish 'Loyalists'" [poem], *A,* LVIII (November 27, 1937), 188.

Fischer, Marjorie. "Angela" [story], *Direction,* II (January-February, 1938), 16-17.

Fremantle, Anne. "Davos-Parsenn" [story], *New Statesman and Nation,* XVII (March 4, 1939), 321-22.

Funaroff, S. "To Federico Garcia Lorca," *Poetry,* LII (July, 1938), 185.

————. "To the Dead of the Lincoln Brigade" [poem], *NM,* XXX (January 3, 1939), 4.

Galvin, James J. "Spanish Alleluja!" [poem], *Spirit,* IV (January, 1938), 169.

Gellhorn, Martha. "Visit to the Wounded," *Story,* XI (October, 1937), 58-61.

Gessner, Robert. "Stand Up, the Lovers of Spain" [poem], *NM,* XXI (December 1, 1936), 6.

Ginsberg, Louis. "Bombs on Barcelona" [poem], *NM,* XXVIII (August 2, 1938), 20.

Gordon, David. "Threnos" [poem], *A,* LX (December 3, 1938), 212.

Gustave, Sister M. "Lament for Spain" [poem], *S,* XVI (January, 1937), 337.

Haggard, Paul. "Castle in Yellow" [story], *Esquire,* XI (March, 1939), 32-33, 120.

————. "Let the Day Perish" [story], *Esquire,* X (August, 1938), 32-33, 130, 135.

————. "The Silver Fleet of Time" [story], *Esquire,* X (September, 1938), 28-29, 157-58.

Harrison, Charles Yale. *Meet Me on the Barricades* [novel]. New York, 1938.

Hellman, Lillian. "A Bleached Lady" [story], *NM,* XXIX (October 11, 1938), 20-21.

Hemingway, Ernest. "The Butterfly and the Tank" [story], *Esquire,* X (December, 1938), 51, 186, 188, 190.

————. "The Denunciation" [story], *Esquire,* X (November, 1938), 39, 111-14.

————. *For Whom the Bell Tolls* [novel]. New York, 1940.

————. "Night before Battle" [story], *Esquire,* XI (February, 1939), 27-29, 91-92, 95, 97.

————. "The Old Man at the Bridge" [story], *Ken,* I (May 19, 1938), 36.

————. *The Short Stories of Ernest Hemingway: The First Forty-Nine Stories and the Play, The Fifth Column.* New York, 1938.

Hepburn, Ethel. "To Ann, on a Street-Car" [poem], *Midwest*, I (December, 1936), 20.

Hope, Edward. "Spanish Omelette" [story], *Cosmopolitan*, CII (April, 1937), 28-31, 130-54, 158-63.

Hopkins, J. G. E. "Cynical Comment" [poem], *A*, LVII (April 17, 1937), 44.

Hughes, Langston. "Air Raid: Barcelona" [poem], *Esquire*, X (October, 1938), 40.

————. "Madrid" [poem], *Fight*, V (July, 1938), 14.

————. "October 16th" [poem], *Volunteer for Liberty*, (October 11, 1937), p. 16.

————. "Post Card from Spain" [poem], *Volunteer for Liberty*, April 9, 1938, p. 4.

Humphries, Rolfe. "A Gay People" [poem], *NR*, XCVIII (April 12, 1939), 275.

————. "On an Official Occasion," *Poetry*, LI (November, 1937), 60.

Jarrell, Randall. *The Rage for the Lost Penny* [poems], in *Five Young American Poets*, ed. James Laughlin, IV. Norfolk, Conn., 1940.

Johnson, Raphael. "The Night of Hope" [story], *S*, XVI (December, 1936), 273-76.

Kaghan, Theodore. *Hello Franco* [play]. New York, n.d.

Keyes, Frances Parkinson. *The Great Tradition* [novel]. New York, 1939.

Komroff, Manuel. "Don Quixote Rides Again" [story], *Esquire*, XI (January, 1939), 36-37, 103-4.

————. "An Easter in Spain" [story], *Esquire*, XI (May, 1939), 68-69, 207-9.

————. "Spanish Episode" [story], *Coronet*, V (January, 1939), 107-10.

Kornblatt, Sam. "Soldier from Spain" [poem], *AF*, I (Spring, 1938), 12.

Leslie, Kenneth. " 'Fifth-Column'-ist" [poem], *Protestant Digest*, I (March, 1939), 24-30.

Kramer, Aaron. "Two Poems," in *Seven Poets in Search of an Answer*, ed. Thomas Yoseloff. New York, 1944, pp. 55-56.

McCarthy, Mary. *The Company She Keeps* [novel]. New York, 1939.

MacLeish, Archibald. *Air Raid* [play]. New York, 1938.

Maher, Jerome. "That Which We Call a Rose" [story], *Columbia*, XVII (October, 1937), 14, 22.

————. " 'Unimpeachable Sources' " [story], *Columbia*, XVII (August, 1937), 5, 24-25.

Mathews, H. "Spanish Volunteer" [story], *Man!*, VI (May, 1938), 7.

Millay, Edna St. Vincent. "Say That We Saw Spain Die" [poem], *Harper's*, CLXXVII (October, 1938), 449.

Merrick, William. *Forgot in the Rains,* in *Columbia Workshop Plays,* ed. Douglas Coulter. New York, 1939.

Munson, Frank W. "Friendly Argument" [story], *Catholic Digest,* I (July, 1937), 14-18.

Neugass, James. "Convoy" [poem], *NM,* XXVII (May 31, 1938), 19.

————. "Give Us This Day" [poem], *Story,* XIII (November-December, 1938), 83-93.

————. "Headlines from Spain" [poem], *NM,* XX (August 4, 1936), 13.

————. "On the Road" [poem], in *Salud!,* ed. Alan Calmer. New York, 1938, pp. 5-12.

Newhouse, Edward. "They Also Serve" [story], in *Salud!,* ed. Alan Calmer. New York, 1938, pp. 32-37.

Nicholson, Helen. *The Painted Bed* [novel]. New York, 1938.

————. *Shelter for the Night,* in *Eight New One-Act Plays of 1937,* ed. William Armstrong. London, 1937.

Norman, Charles. *The Savage Century* [poems]. Prairie City, Ill., 1942.

Nyiradi, Irene. "Spain 1936" [poem], *World Youth,* II (January 30, 1937), 7.

Parker, Dorothy. "Soldiers of the Republic" [story], *NY,* XIII (February 5, 1938), 13-14.

Partnow, Hyde. "Madrid to Manhattan" [story], *NM,* XXV (December 7, 1937), 17-23.

Paull, Irene. "What Price Spain" [play], *Young Communist Review,* II (February, 1937), 12-13.

Pereda, Prudencio de. "The Bullfighter" [story], *NM,* XXII (March 16, 1937), 15-16.

————. "The Denunciation" [story], in *Salud!,* ed. Alan Calmer. New York, 1938, pp. 16-27.

————. "Fascist Lament" [story], *NM,* XXXI (February 28, 1939), 11.

————. "My Brother Goes Back" [story], *NM,* XXVIII (July 26, 1938), 20.

————. "The Spaniard," *Story,* X (March, 1937), 9-18.

Powers, Jessica. "Lament for Spain" [poem], *Commonweal,* XXVIII (September 16, 1938), 523.

Prokosch, Frederic. "Peninsula" [poem], *NM,* XXV (October 19, 1937), 11.

Quin, Mike. "How Much for Spain?" [poem], *AF,* I (Spring, 1938), 18.

————. *On the Drumhead* [collection]. San Francisco, 1948.

Randall, W. J. "Maria's Grand Finale" [story], *S,* XVII (August, 1937), 23-26.

Reed, Jack. "Burgos Jail" [story, 1st of four parts], *Fight,* VI (March, 1939), 16-19, 29-30.

Rexroth, Kenneth. "Requiem for the Dead in Spain" [poem], *NR*, XC (March 24, 1937), 201.

———. "Two Poems," in *Salud!*, ed. Alan Calmer. New York, 1938. pp. 28-30.

Rolfe, Edwin. "Elegy for Our Dead" [poem], in *Salud!*, ed. Alan Calmer, New York, 1938, p. 13.

———. *First Love and Other Poems*. Los Angeles, 1951.

Rollins, William, Jr. *The Wall of Men* [novel]. New York, 1938.

Romancero de los Voluntarios de la Libertad [anthology]. Madrid, 1937.

Rorty, James. "Elegy for the Spanish Dead" [poem], *Modern Monthly*, X (September, 1937), 3.

Rosenberg, Harold. "Spanish Epitaph," in *New Letters in America: 1*, ed. Horace Gregory. New York, 1937, p. 106.

Rosenstein, Joseph. "Twenty of Us" [poem], *Volunteer for Liberty*, February 23, 1938, pp. 4-5.

Rosten, Norman. *The Fourth Decade and Other Poems*. New York, 1943.

———. "Fragments for America" [poem], *NM*, XXVIII (July 12, 1938), 154-56.

———. "The March" [poem], in *Salud!*, ed. Alan Calmer. New York, 1938, p. 31.

———. "Ode to Spring" [poem], *NM*, XXVII (May 31, 1938), 19.

———. "Parade" [poems], *NM*, XXIII (April 20, 1937), 24.

Rukeyser, Muriel. "Mediterranean" [poem], *NM*, XXIV (September 14, 1937), 18-20.

———. *A Turning Wind* [poems]. New York, 1939.

Sachs, David. "Heard from Spain," *Poetry*, LI (January, 1938), 200.

Sarnoff, Lilly. "On the Road" [story], *Man!*, VI (April, 1938), 7.

Scoggins, Nancy. "The Nun Who Met the Rebels" [story], *Liberty*, XIII (October 24, 1936), 32-35.

Sheean, Vincent. "Four Verses," *NM*, XXIX (October 4, 1938), 16.

———. "Puigcerdà" [poem], in *Salud!*, ed. Alan Calmer. New York, 1938, p. 41.

Shepherd, Paul. "The Lincoln Brigade Returns" [poem], *NM*, XXIX (November 29, 1938), 5.

Sherman, George Witter. "Moon Over Spain" [poem], *Frontier and Midland*, XVIII (Spring, 1938), 173-74.

Sholley, Hazel. *Night Falls on Spain* [play]. Boston, 1939.

Sinclair, Jo. "Children at Play" [story], *Esquire*, IX (January, 1938), 45, 124.

Sinclair, Upton. *No Pasaran!* [novel]. Pasadena, 1937.

Stavis, Barrie. *Refuge* [play]. New York, 1939.

Stowe, Leland. "We Call It Peace" [poem], *Fight*, VI (February, 1939), 15.

Sutton, Kathleen. "Women of Spain" [poem], *Man!* V (December,

1936-January, 1937), 7.

Taylor, Penia. "The Tomb" [poem], *NM*, XXII (March 9, 1937), 18.

Terrence, Amherst. *This Little Stream* [play]. Typescript, New York Public Library.

Titus, Bill. "Fighting in the Guadarrama Mountains" [poem], *American Prefaces*, II (May, 1937), 123.

————. "Spain" [poem], *American Prefaces*, II (May, 1937), 122.

Todrin, Boris. *Seven Men* [poems]. New York, 1938.

Virginia, Sister Mary St. "Christ Returns to Barcelona" [poem], *A*, LX, (February 25, 1939), 500.

Williams, Michael. "Spain's Sacrifice" [poem], *Commonweal*, XXVI (May 14, 1937), 71-72.

Wilson, Leon. "Portrait of the Artist in Revolution," *Story*, XI (December, 1937), 24-28.

Wolff, David. "The Defenses" [poem], in *Salud!*, ed. Alan Calmer. New York, 1938, pp. 14-15.

Wurdemann, Audrey. "Spanish Burning" [poem], *Saturday Review of Literature*, XV (January 30, 1937), 10.

Yoseloff, Thomas (ed.). *Seven Poets in Search of an Answer* [anthology]. New York, 1944.

SCULPTURES, PAINTINGS, AND OTHER GRAPHIC MATERIALS. LOCATION OF ILLUSTRATION GIVEN.

Blanche, Lucille. *Afternoon in Spain*. Catalogue of American Artists Congress, *Second Annual Membership Exhibition*. New York, 1938.

Briggs, Judson. *Brunete Sector*. Art Digest, XII (May 15, 1938), 16.

————. *Spanish Landscape*. Magazine of Art, XXXI (June, 1938), 360.

————. *Trenches at Night*. Pictures on Exhibit, I (May, 1938), 15.

Davidson, Jo. *Spanish Portraits* [pamphlet with illustrations of busts made in Spain]. New York, 1938. Also published as *An Exhibit of Sculpture*. New York, 1938.

De Diego, Julio. *Souvenir of Spain*. Art News, XXXVI (September 17, 1938), 10.

Gropper, William. *Air Raid* [water color]. Magazine of Art, XXX (August, 1937), 471.

————. *Bombardment*. Survey Graphic, XXVI (July, 1937), 366.

————. *Casualty*. Survey Graphic, XXVI (July, 1937), 366.

————. *Defenders*. NM, XXII (March 9, 1937), 17.

————. *Foreign Legion*. Esquire, VIII (September, 1937), 106.

————. *Refugees*. Magazine of Art, XXX (August, 1937), 470.

————. *Spanish Landscape*. NM, XXVI (March 15, 1938), 16.

Groth, John. *Moors and Boots.* Catalogue of American Artists Congress, *Second Annual Membership Exhibition.* New York, 1938.

Guston, Philip. *Bombardment. Direction,* II (January-February, 1938), 16.

Harkavy, H. R. *Woman of Madrid* [sculpture]. *NM,* XXII (February 2, 1937), 12.

Harriton, Abraham. *Fighting for Spanish Democracy. NM,* XXII (January 26, 1937), 15.

Hecht, Zoltan. *Air Raid. Fight,* IV (August, 1937), 42.

Hoffman, Arnold. *War. Pictures on Exhibit,* I (January, 1938), 23.

Ishigaki, Eitaro. *Amazons.* Catalogue of American Artists Congress, *First Annual Membership Exhibition.* New York, 1937.

Kruse, Alex Z. *Españolephone.* Catalogue of American Artists Congress, *Second Annual Membership Exhibition.* New York, 1938.

Lenson, Michael. *Iberian Spring.* Catalogue of American Artists Congress, *Second Annual Membership Exhibition.* New York, 1938.

Liberté, Jean. *Mother of Spain. Pictures on Exhibit,* II (March, 1939), 19.

Lux, Gwen. *Spanish Widow. Art News,* XXXVI (December 25, 1937), 14.

Mervin, Jules. *War and the Ivory Towerists. Art News,* XXXVI (December 25, 1937), 14.

Mommer, Paul. *Execution in Spain. Art Front,* II (November, 1936), 11.

Ostrowsky, Ella. *Spanish Refugees.* Catalogue of American Artists Congress, *Second Annual Membership Exhibition.* New York, 1938.

Rabin, Ralph. *Bombardment* [etching]. *NM,* XXII (January 26, 1937), 20.

Refregier, Anton. *Bombers. NM,* XXVII (June 14, 1938), 7.

————. *Fascists over Spain. NM,* XXIII (May 11, 1937), 20.

Ribak, Louis. *Refugees. Magazine of Art,* XXXI (May, 1938), 275.

Robinson, Ione. *Eight Drawings. A Wall to Paint On.* New York, 1946, between pp. 216-17.

————. *Child With Bread, Girl With Grass, Young Republican* (1), *Young Republican* (2). *A Wall to Paint On,* facing p. 328.

Ross, C. B. *Spanish Mother.* Catalogue of American Artists Congress, *Second Annual Membership Exhibition.* New York, 1938.

Simon, Henry. *Madrid* [lithograph]. *NM,* XXV (November 23, 1937), 15.

Soyer, Isaac. *What Next? Art Digest,* XII (May 15, 1938), 6.

Soyer, Moses. *Spanish Refugees. Magazine of Art,* XXXI (May, 1938), 275.

————. *A Victim of Fascism. Fight,* IV (August, 1937), 42.

————. *Wife and Children of a Worker-Soldier. NM,* XXII (January 12, 1937), 4.

Soyer, Raphael. *Workers Armed. NM,* XXI (December 1, 1936), 3.

Szucs, Victor. *Loyalist Defenders* [etching]. *NM,* XXII (January 26, 1937), 18.

Wald, Sylvia. *Air Raid. NM,* XXIII (April 13, 1937), 11.

Werner, Nat. *Tragedy of Spain* [sculpture]. *Art Front,* III (March, 1937), 5.

White, Bob. *General Mola Salutes the People* [etching]. *Midwest,* I (November, 1936), 9.

FILMS SHOWN IN
THE UNITED STATES

Blockade [feature]. Walter Wanger-United Artists, 1938. Screenplay by John Howard Lawson.

Fury over Spain [documentary]. Modern Film Corporation, 1937.

The Heart of Spain. See *Return to Life.*

Last Train from Madrid [feature]. Paramount, 1937.

Love under Fire [feature]. 20th Century-Fox, 1937.

Return to Life [documentary]. Medical Bureau and North American Committee to Aid Spanish Democracy, 1938.

The River Is Blue. See *Blockade.*

Spain in Arms [documentary]. Filmfacts, 1938.

Spain in Flames [documentary]. Amkino, 1937.

The Spanish Earth [documentary]. Contemporary Historians, 1937. Commentary and voice by Ernest Hemingway; direction by Joris Ivens.

Will of a People: Spain Fights On [documentary]. Louis Frank, 1939.

MUSIC AND DANCE

Blitzstein, Marc. See Virgil Thomson.

Cowell, Henry. Music for Martha Graham, *Deep Song* and *Immediate Tragedy.*

Enters, Angna. *Flesh-Possessed Saint: Red Malaga* [dance].

_____. *Spain Says "Salud!"* [dance].

Graham, Martha. *Deep Song* [dance].

_____. *Immediate Tragedy* [dance].

Six Songs for Democracy. Asch Recording.

Songs of the Lincoln Brigade. Asch-Stinson Recording.

Soyer, Ida. *War Face* [dance].

Thomson, Virgil, and Marc Blitzstein. Music for documentary film, *The Spanish Earth.*

INDEX

Orlov, Alexander planted many Jew Communist moles in America, eg, the Robert Oppenheimers